Natural Reason

Essays in Honor of Joseph Norio Uemura

Edited by
Duane L. Cady
and
Ronald E. Beanblossom

Hamline University
St. Paul, Minnesota

Published in 1992 by
Hamline University
Philosophy Department
1536 Hewitt Avenue
St. Paul, Minnesota 55104

Library of Congress Catalog Card Number: 92-72687
Paperback edition ISBN: 0-9633686-0-5
Hardcover edition ISBN: 0-9633686-1-3

Natural Reason

Essays in Honor of
Joseph Norio Uemura

Dedicated to the memories of

Kenneth E. Haas

and

Mark E. Kispert

Contents

Preface ix

Introduction...xi

1. On Forms
    Peter W. Wakefield 1

2. *Phaedo* 72e-74a: What Is the Point?
    Martha Phillips 13

3. The Positive Argument in Plato's *Theaetetus*
    Duane L. Cady..31

4. The Ethics of Being
    Albert A. Anderson 43

5. The Developmental Relationship Between Moral Reasoning and Motivation
    Richard Kyte..55

6. Rachels' Defense of Active Euthanasia: A Critique
    Robert N. Hull 67

7. Ethical Perception and Managerial Decision Making:
    A Conceptual and Empirical Exploration
    Dennis Wittmer 75

8. Retention and Advising: Paternalism, Agency and Contract
    Christopher Dreisbach 97

9. Dewey's Theory of Aesthetics and Art
    Thomas A. Wilson 105

10. James and Reid: Meliorism *vs* Metaphysics
    Ronald E. Beanblossom 121

11. Seeing a Donkey's Jaw, Drinking Green Tea:
    Self and Ordinariness in Ecophilosophy
    Deane Curtin...137

12. The Necessity of the Ontological Argument
    Joseph N. Uemura 153

A Decalogue for a Pedagogue
    Joseph N. Uemura 161

Contributors 163

Notes 166

Preface

⁀

Although Joseph Norio Uemura rejects the claim that "man is the measure of all things," I will risk his protestations to consider some of the things which are the measure of this man. How does one measure a man? There are those who measure a man by his reputation, by how much his colleagues, friends, and neighbors respect him. To be sure, Joe enjoys the respect of those who know him. Yet, one need only remember the *Republic* to be mindful of the inadequacy of such a measure. Some people measure a man by what he does or has done; others do so by what he thinks; and still others profess to measure a man by what he is in the sense of a combination of the two. It may seem that in this case all three measures are appropriate despite concerns that might be raised about acting without thinking or thinking without acting.

It does appear that the measure of Joe can be taken in terms of what he has done. For, like Socrates, Joe can be accused of corrupting the young (and not so young). Notwithstanding the typical Socratic defenses, consider the astonishing number - a number too great for mere coincidence - of his former students who have eschewed sensible occupations in order to become professional "lovers of wisdom": Al Anderson, Gerry Anderson, Ron Beanblossom, Duane Cady, Deane Curtin, Chris Dreisbach, Tom Gilbert, Ken Haas, Rob Hull, Dale Jensen, Mark Kispert, Susan Krantz, Rick Kyte, Ron Messerich, David Miller, Martha Phillips, Peter Wakefield, Gordy Wax, Tom Wilson, Dennis Wittmer.

Yet, in citing what he has done in this case we are not dealing with some thoughtless act, as if he could plead innocent on the grounds that he did not know what he was doing. My evidence is Joe's "A Decalogue for a Pedagogue" which states that "thou shalt create a devotion to thy science ...." Clearly he succeeded in what he set out to do as evidenced by the students listed above as well as many others who pursued their interest in philosophy after graduating from college.

In attempting to measure Joe by his thoughts where should I begin?

More importantly, where would I end? Joe has prided himself on being a generalist. Should I consider his thoughts on various issues in metaphysics, epistemology, ethics, aesthetics, or logic? Should I consider his views on Socrates, or Spinoza, or Dewey, or Rorty? Perhaps it is best not to begin. But even these unstated thoughts are related to his actions. My evidence is this volume of articles by his former students. They exhibit a wide variety of interests and views topically, historically, and methodologically. This diversity of interests and views is due in no small measure to Joe.

Perhaps, then, the final measure of this man is best taken by considering what he is in terms of the unity of thought and action. The appropriateness of this approach is especially compelling after our many discussions about the relation of form and content in beautiful art. True to his thoughts on this matter, Joe's calligraphic efforts are always contentful and thought provoking. One in particular which comes to mind is taken from Aristotle's *Nicomachean Ethics*, VIII, 3: "Perfect friendship is the friendship of those who are good and alike in virtue; for these wish well alike to each other *qua* good ... and goodness is an enduring thing." Joe takes seriously the virtues of which Aristotle speaks and has always wished his students well. I feel very fortunate, as do many others, to have known Joe not only as a teacher but also as a friend.

Ronald E. Beanblossom

Introduction

In mid December of 1990 I received a Christmas card from Al Anderson which contained, in Al's words, "a bold proposal:"

> Joe will turn 65 in July, so that seems to be a
> good time for those of us who owe him so much
> (and there are many) to say thanks. How about a
> *Festschrift?*

From Al's bold proposal plus the encouragement of several of the contributors below, Al, Ron and I conspired to gather those of Joe's former students who persisted through graduate degrees in philosophy and were teaching at colleges and universities. Our hope was to honor Joe for his influence on our careers and to meet one another to talk philosophy and swap Uemura stories. We thought we might present papers to one another and later collect them for a volume in Joe's honor.

We planned a gathering for July of 1991 but postponed the occasion because Maye broke her hip during the Uemura's trip to Japan earlier in the summer. Since Maye was essential in our effort to surprise Joe, we rescheduled the gathering for June of 1992 and got to work on the *Festschrift* thinking that we could get it together before the rescheduled celebration and present it to Joe as a tribute.

Joe has countless former students who have continued in philosophy in one way or another; some are teaching, some writing, some in graduate schools, others have gone into law, medicine, the ministry, a wide variety of professions throughout the country. Always their experiences with Joe have stayed with them and have made philosophy an important and vital aspect of their lives and work.

For the purpose of this volume we invited submissions from the twenty or so of Joe's former students who were undergraduate philosophy majors, did graduate degrees in philosophy and are currently teaching. The essays anthologized here reflect—but certainly do not exhaust—the range of interests and influence Joe Uemura has had. The invitation was for essays reflective of the work of each author; there were no thematic restrictions.

As might be expected, several of the submissions address issues in ancient philosophy. The collection opens with three essays each concerned with interpreting important arguments in Plato (Wakefield, Phillips, Cady). The next five papers fall into another area important to Joe's teaching: ethics. Both theoretical (Anderson, Kyte) and applied (Hull, Wittmer, Dreisbach) issues are addressed. These are followed by two papers (Wilson, Beanblossom) interpreting major American philosophers, another of Joe's interests. The volume closes with two essays in metaphysics, the first on the self (Curtin) and the final essay, from our honoree, on the ontological argument. We have included Joe's "A Decalogue for a Pedagogue" and notes on the contributors at the end of the book.

It would not have been possible to move from Al's "bold proposal" to the completion of this *Festschrift* without a great deal of help. I want to thank Mary C. Smith, Humanities Division Secretary at Hamline University, for her time, patience and skills in preparing the unified typescript. Thanks also to Dan Loritz, Vice President for University Relations and Jennefer Hill, Associate Director of Publications, both at Hamline University for their timely support in seeing this project through to publication. I am grateful to the contributors for meeting the various deadlines I needed to impose (although Al stretched them sufficiently to keep me worried). Finally, I want to thank Rose West for creating the Mark Kispert Memorial Endowment at Hamline University to honor her son. Mark had grown to love philosophy in Joe Uemura's classes at Hamline. After he was tragically killed in an accident while working on a Ph.D. in philosophy at Claremont, Rose West donated Mark's books to Hamline and established a fund to support philosophy. Her generosity has enriched the lives of philosophy students at Hamline. And it has helped to make this volume possible.

Duane L. Cady

On Forms

Peter W. Wakefield

*H*aving now spent the majority of my adult life studying Plato and Aristotle, I have often had the occasion to ask what quirks of fate lead me to such a rich, yet socially aberrant pursuit. Who turned me into this odd type, an ancient scholar? And when I ask such questions, one image rushes to the fore in my mind; it is that of a short and mirthful man, rubbing his eyeballs, giggling and goading, and all the while seriously challenging me and my classmates to defend claims that we had always taken as obvious. It is the image of Professor Joseph Uemura, encouraging me in opinions I had not previously explored, mocking me when I became too complacent, answering in riddles when I needed to find the answer myself, acting so odd that I could not help but find the life of philosophy intriguing.

And when it came to the specifics of philosophy, there was nothing odder than Professor Uemura's interpretations of the Platonic dialogues. What appeared on the surface, Professor Uemura would reveal as a riddle or a joke. What scholars took to be Plato's point, Professor Uemura would find reason to doubt. And that view or theory—whether concerned with justice or politics or the afterlife—that view which one might independently take to be the most promising and reasonable would be the one that Professor Uemura would find in the Platonic text. To hear it from Professor Uemura, Plato was a wise man who had anticipated his detractors and was laughing at them. To read Plato with Professor Uemura was to encounter an ancient mind that was nonetheless alive in its cynicism and its relevance. The wisdom and playfulness that Professor Uemura revealed in Plato defied the dryness of scholarship and affirmed the vital importance of philosophy.

In no text was this more true than in the *Republic.* Far from an ideal state, Professor Uemura insisted, Plato here presents us with "an antidote to all future utopias." How could this be true? As I took this controversial interpretation beyond Professor Uemura's classroom and attempted to explore it with other scholars I discovered that the implications of this reading collided with several points of Platonic orthodoxy. If Plato weren't concerned with an ideal state, why does the *Seventh Letter* reveal that he actually tried to institute something like the *Republic*'s ideal state in Syracuse? Again, if Plato didn't believe that philosophers could be authoritative rulers, why did he spend so much time in the middle books articulating a theory of separate forms, which, by their transcendence, would lend those who could rise up and encounter them absolute knowledge of goodness, justice and the other properties—the knowledge which is necessary to the good governing of others? If you throw out utopia, I was told, you undercut the motivations for one of the best attested aspects of Plato's theory, namely the separation of the forms. The forms must be separate, I heard. Aristotle himself states this, then goes on to argue at length against the impossibility of such separation. Aristotle was Plato's student and thus his most authoritative critic. If Aristotle says forms are separate, we must take this as "pukka" Platonic doctrine. So, forms are separate, and, I was taught, one main reason for separate forms is Plato's desire to render philosophical knowledge absolute, non-subjective and authoritative.

It was in the face of this argument, and with traces of Uemurian *chutzpa*, that I came to question the separation of the forms. Maybe Aristotle was wrong and Plato didn't separate forms after all. Or maybe he at least didn't separate them in the damaging way Aristotle thought; didn't separate them in the dualistic way assumed by those who also assume that Plato set out to justify philosophical authoritarianism. In a nutshell, this is the question, inspired by Professor Uemura, which has come to intrigue and plague me for these many years.

Suffice it to say it is a long argument. In what follows I will omit most of that long argument and go right to the heart of the matter. If forms aren't separate—if they are not independent entities existing in a realm different than the sublunary one which is revealed to us by our senses—then what are forms? Is there any evidence in the dialogues that the forms might be less problematic and more closely tied to the perceptual world than Aristotle leads us to believe?

Posing the Question in Platonic Terms

First, let us make these broad questions more precise. In *Republic* V - VII and the *Phaedo*, Plato clearly says that that which we perceive is inferior to the forms which we have knowledge of. The things we perceive are both double and half, both equal and not equal—in short, both F and not F. Aristotle captures this by saying that Plato subscribed to the Heracleitean view that the perceptual world is in flux. How is the flux, or unknowability, of the many Fs which we perceive meant to ground a theory which takes universals to be the objects of knowledge, superior in their reality to what we perceive?

Again, Aristotle tells us, apparently correctly, that Plato was insisting on the importance of investigating universal properties. But Aristotle also asserts that it was this concern with universals, combined with their separation, that led to the irrelevance of the theory of forms—one doesn't need forms to explain the things Plato wanted to explain, complains Aristotle; universals are in the things we perceive, not separate from them. Thus, we must ask, how can a theory of universal substance possibly be *directly* serviceable to *human* life. Our lives seem to revolve around particular, worldly items. How are forms related to these things? And how are we to describe these universals? How do we individuate them? How do we explain epistemological hierarchies amongst them? Finally, if we deny the separation of forms and claim, as I want to, that forms are *in* the particulars things which we perceive, don't particulars become similar to Human "bundles" of properties, given that Plato felt that universals, not particulars were true substances? How, if this is the case, do we individuate these complex "bundles" of properties?

And if one were to look to the scholarship on Plato's theory of forms, various other questions would arise concerning certain properties which forms are said to bear, many of which are felt to lead indirectly to the separation of forms. What is the fundamental principle of Plato's theory? (Is his language of paradeigmatism the primitive intuition of the theory, or is the talk of paradigms an illustration of something else?) Concerning the nature of forms, how do we explain their being F, but not not-F? (Are they non-relative relatives?) How do we explain their being "really real"? How their self-predication, their independence, eternality, immutability, and satisfactoriness for happiness? How do we explain the purchase forms give us on the world of perception? For that matter, what *are* particulars, and how are *they*, correspondingly, F and not-F, inferior, and never the same?

These are the questions. Now for some tentative answers.

The Fundamental Intuition of the Theory

Plato's views on forms spring from the principle that knowledge governs metaphysics, in the sense that a study of the world must begin with a study of mind. That is, in order to understand the way the world is—the world which any rational creature will have to deal with, the world as it is *presented* to us—we must obtain *knowledge* of the world. Knowledge is the mind's grasp of what is true. To be certain we don't mistake true belief for knowledge we must investigate what knowledge is. For Plato, knowledge is exemplified, encountered and identified in certain characteristic mental experiences. We know, for example, that three is odd, and that justice is good. Thus, we must study the mind—specifically what is involved in the mind's knowing something—in order to give an account which is true and therefore descriptive of some real element of the world. The real world is the one described by human truths. This is true either because "the world as it is presented to us" is so comprehensive and useful a notion that any parts of the world which might escape the purview of rational creatures need not be considered, or because the mind is fortuitously (or by divine grace) "in tune" with the way the universe is.[1]

Here, Julia Annas'[2] comment reveals, the discussion of *Republic* V, which is acknowledged as a *locus classicus* for the foundational arguments of theory of forms, Plato proceeds from intuitions about knowledge to draw conclusions about the structure of the world. All subsequent elaborations of the theory are subordinate to the discussion of *Republic* V, where Plato offers his most explicit and direct arguments concerning the nature of knowledge.

In this passage it becomes clear that because we are talking about "the world" as it is relevant to us rational creatures. For example, because the love of the philosopher is the "sight" of *truth* (475e4), "what is" in the world is identical to what is *known* by rational minds, or to what is true. We focus on our immediate and straightforward intuitions—those which are useful and explicable, yet so clear that they can't be doubted. These intuitions are knowledge. And in these intuitions we grasp reality.

The crucial point to observe is the order of the argument. When we can say that we *know* something, we can also say how the world *is*. By discovering what we can and do know, we discover the nature of the world. Plato calls any form "what is." But if one is to understand the nature of forms, it is crucial to remember that the form is real only insofar as it is known. Forms are first the entities the mind encounters when it *knows*. Because they are objects of knowledge, they also imply a "reality." But Plato's main concern is not to construct a dualistic ontology. For Plato there need by only one world—it's the one we grasp when we know, and its basic elements (its substances) are the basic elements of knowledge—viz. universal properties, or forms.

Viewed in this way, one can see why, contrary to Aristotle's claim that Plato's theory of forms had nothing to do with practical daily life (cf. *Met.* 992b8-9), forms are essential to human thought, and so to human life. They are essential insofar as they are the basic elements of propositions, which in turn are the stuff of knowledge. Hence, we can also say that forms are essential insofar as they constitute (or, in a metaphysical sense, *are*) the world which we do and can encounter, and with which we deal every day. When we look at the world and try to understand it, we do so by analyzing and dealing with the universal properties which are presented to the senses and hence to the mind. From this point of view we might say that forms are the world *for* us. But this is no subjectivism, for no rational creature will ever encounter any other world than the one revealed in knowledge, through forms. At the most fundamental level, forms are therefore in no way given to the "superhuman" nonsense of postulating a superfluous, transcendent realm—Aristotle's frequent criticism. Plato's theory, like Aristotle's, answers to "*phainomena.*" But, unlike Aristotle, Plato's fundamental intuition is that the world is revealed to us in what we know. By contrast, Aristotle starts with the intuition that the things we can point to are most real; then he must ask how such things can be known. Thus, Aristotle's problem is to define concrete individuals, whereas for Plato, the perennial questions concern how a mind can get to the truth or how much can be known.

The Nature of Forms

My points so far have been that Plato begins with an intuition about the one-to-one relation between knowledge and reality, then picks out certain paradigm cases of knowledge and finally by analysis specifies that knowledge is a matter of grasping the relations between forms. If I am right about this, I can now be more precise and infer that Forms are *definienda*.

First support of this claim comes from Plato's fundamental terms for them: "the F, itself" and "what each (thing) is." G.E.L. Owen describes how Plato intended to "bracket a term" in its context, then ask precisely what that term means, by itself, independent of its context.[3] Though Owen would reject my interpretation of forms, he is correct about Plato's method, and that method fits neatly with my interpretation. We can say that, as definienda, forms or relatives can be at the same time both relative (i.e. they include relativity in their nature, in their definiens) and *kath' hauto*, (i.e. they are properties considered by themselves—comprehensively, in the abstract, logically and analytically). Thus, there need be only one realm, only one world for Plato. We encounter the world through the senses, but if we are to know it (in other words, if we are to describe it as it is) we must break out experience of the world into its constituent parts—into the universal properties which we experience. Then we must define each of these parts, thinking of it by itself—not restricted to any specific contexts in which it might occur. And if this is the nature of forms, there is nothing controversial in saying that forms are *in* particulars. Forms are the basic elements of what we know about the world. Through defining a form properly we know the world. Taken together, forms exhaust what we can know about the concrete world around us. A form is an aspect of the perceived world as *clearly conceived*.

Complete knowledge of a form will involve knowing the basic property, the universal, which is the form. This knowledge of the form will involve knowing all of the form's relations to other forms. The latter will possibly entail some knowledge of all forms, and so of all particulars (see below). If this seems formidable, it is mitigated by; the fact that limited knowledge of forms is possible (and usually more useful), given the relevance or irrelevance of certain aspects of the form to the context of the investigation at hand. This is why knowledge of the Good (in *Republic* VI) gives Socrates pause, and why he is modest in his claims to wisdom: there may be an aspect of forms we haven't considered in the context we discussed today, which yet overrules the conclusions we have reached. On the other hand, the possibility of limited knowledge of forms explains why Socrates does not shy from certain knowledge-claims: justice is holy (*Prot.* 331a-b), justice is each part of the soul doing its own (cf. *Rep.* 443b ff., esp. 443e-444a), a just person is happier than the unjust (*Rep. passim*, e.g. 587e, 591b-c), and a just person does not escape from prison if his or her situation is similar to Socrates'.

Knowledge of Particulars

This is a trickier matter, since our common sense notions have to be revised when we see that we only know these "individuals" as a collection of properties, or of forms. Once again, the governing intuition is the difference between the way we perceive, and the way we know, *the* world. A particular, then, is a collection of forms, at a specified time, bearing (obviously) complex relations to all other properties, or forms (or, what is the same, to all other "particulars") at the time. The "size" or "identity" of such a particular-bundle, i.e. the extent to which any of its apparent properties can be reduced to other more basic forms or simply ignored, is governed by considerations of relevance. To know the particular as F (e.g. to know Simmias as tall, to know that he is tall, or, again the same thing, to know the tallness-in-Simmias) would involve a complex specification of the sense in which the particular is F. The magnitude of the task, and the fact that "particulars" appear as constructions, seems to have led Plato away from use of the notion of particulars and away from the study of particulars as a first step to wisdom. Thus, in the *Phaedo*, we move from the particular, "Simmias," to one aspect of Simmias, "the F in Simmias" (about which Socrates may not have knowledge, but is at least more confident in making significant claims), in order to clarify our investigation of the world. The *Republic* continues this move (or perhaps tries a new one—the notion seems to have been elusive to Plato, as to us) by simply speaking of "the many," and emphasizing how vague and shaky our knowledge of these complex collections is. Since our knowledge is limited we can't *say* whether they are or are not F. This limited knowledge and perception shows us a world which is (i.e. *appears,—phainesthai,* 479b) never the same.

Perception generally leads us to be concerned with "particulars." But Plato bucks this habit on the grounds that perception is confused, whereas knowledge is not only clearer, but also shows us the world as it is. In reinforcing the epistemological superiority of knowledge and its elements, forms, over the habitual perceptual concerns of most humans, Plato finally resorts to the metaphors of paradigms, and of images and dreams. But such terminology is nothing more than a graphic description of the two different aspects of our experience which Plato has discerned. The metaphors only serve to illustrate the epistemological distinction, they do not constitute a metaphysics.

Note that knowledge of particulars is not impossible. *Republic* 520c states that knowledge of the forms will allow those who have obtained it to go back down into the cave, into the world of perceived particulars, and to know what those particulars are, and of what (in regard to their of clarity) they are merely images. *Republic* 438b, meanwhile, suggests that Plato is well aware of the logic of relative terms. To *know* a relative property, one must be able to specify the context in which the property applies—e.g. Simmias is large in these respects, but short in these. Such a specification, if it is to be comprehensive, would certainly be difficult, but not impossible.

Moreover, such comprehensive knowledge need not always be impractical. As we can easily list all the possible two-place relations of three properties, A, B, C, (that is: A-B, A-C, B-C), so the *relevant* properties of a particular situation—e.g. justice, as it relates to escaping with Crito—might come into our purview in a single discussion in such a way that the matter is obvious to us (i.e. we know it would be useless to plumb for possible oversights; cf. *Crito* 54d-e).

"Self-Predication"

On Aristotle's interpretation, this is the fault that leads to the "Third Man Argument." But problems only arise if we assume any given universal term applies to the form in the same way it applies to particulars. Since any given form is only a constituent of particulars, this can't be the case. Yet the dialogues contain suggestions of self-predication. What intuition is reflected in these passages?

Anything is holy to which the definition of holiness applies. Thus, the definition applies (i.e. stands on the other side of the copulative "is") to the definiendum (holiness) in the same sense it applies to particulars, though a smaller portion of the definition may be relevant to the given particular. "A smaller portion," because if we only want to know about the large in Simmias in order to answer a limited question, we will not need the entire comprehensive definition of "large, itself." The extent to which a definition applies in practice is a matter of practically determined relevance. Yet, the definiendum is not another holy "thing," for then it would be described as both the whole and a part of the definiens of holiness, which would be logically impossible. So the TMA is defused. There *is* an equivocation here—on the way the definiens "applies," or in the way the form and concrete examples "are" whatever they are. But it is not a pointless or destructive equivocation, for this is a natural and informative way to talk about definienda. Further, this view makes obvious Socrates' claim that "hardly anything else could be holy, if holiness is not": if we cannot even define holiness, how are we to call anything holy?

Eternality, Perfection, Single-naturedness, etc.

Since forms are comprehensive of all the relations in which they stand, we conceive of them as describing all of reality through all of time. They stand in a comprehensive order, "fixed in nature," to borrow from Richard Patterson.[4] In this sense they are changeless and eternal; they supersede time, which is a function of the world as we perceive (not know) it. And in this sense they are perfect, for they lack nothing, and stand always in the same (comprehensive) relation(s), not receiving things into themselves, not going out into anything else (cf. *Timaeus* 52a). As remaining the same, forms are single natured. Since knowledge of such a form, analogously, will remain the same, it can be said to satisfy us more than other desire-satisfactions.

Mutability of Perceptibles

What is not known, but only believed or perceived, will *appear* to fluctuate because we cannot specify comprehensively the "what" that we are talking about. Perceptibles (i.e. the world as perceived), and so particulars, are in the same fixed order as forms (there is only one order), and so, would not be thought to change, *if* they were fully understood. (Of course, then, it would be inaccurate to call them mere perceptibles.) Perception is viewed by Plato as an immediate act: we perceive equals as equals, but make no other reflections on what the equals are equal to, in what respect they are equal, etc. As soon as we begin to reflect on such questions, forms come into play, the world takes on greater stability and we begin to understand. This view of perception perhaps strikes many today as odd, but it seems to underlie his denigration of perception and the conclusions he draws from the *contextual* mutability of the so-called "perceptibles;" in other words, of the world, as it is presented in confused, unanalyzed perception.

Causation and Forms as Explanations

On this point one can usefully follow the suggestions of Gregory Vlastos and Richard Patterson, among others. Their point is that forms are formal explanations. But, since Plato urges us to revise our view of reality, such that what is known (what is true) alone can be said to *be* (not some unknowable matter, or indescribable individual, as Aristotle suggests), these "formal" explanations take on new force. In a literal sense, forms "make" particulars what they are for us, since the latter are only known as bundles of properties, or forms. As we said, this will also play a role in what is called causation, since the total state of a "particular" at t_{x+1} is determined by its previous state, at t_x, and these "states" are nothing but the relations between forms. Thus, forms can be said to play a role in temporal causation, though it is important to remember that this notion of temporal causation is always a function of limited knowledge, not of reality. Since the relations among forms are immutable and fixed, from God's point of view nothing ever changes. (Somewhat problematically, in Plato's writings only the human will is implicitly recognized as free, to question or not to question—a point which leads beyond our scope.)

"Relevance" and the Independence of Forms (Plato's "Mechanism")

We come to the most controversial aspect of our interpretation, but it is also necessary. Against what we have said, one might object that we have left Plato open to the charge of sloppy subjectivism, a subjectivism which lets what one thinks, or knows, determine what is. Suppose human beings think wrong, or suppose that they are systematically deluded about what they know, in what sense can this "knowledge" then be said to determine what is? We need some explanation of how knowledge can be a standard, independent of, yet accessible to, any knower.

The concept which seems to underlie Plato's philosophy, in answer to this problem and others, is that of Mind, or rationality, considered universally and abstractly. That is, Plato seems to have a view of how rationality ideally would (or does) view the world in any particular case. In our investigations it is this (infallible) rationality which we try to approximate.[5] Mind in this normative and universal sense must include both the laws of logic, as well as some principles, akin to those of an ideal will or an ideal set of interests, which allow us to scrutinize claims of what is truly relevant or important to us as rational creatures in this world.

The notion is extremely convenient. It at once makes reality both directly accessible to thinkers and independent of them. It also allows Plato some leeway in determining the relevance of certain aspects of forms to a pursuit; leeway also in determining the relevance or worth of recognizing certain forms. "Given our ends, now, what would a rational person (*tis noun echon*, e.g. *Republic* 477e) say is relevant; what forms are we dealing with, and what aspects of them?" It is also this aspect of relevance which allows Plato to *identify* a form, or a particular, as such and so. (Thus, we can pick out a particular bundle, e.g. by speaking of those properties of Simmias relevant to our investigation of his tallness, even though this "individual" might not be as unique and unrepeatable as Aristotle might wish. What is crucial is that we fix the topics securely enough for our discourse at the moment.) A form, we might say, is an individual aspect of the world as Mind conceives it. The task is to understand how Mind does conceive the world. The route to this is dialectical discussion. This is to say that forms are specifiable and identifiable, non-arbitrary, even though they are also universal. Thus we have provided Plato's response to the suggestion we considered in Aristotle, that forms aren't the *kinds* of things that can be identified (and so discussed) non-arbitrarily.

Backed by this flexible (and, in another sense, rigid) notion of Mind, Plato seems quite comfortable treating 'being' as a form in one context, despite his concentration on forms which are obviously aspects of 'being' in other contexts. He is comfortable in *Republic* X saying he recognizes a form for every predicate, but then, in *Statesman*, ruling out 'barbarian' because it does not serve, rather only confuses, the ends of the discussion in that context; Mind conceives the world clearly. It recognizes only true predicates. But to see what this means we may have to pursue questioning in a certain context, and be confused by our aberrations, before we approximate to the rational view of the world.

So, Mind renders truth independence from the many minds, but allows for (apparent) flexibility in relevance between contexts—a flexibility which, if we are to remain consistent, must itself be explainable and understandable. This may involve no more than saying why it is important to investigate justice or weaving, or it may involve some "will" in the notion of Mind. I tend to think Plato would have pressed the former of these explanations, but I raise the problems and the speculation to bring us back to the controversy of this notion of Mind. The controversy is probably not so much in its force or articulation, as in the ascription of this "mechanism" to Plato. This is an aspect of Plato's theory which is assumed more often than it is articulated, or even mentioned. With this admission, however, we must present our documentation for crediting Plato with the view.

My mention of passages will be brief, for I think the notion is most often found in the form of innuendo, and this is something readers must find for themselves at each step of the dialogues; something which depends heavily on how one interprets certain key terms. To speak to this latter point, however, we can identify the main clues of this notion in Plato. They are (1) the notion that Mind (*nous*) orders things for the good; (2) the notion that truth, or being, in any context depends on the good; and (3) the notion that this true or good order is divine—i.e. identical with God. If these principles can ground the notion of Mind as a universal, abstract and normative standard, then the reader will already, I think, see where documentation can be found.

Whatever it says about Anaxagoras, *Phaedo* 97b-c clearly tells us that Socrates was fascinated with Anaxagoras' book *because* it said that *nous* "ordered and caused" all things. *Republic* VI is famous for its statement that the Good is the father of all knowledge and being, that is, I submit, of all rational order. When Socrates speaks of desiring the good, and of philosophy as the best of activities, we might argue, he has in mind the attainment of truth through approximation of *the* rational view of the world. The relation of the Platonic view of divinity to all this is yet more controversial.

If the praises sung to the Good in *Republic* VI are not enough to show its assimilation to the divine, to God, and so to an abstract and normative concept of mind, I would cite passages such as *Republic* 590c-d (where the reasoning element of the true philosopher is called divine), 492a (where reason in a bad environment will only be saved by some god), all the passages where Socrates calls his own knack for reasonable action a *daimon*, and the many others where true *logoi* and philosophy are intimated to be akin to godliness—i.e. they are akin to *the* rational order, the truth; akin to Mind.[6]

Separation

At long last we are in a position to see what Plato's demanding, leading language has forced many scholars to think through and argue about. Contrary to Aristotle and many others, we can now assert with some justification that forms are not separate in the way that particulars are separate from each other (i.e. spatially, or in a way discernable by perception). Further, forms are not independent of the world we live in, not in another realm. Forms are separate and different from "particulars" just in that the world conceived clearly and truly (i.e. *conceived* as it *is*) is "separate" and different from the world conceived doubtfully and vaguely (i.e. *perceived* as both F and not F).

Forms would lend us authoritative knowledge of the world, if we could attain complete knowledge of forms. But this is highly unlikely for anyone except a god. Since forms are in essence epistemologically clear, knowledge of forms comes only through life-long devotion to dialectical discussion, discussion which is constantly open to the challenge of reviewing and re-explaining old conclusions. Thus, knowledge of forms is more relevant to the daily actions of most of us in its elusiveness, than in its possession. The fact that we don't know the form of justice adequately should keep us from politics, not urge us to take up the rudder of state. This is the real lesson behind the separation of the forms. And this is the real paradox of the philosopher-king.

Or, so at least, Professor Uemura's provocative questions have led me to conclude. If there are still points to be discussed, still assertions to be clarified, still more philosophy to be done, I suspect that Professor Uemura, if not also Plato himself, will feel that his job has been well done. ≈

Phaedo 72E - 74a:
What Is the Point?

≈⏑≈

Martha Phillips

*T*he focus of this paper will be *Phaedo* 72e-74a, beginning with Cebes' suggestion that the theory of learning as recollection can lead to a proof for the soul's immortality and ending with Socrates' introduction of the concept equality (*auto to ison*). Cebes begins this section by presenting a valid argument for how learning as recollection can lead to the immortality of the soul. Simmias then takes over and asks, "What is recollection?" At 74c, Socrates provides two significantly different criteria, both of which would be necessary for a definition of recollection which could lead to a proof for immortality. The last part of this section contains a number of examples.

At first glance this section seems to be at least pointless, if not completely ridiculous. This is because neither of the criteria for recollection nor any of the examples presented here provide any meaningful support for a proof of immortality based on recollection. Why not? Anyone who attempts to use the human soul's capacity for recollection as evidence for the soul's immortality has to begin by showing that the human soul, in fact, has the capacity to recollect a form. One will further have to prove that the nature of the forms implies necessarily their existence in another world. From those two premises, the soul's knowledge of the forms and the separate existence of the forms, one can infer that the soul is capable of recollecting forms because it existed in the world of forms before it was born into·this world. The soul's ability to recollect forms, then, is necessary, although not sufficient, for eventually proving the soul's immortality in the sense in which immortality is supposed to be proven in this section of the dialogue. The two criteria for recollection presented here, however, do not include the necessary condition that recollection be defined as recollection of a form. Why, then, did Socrates present these two criteria and this set of examples? How does this section of the dialogue serve to improve and complete, rather than just distract from, the argument? In other words: what is the point?

In this paper, I will argue that each step in the discussion serves to move the argument forward. This is not, however, because Cebes' argument, or the two criteria, or the examples, provide any evidence for the immortality of the soul. Rather, the process here is via negativa: Socrates is providing possible criteria for and examples of recollection which could not possibly prove the immortality of the soul. The criteria and examples, in turn, demonstrate that some of the premises in Cebes' argument are false. However, by the end of this section the possibility is still left open for exploring some different examples which would avoid the pitfalls of these examples and lead to a more precise definition of recollection which might be able to provide evidence for immortality. The example of equality (*auto to ison*) is a more appropriate example and leads to a new, more refined notion of recollection. Socrates' purpose here, then, is to point out to Cebes the need to refine his argument, to point out to Simmias the need to find more precise criteria for defining recollection, and to provide examples of mental activities which Simmias and Cebes both call recollection but which could not possibly prove immortality.

Let me turn now to Cebes' argument as he presents it at 72e:

> ...there is that theory which you often described to us—that what we call learning is really just recollection. If that is true, then surely what we recollect now we must have learned at some time before, which is impossible unless our souls existed somewhere before they entered this human shape. So in that way too it seems likely that the soul is immortal.

The logical structure is this:

> 1. Socrates says, learning is recollection (L is R);
> 2. If learning is recollection, then what we recollect now we must have learned at some time before (If L is R, then RN-LTB);
> 3. If our souls did not exist somewhere before they entered human shape, then it would not be the case that what we recollect now we must have learned at some time before (If -[SEBHS], then -[RN-LTB];

> #3 is logically equivalent to:
> If what we recollect now we must have learned at some time before, then our souls must have existed somewhere before they

entered human shape (If RN-LTB, then SEBHS);

4. If our souls existed somewhere before they entered human shape, then our souls are immortal (If SEHBHS, then SI).

In order to grasp the form more clearly, here is the argument in abbreviated form:

1. L is R;
2. If L is R, then RN-LTB;
3. If RN-LTB, then SEBHS;
4. If SEBHS, then SI;
5. Therefore, SI.

The argument is obviously logically valid. That is, the conclusion is necessarily true if the premises are true. I will argue that the discussion from 72e-74a succeeds in showing that premises #2 and #3 are not always true, or not necessarily true. Therefore, logically speaking, they are false. Or, to put it another way, the arguments from 72e-74a show that for both premises #2 and #3, which are conditional propositions, it is possible for the antecedents to be true and the consequents false, thereby making the propositions false. The section from 73c1-73d1, which concerns the criteria necessary for an adequate definition of recollection, shows implicitly the falsity of proposition #2. The section from 73d2-74a1, which includes all of the examples, shows implicitly the falsity of proposition #3. At the end of the entire argument for immortality based on recollection, at 77b, Simmias and Cebes themselves question the truth of proposition #4. They recognize that the soul could exist before birth without it necessarily existing after death. But this is beyond the scope of the discussion here.

Let me turn, then, to the first proposition of the argument, "learning is recollection." The first point to notice is that the proposition, as given in the dialogue, is not quantified. We cannot tell if Cebes, or anyone trying to argue for immortality based on recollection, is making the claim that all learning is recollection or that only some learning is recollection. In order to provide support for immortality, only the second, weaker, claim is necessary: one has to show only that some instances of learning involve the recollection of a form in another world in order to support the claim that the soul existed in this world of forms before birth. One does not have to show that all learning involves recollection of a form in order to argue for immortality.

Second, it is important to notice that Cebes uses the term *mathesis* when he says, "learning is nothing but recollection." He does not use the word *episteme*. This is significant, because *episteme* would more appropriately be translated "knowledge." *Mathesis* implies a larger class: one could learn something through recollection, in some sense of the term recollection, without necessarily recollecting a form. On the other hand, if *episteme* is used systematically, every case of gaining knowledge through recollection would require the recollection of a form. This is the case because Socrates has presented the view through his dialogues that all of our real knowledge is, or at least includes, knowledge of a form. One will have to observe how these two terms are juxtaposed in the discussion to see if Socrates is suggesting the possibility that knowledge as recollection is a subclass of learning as recollection.

Third, in order for the argument to work, the first premise, "learning is recollection" must be true. At this point in the discussion, however, this is an ad hominem claim: Cebes introduces it as true because Socrates himself has often said it. It is certainly undeniable that Socrates has made this claim. Cebes is simply quoting what he has heard Socrates say, and the reader of Plato's dialogues is aware that Socrates has, indeed, made this claim, particularly in the *Meno*. It would be possible to go back to the *Meno* and examine carefully if Socrates seems to indicate whether or not he thinks the theory of learning as recollection actually proves the soul's immortality. But this would lead us away from our task here. The issue at this point in the *Phaedo* is to examine what Cebes believes Socrates actually means when he says, "learning is recollection."

The first premise in the argument, then, leads the reader to ask, "What is learning?" What is the relationship between learning and knowledge?" Are there cases of learning which are not instances of gaining knowledge?"

The second premise in the argument, to which I will now turn, focuses on the next question, "What is recollection?" Since the notion of recollection seems so crucial for making the connection between learning and immortality, let me first examine more carefully what recollection is. Recollection, by definition, includes minimally a kind of mental activity in which the human soul has some sensory experience, by which I mean, it takes in some data through one or more of the five senses, and this causes the soul to remember, or "recollect," something else. This is the most generic definition.

This kind of mental activity, that is, sensing one object and remembering another, certainly does not prove the soul's immortality. For example, I might look at my watch and recollect that I have to pick up my daughter at school in 15 minutes. This hardly proves my soul is immortal. Or, if one wants to include an example of learning as recollection, I could point to a yellow bowl and say, "yellow," point to a ripe banana and say "yellow," and point to a number of different yellow objects and say, "yellow," and after awhile my 2-year-old niece will remember, or "recollect" the association between the visual image and the word and will point to a ripe banana and say, "yellow." One could say that not only has she learned what the word "yellow" means, she has also gained knowledge of the meaning of the word yellow, in some sense of the term, "knowledge." However, this hardly proves her soul is immortal.

As I said earlier, in order for the human soul's capacity for recollection to prove immortality, two claims need to be proven: a) that the human soul, indeed, recollects forms; and b) that forms in the sense of the forms as objects of knowledge cannot exist in any form in this world. From there one can infer that forms exist elsewhere and that the soul also existed there before birth. In at least some cases of recollection, then, the soul is recollecting a form which it gained knowledge of before it was born into this world.

Cebes' second premise focuses directly on this issue, because it implies a certain definition, or at least a necessary criterion, for recollection,

> If learning is recollection, then what we recollect now we must
> have learned at some time before. (72e)

Cebes' assumed criterion here is that all cases of recollection are cases where the object being recollected was learned at some previous time. In this sense, Cebes is correct: temporal sequence is necessary to prove the soul's prenatal existence in a separate world of forms. Otherwise, if one eliminates temporal sequence and claims that the soul can recollect a form which it did not learn at a previous time, but which it is learning about at the very same time it is perceiving the world of sensible objects, then the soul's preexistence and a separate world of forms would not be necessary and would not be proven. Temporal sequence, then, is a necessary criterion for, or property of, the kind of recollection that proves immortality.

In the next interchange, at 73c, Socrates proposes two distinct criteria for a definition of recollection, a move which focuses the discussion directly onto the issue of temporal sequence. Socrates implicitly challenges whether recollection has to include temporal sequence when he presents a second description of recollection which eliminates it. Socrates' first description of recollection includes the necessity of temporal sequence which was implied in Cebes' second premise,

> ...if a person is to be reminded of anything, s/he must first know
> it at some time or another? (73c1)

But then Socrates goes on to present a "clarification" which is really another, more inclusive, criterion for recollection:

> Are we also agreed in calling it recollection when knowledge
> comes in a particular way? I will explain what I mean: Suppose
> that a person on seeing or hearing or otherwise noticing one
> thing not only becomes conscious of that thing but also thinks
> of a something else which is an object of a different sort of
> knowledge. Are we not justified in saying that he was reminded
> of the object which he thought of? (73c3-d1)

In the dialogue, Simmias indicates he is lost and Socrates goes on to present some examples.

What I would like to suggest is that this second criterion necessary for an adequate definition of recollection is significantly different from the first. It is no surprise that Simmias is lost. Not only is it a different criterion, it is different in ways which have a significant impact on whether the activity of recollection leads necessarily to a proof of the soul's immortality. The first criterion required that the object being recollected had to be known "at a previous time." Temporal sequence was necessary. In this "clarification," which is really a second criterion because of its significant difference from the first, temporal sequence is not necessary for a legitimate recollection to occur. Instead, the only necessary condition here is that the object being recollected is known "in a different way" than the object being sensed.

Another point to notice is that when presenting these two criteria, Socrates has now shifted from using *mathein* (to learn) to *epistasthai* (to know). The recollected object is not learned at a previous time and/or in a different way; rather, the recollected object is now described as known, either at a previous time or in a different way. I think it is important to note that Socrates made the shift without any reaction from the interlocutors, and this shift implies that the logical and ontological issues involved here do, in fact, apply to those instances of recollection which involve knowledge, or the recollection of a form. Throughout the rest of this analysis, I will point out places where I think Socrates' use of *episteme* has significant implications for the argument.

Socrates' presentation of two criteria necessary for a legitimate recollection leads to a closer analysis of all of the criteria necessary for recollection to occur. The activity of recollecting involves two distinct objects and two distinct mental processes. Every act of recollection involves one object from the world of sensibles, perceived by the soul through one or more of the five senses, and another object, the object recollected by the soul, along with the mental activity which brings that object to mind. This second mental activity, when it is referred to simply as "recollection," could be a variety of different kinds of mental processes: it could be the memory of an object one has learned about through perception at an earlier time, i.e. the ripe bananas, or it could be knowledge of a form, whatever that means.

Even if we narrowed our definition to include only those instances of recollection which involve knowledge of a form rather than mere memory of a perception, which Socrates seems to imply by using the word *episteme*, such a case could satisfy the conditions of the second criterion without requiring that the form exist in a separate world. The soul could recollect a form without having preexisted in a separate world of forms before birth. This is true because the second criterion leaves open the possibility that the soul could engage in both mental activities required for recollection, perception of a sensible object and knowledge of a form, simultaneously, while encased in a body and alive in this world. When recollection is understood merely as knowing something "in a different way" from the way one perceives sensibles, it does not necessarily entail the existence of the forms in another world and the prenatal existence of the soul in that world of forms.

I think Socrates' expanded view of recollection reveals the interlocutors' confusion and their inability to recognize exactly what criteria are necessary to define recollection in a way which will prove immortality. The expanded definition, if taken as true, refutes the truth of Cebes' second proposition:

> If learning is recollection, then what we recollect now we must
> have learned at some time before. (72e)

The antecedent of this proposition can be true and the consequent false. Suppose learning is defined as a kind of recollection and recollection is understood as gaining knowledge of the recollected object "in a different way" from the way one perceives the object which triggered the recollection. Given these assumptions, which are, indeed, what we have been given in Socrates' second criterion, one does not necessarily have to have already learned or gained knowledge of the object being recollected at some previous time. Using the second criterion, temporal sequence in the sense I have been using it, that is, the knowledge of the recollected object being temporally anterior to the object perceived, is not a necessary condition for recollection of a form.

Socrates then turns to a series of examples. His aim is to clarify the nature of recollection. In these examples, Socrates adheres to the condition of temporal sequence. In each case, the object perceived leads the soul to recollect another object which it knew at a previous time. Yet the examples still fail to prove immortality. In other words, the requirement that the object recollected be known at some particular time before the object perceived is not a sufficient condition for proving immortality based on recollection. This part of the discussion implicitly shows, therefore, that Cebes' third premise is false, because the proposition is based on a necessary connection between knowing the recollected object previously in time and the soul's immortality:

> If what we recollect now we learned at a previous time, then our
> souls existed somewhere before they took on human shape.

The examples Socrates chooses serve to make the antecedent true and the consequent false: in every example, on the one hand, the object being recollected was, indeed, known at a previous time, and, on the other hand, the nature of that object is such that the human soul must have come to know it after it took on a human shape; the soul could not have known it in a separate world of forms. Let me turn to the examples to show how this occurs.

I will begin by reintroducing Socrates' earlier discussion of the two criteria, showing each of the parts Socrates thinks are necessary in every instance of a legitimate recollection. Then I will analyze each example according to whether or not it satisfies all of these criteria. Particular emphasis will be placed on whether the examples satisfy the criterion of temporal sequence, the criterion of knowing the recollected object "in a different way," or both. First, I will repeat Socrates' presentation of these two criteria,

> ...if a person is to be reminded of anything, s/he must first know it at some time or other? (73c1)

> Are we also agreed in calling it recollection when knowledge come in a particular way? I will explain what I mean: Suppose that a person on seeing or hearing or otherwise noticing one thing not only becomes conscious of that thing but also thinks of a something else which is an object of a different sort of knowledge. Are we not justified in saying that s/he was reminded of the object which s/he thought of? (73c3-d1)

Here are the parts of every case of recollection:

> a) a person sees or hears or otherwise notices an object, x;
> b) s/he knows x;
> c) s/he knows another object, y;
> d) the knowledge of y is different from the knowledge of x, either because y was known at a previous time (criterion #1), or because y was known in a different way (criterion #2).

On the one hand, if there exist instances of the human soul's recollection of a form from a separate world of forms, such an example would, indeed, fit all of the conditions for a legitimate recollection presented here in the *Phaedo*. However, on the other hand I will show that it is also possible to give examples of recollections which fit all of the conditions given above without thereby proving the separate existence of forms and the soul's preexistence in the world of forms. The criteria set forth here, then, even both combined, are necessary but not sufficient for proving the soul's immortality from the nature of human recollection.

This leads to a further distinction. For the argument from recollection to work, the only cases of recollection which might lead to a proof for immortality would be those cases in which the object being recollected is a form. Only when the object recollected is a form would it be possible to go on to argue for the separate existence of forms and the soul's preexistence, although this would require further argumentation. When examining each example, then, the reader needs to ask if the object being recollected is, indeed, a form or not. If it is not, then the example will not prove immortality. If the example satisfies all the conditions of both definitions and yet the object being recollected is not a form, then we must conclude that the definitions are inadequate.

I think the text indicates that Socrates wants the reader to keep in mind that the argument from recollection is about how the soul gains knowledge, and knowledge is by definition knowledge of the forms, because he prefaces the first example by saying,

> A human being and a musical instrument, I suppose you will agree, are different objects of knowledge (*episteme*). (73d)

Socrates' choice of the word knowledge (*episteme*) here is very deliberate. Socrates' comment here seems to imply that it is possible to have knowledge of "a man" and "a musical instrument" which, because they are particular objects of perception, are not forms. At the end of the proof for immortality based on recollection, Socrates gives another account of what it means to know, an account which could be applied to particular objects,

> When a person knows, can s/he give an account (*logos*) of what s/he knows or not?
>
> Certainly s/he can, Socrates.
>
> Given this definition of what it means to know something, how could we apply it back to the example of knowing a human being and knowing a musical instrument?

Knowing a human being might mean being able to give an account of him. As is shown throughout the Platonic dialogues, Socrates gains knowledge of the people he meets by talking to them and finding out their thoughts, emotions, and character traits. If the definition of a human being is to seek wisdom, or knowledge of the forms, then the knowledge of any particular human being would be the knowledge of what he knows and does not know, and what he thinks he knows but does not really know. This is a fairly accurate description of what Socrates is doing here in the *Phaedo* and elsewhere. Given Plato's dialogues, then, this seems to be a reasonable interpretation of what it would mean to have "knowledge of a human being."

On the other hand, "knowledge of a lyre" would have to be different. Certainly knowing a lyre would include knowing what it is made of, perhaps, but most importantly it would have to include what kind of music it makes, since that is the purpose for which the lyre was made. "Knowledge of a lyre," then, would have to include most of all a critical evaluation of the quality of the sound it makes, just as knowledge of a human being, above all, must include a critical evaluation of what s/he knows and does not know, since knowledge is the unique purpose of human life.

Although this is only speculation, I have presented it in order to make clear the surprising difference between what a reasonable, Socratic interpretation of what knowledge of a person and knowledge of a musical instrument might mean and what Socrates actually says at this point in the discussion:

> Well, you know that a lover when he sees a lyre or a cloak or anything else which his beloved is wont to use, perceives the lyre and in his mind receives an image of the boy to whom the lyre belongs, do you not? (73d6)

This example is not even remotely an instance of knowledge of the lyre or knowledge of the person in the sense of being able to give an account of either. Let me break down the example into its parts to see more clearly exactly what it is an example of:

> a) the object perceived is a lyre, not the music the lyre makes, but only the physical object. The lover is not listening to the lyre, but rather is looking at it. What it looks like, however, is only indirectly related to its nature, and being able to give an account of what it looks like would not enable one to know anything about the kind of music it makes.
> b) the object being recollected is a young boy. The knowledge of the boy involved here is that the lover must have seen the boy play this lyre before. The lover looks at the lyre and recollects the boy.
> c) this example fits both criterion for recollection, because, 1) the lover's knowledge of the boy is, indeed, different from his knowledge of the lyre; 2) the lover must have known the boy before he saw the lyre (satisfying criterion #1); and 3) the lover knows the boy in a different way then he knows the lyre because he is looking at the lyre but he is only remembering the boy (satisfying criterion #2).

What we need to consider most carefully, however, is whether this example can qualify as knowledge in any sense. The lover looks at a lyre and recollects the boy. The boy, clearly, is not a form. This is not a case of the human soul perceiving one object and being reminded of one of the separately existing forms. Further, the connection between the lyre and the boy is purely accidental: there is nothing in the nature of the lyre which would lead to an association to the boy.

Rather, this man makes the association between the lyre and the boy because he happens to have seen the boy play it before and also because he happens to be in love with the boy. Someone else will not make the association because they have not seen the boy play it, or they might have seen the boy play it before, but they do not make the association because they are not in love with the boy and, therefore, do not think of him every time they see any object he has used before.

Socrates uses a play on the word "form" (*eidos*) here. He says that the lover is reminded of the form (*eidos*) of the boy which he has in his mind (*en dianoia*). I do not think Socrates uses the word in order to argue that the boy is, indeed, a form. Rather, he points out the different ways the word form is used in Greek and the need to distinguish between what "form" means in this context and what "form" as the object of knowledge means. Even if one were to argue that there exist human beings in Hades, and this is what Socrates meant, it is certainly not the case that one can fall passionately in love with the shadows in Hades. The association being made here between the lyre and the boy is based purely on erotic passion, something that exists only when the soul is encased in a body. It is an arbitrary association and a temporary association: maybe next week, if the lover is no longer in love with the boy, he will look at the lyre and not think of him.

If this is so clearly an example of recollection which does not support, much less prove, the soul's immortality, why would Socrates use it? There are a number of reasons, I think. First, Socrates wants to see if Simmias and Cebes are thinking critically or if, instead, they believe whatever Socrates says. Next, Socrates wants to know whether Simmias and Cebes understand the implications of the definitions. Do they recognize that the definitions can be satisfied without establishing the soul's ability to recollect forms from another world? Third, the example makes some very important logical and ontological points. It points out the inadequacy of the two criteria. It points out the inadequacy of the words "form" (*eidos*) and "thought" (*dianoia*) for proving immortality from recollection, since both words can be used to describe cases of recollection which do not prove immortality. One needs either to find other words or to make a distinction between a systematic and a non-systematic use of these terms. The systematic use would refer only to the forms (*eide*) as objects of knowledge and thought (*dianoia*) would refer only to those mental activities which lead the mind to some sort of objective truth. This example, however, points out the confusion which results when one does not make this distinction. Finally, this example serves to point out that even though one might still be able to argue that all learning requires the soul's transition from the perception of a material, sensible object to the recollected knowledge of a form, it is clearly also the case that some mental associations which are commonly called recollection clearly do not fit these criteria. Learning in the technical sense of going from perception to knowledge, is only one subset of the class of recollections.

The second example brings the discussion one step further along:

...just as when one sees Simmias, one often remembers Cebes. (73d)

This example satisfies all of the conditions of both definitions:

    a) a person sees Simmias and recognizes him;

    b) she is reminded of Cebes, whom she also knows;

    c) her knowledge of Cebes in so far as she is being reminded of him, is different from her knowledge of Simmias, at whom she is looking. Therefore, she is reminded of Cebes because she knew Cebes at a previous time (satisfying criterion #1) and she knows Cebes in a different way than she knows Simmias (satisfying criterion #2).

This example is ambiguous is some very significant ways. The important issue here is why someone would see Simmias and be reminded of Cebes. Where the reason for the connection was made explicit in the first example, it is left to the reader to speculate in this second example. Certainly the connection could be based on erotic passion, as was the case in the first example. Simmias and Cebes might be lovers, or the person seeing Simmias might even be reminded of Cebes because s/he is passionately in love with both of them. These alternatives are possible, but they are not the only possibilities. It might be the case that Cebes looks like Simmias, so seeing Simmias reminds the observer of Cebes. Or, the association could be based on the fact that Simmias and Cebes are friends and are often seen together, so seeing Simmias would lead anyone who knows them to think of Cebes.

There is another factor, however, which makes this example interesting and important. If we substitute either "Socrates" or "the reader of the *Phaedo*" for the person who first sees Simmias and then is reminded of Cebes, the example leaves open the possibility for a more sophisticated kind of mental association than we have discussed thus far. Simply from reading this far into the *Phaedo* dialogue, one could begin to understand how seeing Simmias might remind one of Cebes. One would have to interpret "seeing Simmias" more broadly, however. Assuming "seeing Simmias" can mean not only looking at him, but also talking to him, there are many instances thus far in the *Phaedo* dialogue where what Simmias says reminds the reader, and presumably Socrates also, of Cebes. For example, when one of them expresses anger over the fact that Socrates does not seem to be afraid of death, the reader is reminded of the other, because they both feel the same way. Also, throughout the dialogue, intellectually, they both accept the existence of the forms, without critically examining the nature of the forms or how their existence can be proven.

Without going into the dialogue, however, one can argue that Plato has given his reader "images in speech," rather than visual images, of both Simmias and Cebes. The reader of the *Phaedo* can read what Simmias says at one point and be reminded of Cebes, because they have similar emotions or similar thoughts. If the reader can make these kinds of associations, surely Socrates, who presumably knows them better than the reader does, can make even more complicated associations between them based on their emotions and knowledge. These kinds of associations would be closer to the forms, because they would be based on what Simmias and Cebes know and do not know, or each man's relative exposure to, or ability to recollect, the forms. However, the object being recollected in this example, Cebes, is still not a form.

In the first example, then, someone looked at an object and was reminded of someone with whom they were in love. The cause of the association was erotic passion. The example satisfied both criteria even though it failed to prove the soul's previous existence in a world of forms. In the second example, one person reminds someone of another person. The cause of the association is left ambiguous: it could be because they look alike, but the particular example chosen, Simmias reminding one of Cebes, leads the reader naturally to think about the kinds of associations between Simmias and Cebes which Socrates would be able to make, based on his knowledge of their souls. Also, it makes the reader aware of the kinds of associations s/he can make based simply on the image in speech presented of each person here in the *Phaedo*. Does this second interpretation, a mental association between two people based on the nature of their souls, satisfy the criteria Socrates presented earlier?

In the case of Socrates' association based on his previous encounters with Simmias and Cebes, the recollection would satisfy both of the criteria: Socrates is reminded of Cebes because he knew him at a previous time (criterion #1) and Socrates knows Cebes in a different way, because he is talking to Simmias and only thinking of Cebes (criterion #2). Ironically enough, however, in the case of the reader of the *Phaedo*, even though this association is more closely related to the human capacity for knowledge, hence to some view of the forms as what the human soul knows, the associations the reader can begin to make between Simmias and Cebes do not fit either of the definitions. The reader is not reminded of Cebes because s/he knew him at a previous time. Rather, the reader is being introduced to both Simmias and Cebes at the same time (fails to satisfy criterion #1).[1] The only perception in this case is the visual image of letters on a page leading to the formulation of a notion of Simmias' and Cebes" souls, their hopes and fears, their knowledge and ignorance. Although these are presumably the characteristics of a human being which would be included in their soul's immortality, this example of recollection does not fit the criteria. Rather than reject this kind of mental association between human beings based on the nature of their souls, however, I think the implied suggestion is that there is something wrong with the criteria.

Even though the second example leads the reader to a more sophisticated kind of mental association one might call recollection, the object recollected is still a particular person, not a form. Hence, this kind of recollection is not the kind of knowledge which can support an argument for the soul's immortality. Socrates could make many associations between Simmias and Cebes, he could know them in the sense of being able to give an account of them, and the reader could also think about how Simmias's and Cebes's souls are related without, thereby, proving the immortality of the soul. I think this is what Socrates is indirectly alluding to when he makes the next remark:

> ...and I could cite countless such examples. (73d)

Socrates is pointing out that the examples cited thus far are all based on the particular existential circumstances of an individual human being's life. They are associations from one particular object or person to another particular person, rather than an association between a particular object and a form. That is why there are "countless" such associations: we are born into a world of sensible objects and we learn about them through the use of our five senses. We can associate these objects in any way; the associations are not necessarily based on any kind of knowledge. They might be based on a short-lived passion or purely on coincidence. For example, if I got hit by a blue car, I might begin to hate the color blue. These kinds of associations are never wrong: no one can tell me I do not hate the color blue. I am merely describing my mental associations. These kinds of associations fit the definition of recollection without providing any support, much less proof, for the immortality of the soul.

In his next set of examples, instead of focusing on a subset of recollections that are closer to knowledge, Socrates goes in the other direction: the mental associations between the object perceived and the object recollected are farther removed from knowledge:

> ...can a person on seeing a picture of a horse or a lyre be remind-
> ed of a man, or on seeing a picture of Simmias be reminded of
> Cebes? (73e5)

These examples are all variations of the first two examples, but they are farther removed from knowledge. Let me break these examples down into parts:

a) the object originally perceived, in all three cases, is a picture, either of a horse, a lyre or of Simmias;

b) the object being recollected is a human being, either "a man" in the first two cases, or Cebes in the third case;

c) the examples satisfy both definitions because in all three cases, the person recollecting had to have known the person they are recollecting at a previous time (satisfying criterion #1) and they know the person they are recollecting in a different way, simply because they are not looking directly at them (criterion #2).

However, these examples are farther removed from knowledge than the earlier examples for a number of reasons. First, the picture of something is a visual image of a sensible object. Since seeing consists of taking into one's mind the visual image of a sensible object, seeing a picture consists in taking into one's mind the visual image of the visual image of a sensible object. Plato discusses this further in the *Republic*. In the *Republic*, Plato goes on to distinguish between the lowest level of being, represented by pictures and mirror images of sensible objects, the level he calls *eikasia*, and the level of being which consists of sensible objects, which he calls *pestis*. That distinction is implicit in this series of examples, although it is not clear, and it does not really matter, for the purposes of this argument, whether or not Plato had the Divided Line in mind when he wrote this section of the *Phaedo*. These examples are also farther removed from knowledge because the cause of the association between the object seen and the person recollected is so vague as to be completely ambiguous: the picture of a horse or the picture of a lyre could remind a person of "a man" for any number of reasons, or for no reason at all.

Even though they do not represent examples of recollecting forms, however, these examples serve to further the argument in a number of ways. Again, they point out problems with the original criteria.

Again, they show another subclass of mental associations which are called recollections but which are not recollections of the forms and which do not provide any support for the immortality of the soul. The most important purpose of these examples, is to introduce a class of recollections which begin at a level of reality farther removed from the forms, the sense-image of what is itself an image of a sensible thing, to the recollection, or memory-image, of a living human being, a level of reality one stop closer to the forms. This is important because if the argument ever arrives at a class of recollections which are, indeed, recollections of the forms, the process of recollecting will have to proceed from what is to Socrates a less real level of being, the world of sensibles, to what is to Socrates a more real level of being, the forms. These examples, then, advance the argument by defining another subclass of recollections from the perception of objects at a lower level of being to the recollection of an object at a higher level of being.

Socrates' last example prepares the way for the next step in the argument, the discussion of equality. The example is this:

And on seeing a picture of Simmias he can be reminded of
Simmias himself? (73e)

This final example advances the argument because it includes everything which was true of the previous examples but also includes two additional distinctions which are extremely important for cases of recollection which include the forms.

First, as was true of the first example, this is a case of seeing one object and being reminded of a person. The nature of the association, however, is clearly not based on erotic desire here, as it was in the first example. Second, as was true of the second example, this example is a case of recollection from one human being to another human being. In the earlier example, the human being who was perceived was different from the human being being recollected; in the example here they are the same human being. I suggested in the earlier example that the mental association involved might be based on what the two people look like, but it might also be based on something related to their souls: their emotions or thoughts. In the example here, when one looks at a picture of Simmias and is reminded of Simmias, the same ambiguity exists in the nature of the mental association involved. Although one is looking at an image of the physical image of Simmias, one might not be recollecting simply the physical image of Simmias. Rather, the person recollecting might be thinking about Simmias' soul, his emotions and thoughts. In general, when we look at a picture of someone and are reminded of them, it is probably more common to think of something more than simply what they look like, simply the physical resemblance. Third, like the third set of three examples, the example here is a case of recollection from the image of the physical image of Simmias to a memory-image of Simmias, either of what he looks like, or how he thinks, or some other aspect of his character.

Fourth, and most importantly, we need to examine more closely the nature of the association between the picture of Simmias and Simmias himself. Although this example allows for some ambiguity about whether the person recollecting Simmias is thinking only of what he looks like, or is thinking also of what he is like as a human being, there is one respect in which the example is unambiguous. This is the sense in which the association made is between the picture of a person and the person of whom it is the picture. This is very significant because this is the first example so far in this series of examples where there exists a natural and necessary connection between the object being perceived and the object being recollected. In the preceding examples, the associations made could have been entirely arbitrary: although one might have good reasons for seeing Simmias and being reminded of Cebes, one might also have bad reasons, or no reasons at all for making the association, and the recollection would still have satisfied the definitions given of recollection.

In this last example, however, one cannot merely "free associate." Rather the only people who can look at a picture of Simmias and be reminded of him are those who know him. On the other hand, one might look at the picture and be mistaken about who is supposed to be pictured there. In their words, it is possible to look at the picture, think of someone who one believes it is the picture of, and be wrong. In this example, there is only one correct association to make between the picture and of whom it is; all other claims are wrong. Those who can make the correct association are those who know Simmias, in some sense of the word "know," whether one means a casual acquaintance or a life-long friendship with

him. Although this is not an example of recollection from the perception of one
sensible object to the knowledge of a form, because Simmias is not a form, it is a
case of a recollection based on some kind of knowledge.

This is the reason this example leads us closer to the class of recollections
of forms than any of the other examples thus far: in the case of the recollection of
forms, there must be some natural connection between the object being perceived
and the form which the soul recollects. If there were no natural connection
between the object of perception and the object of recollection, the form, then anyone could associate any object of perception with any form and there would be no
difference between wisdom and ignorance. One person cannot look at a pair of
apples and be reminded of "two" while another person looks at the same pair of
apples and recollects "three" and they are both equally correct. The cases of recollection which include the recollection of a form, therefore, must include this condition: there must be a natural connection between the object perceived and the
object recollected. This is a necessary condition for an adequate definition of the
recollection of a form.

Finally, precisely because the picture of Simmias reminds someone of
Simmias himself, the person recollecting can make the claim that the picture is trying to look like Simmias and can evaluate the picture on the basis of whether it falls
short of a perfect likeness. These are distinctions which Socrates focuses on much
more carefully in the section on equality. I would like to make a few points here,
however, to show how the example of a picture of Simmias reminding someone of
Simmias leads into the issues Socrates focuses upon in the section on equality.

It is only the last example in which the object perceived is "trying to be
like" the object recollected. None of the other examples necessarily include such a
qualification and some, such as a lyre reminding someone of their beloved, don't
come close to fitting such a model: the lover does not want his beloved to resemble
a lyre. The condition of the object perceived "trying to be like" the object recollected, however, is very important for cases of recollection involving the forms. In
every case of recollection involving a form, the object perceived is, indeed, "trying
to be like a form" in some sense. Not only are objects of perception trying to be
like forms, but they also in some sense, "fall short" of being like forms, just as the
picture of Simmias falls short of being Simmias.

It is very important, however, to distinguish between two different senses,
or two different reasons, for why the objects perceived fall short of the objects recollected in all of these cases. In the case of the picture of Simmias falling short of
Simmias himself, the reason the picture falls short might be either a) because it is
not a very representational picture: it might be an impressionistic work or a
blurred photograph; or b) the picture falls short, even if it looks a great deal like
Simmias, simply because it is a picture and not Simmias himself. The picture does
not eat, breathe or think, no matter how much it may look like Simmias.

This is crucial for the examination of the difference between equal sticks and stones and the form equality. One might argue that the equal sticks and stones fall short of the form equality because the form equality is perfectly equal, while the sticks and stones are only approximately equal, or they appear equal at one time and unequal at another time, or they are equal in one respect, say weight, but not in another respect, say shape. On this view, one might go on to say that human beings never perceive cases of perfect equality in the world of sensible objects. Then where did they get this notion? From the soul's previous existence in a world of separate forms. On the other hand, if sticks and stones fall short of the form equality simply because they are sticks and stones and are not forms, it would be possible to go on to show that the human soul is capable of engaging in the activities of perceiving sensible objects and knowing forms simultaneously, without positing a separate world for the forms or a prenatal existence of the soul in this separate world. Any closer examination of this problem, however, leads necessarily into the section on equality and beyond the scope of this paper. At any rate, it is clear that at the end of this section, 74a, the reader is prepared to explore more closely the example of sticks and stones leading to a recollection of the form equality.

What, then, is the point of the discussion from 72e-74? As I have tried to argue throughout this paper, I think the definitions and examples discussed in this section, although they do not come close to proving or even providing evidence for the immortality of the soul, are important in advancing the argument. Although Cebes' argument is logically valid, its conclusion is not established as true, because two of the premises were shown to be false. The two criteria for recollection implicit in Cebes' argument that the recollected object must have been known at a previous time, and that it must have been known in a different way from the perceived object which initiated the recollection, seem to correspond to the unsystematic way the word "recollection" is used in Greek conversation, but were shown to be inadequate if one wants to use the soul's ability to recollect as proof for its immortality. The examples selected led one to understand the class of instances of recollection as containing a number of subsets, many of which are not cases of recollection which end in the knowledge of a form.

The entire discussion led the reader to examine the kinds of mental associations they make and to distinguish between: a) those which are accidental, arbitrary, or related to only one individual, and do not lead to common knowledge of any kind; and b) those which involve the soul's transition from the perception of one material object to the knowledge of a form. This, in turn, leads the reader to be more aware of the criteria necessary for a definition of recollection which will be limited to knowledge of a form. This also leads the reader to examine more precisely whether there are any mental associations they make which they would classify as knowledge of forms. After reading this section carefully, then, the reader is much better prepared for knowing what to look for in the discussion of the example of equality and knowing what kind of definition one must have in order for learning as recollection to provide evidence, and even proof, for the immortality of the soul. ∾

The Positive Argument in Plato's *Theaetetus*[1]

Duane L. Cady

*C*hances are that any student of Plato who turns to a secondary source for help in understanding the *Theaetetus* will be told that it is a "negative" dialogue. Father Copleston tells us that Plato's treatment of the problem of knowledge is "negative and critical,"[2] Frazer tells us that the conclusion of the dialogue is "negative,"[3] Bluck says the argument is "negative,"[4] and Crombie calls the result of the dialogue "negative."[5] The list of those who consider Plato's *Theaetetus* a piece of "negative" philosophy could go on and on. In fact, that this dialogue is "negative" seems to be the one thing about which most commentators of Plato agree. Glenn Morrow remains consistent with the tradition of interpreting the Theaetetus as negative when he argues that Plato, at the time the *Theaetetus* was written, "was not willing yet to show his hand... he was facing a problem that he did not yet know how to solve."[6] In this paper I will draw quite the opposite conclusion, namely that Plato laid his cards on the table. Far from being a "negative" dialogue, the *Theaetetus* shows us *why* it is futile to maintain dogmatically any doctrine meant to "capture" knowledge. We shouldn't expect Plato to come to a definition of knowledge in the *Theaetetus* because the point of the dialogue, and especially of the dream passage and the discussion following it, is to cure us of seeking and holding doctrines that purport to capture knowledge, not to indoctrinate us. That this is a justifiable position should become clear in what follows.

Having considered and rejected both the thesis that knowledge is perception and the thesis that knowledge is true opinion, Socrates and Theaetetus test another proposed answer to the question 'What is knowledge?'. This proposal again comes from Theaetetus:

> Oh yes, I remember now, Socrates, having heard someone make the distinction, but I had forgotten it. He said that knowledge was true opinion accompanied by reason, but that unreasoning true opinion was outside the sphere of knowledge; and matters of which there is not a rational explanation are unknowable—yes, that is what he called them—and those of which there is are knowable.[7]

There is considerable difficulty in translating the Greek (*logos*), translated above by Fowler as "reason" thus making Theaetetus' third proposed definition of knowledge read "Knowledge is true opinion accompanied by reason." This difficulty over the meaning of logos is readily admitted by most translators and interpreters of Plato. Cornford translates the controversial passage as "true belief with the addition of an account (*logos*),"[8] leaving the Greek term in parenthesis to indicate that there are several meanings of the term, while Jowett renders the passage as "true opinion combined with reason."[9] Indeed Plato himself indicates that the term has various meanings since at Theaetetus 206c Socrates asks, "Well then, what is this term '*logos*' [Cornford: "account"; Fowler: "rational explanation"; Jowett: "explanation"] intended to convey to us? I think that it must mean one of three things."[10] But it is just this fact that logos has several meanings that makes us skeptical of Socrates' neat refutation of Theaetetus' third proposal.

As Morrow points out, we weren't particularly surprised to see Socrates reject the thesis that knowledge is perception. His accepting it would have been inconsistent with his position in the *Phaedo* and the *Republic*. We never really expect Socrates to accept Theaetetus' definition of knowledge as true opinion either. To do that would have been to reject an earlier distinction made in the *Meno* (97), *Gorgias* (454d), and *Republic* (477e-478a).

> But when Theaetetus proposes that knowledge be defined as true belief accompanied by logos, we seem at last to be on Platonic ground. It at once recalls the statement in the *Meno* (98a) that true belief becomes knowledge when it has been fastened by reasoning. There is no obvious difference in meaning between saying that knowledge is belief "bound by reasoning (*logismoi*)" and saying that it is belief "accompanied by logos (*meta logos*)." Yet this last proposal is as decisively rejected as the two previous ones have been.[11]

But even more surprising than Socrates' rejection of Theaetetus' third proposal is the matter-of-fact way that it is rejected. Socrates takes up each of the three meanings that he says are "possible" only to find that none will make the third formula for knowledge an adequate one. The first possible meaning, Socrates tells us, would be "making one's own thought clear through speech by means of verbs and nouns...."[12] But this meaning will not do for it fails to distinguish knowledge from true opinion. After all, anyone, Socrates says, can put his thoughts into clear speech sooner or later; "he can show what he thinks about anything unless he is deaf or dumb from the first;"[13] and so adopting this meaning for *logos* will make all true opinion indistinguishable from knowledge. Secondly, *logos* might mean listing the parts or elements of a thing known. But one might guess correctly in enumerating the parts of a thing and surely we wouldn't want to say s/he had knowledge. The third and final meaning of *logos* considered in the *Theaetetus* is "the ability to tell some characteristic by which the object in question differs from all others."[14] But this clearly will not do since "having a true opinion about something entails, to some extent at least, being able to give the characteristics that mark that thing off from other things."[15] If we require that one *knows* the differentia, then knowledge is defined as true opinion plus knowledge (of a differentia), an obvious circularity.

If we assume all of these objections to the possible meanings of *logos* are air-tight, they still do not decisively refute Theaetetus' third proposed definition of knowledge as true opinion plus a *logos* unless, as Morrow points out, it is clearly demonstrated that these are the only possible meanings of *logos*. And this demonstration, a necessary link in the argument against the third proposed definition, is wanting.

> ...Socrates' enumeration is clearly not exhaustive and it is hard to believe that Plato thought it was. The word *logos* has a signification more varied than that of almost any other term in Greek philosophy. Even in Plato's own dialogues there are examples of its use in many meanings other than the three mentioned here. It sometimes means definition; sometimes proposition, or statement; sometimes theory; sometimes argument or dialogue; sometimes thinking or inner dialogue; and sometimes mathematical proportion. There are examples of most of these in the Theaetetus itself....[16]

In light of this, we surely ought to be a bit skeptical of Socrates' "exhaustion" of the possibilities and the concluding rejection of Theaetetus' third proposal.

It is most interesting to note that Socrates' dream immediately follows Theaetetus' introduction of the third proposed definition of knowledge, and that Socrates offers it as an alternative statement of that third view. But in his refutation of Theaetetus' third proposal by rejecting each of the three "possible" meanings of *logos*, the dream and the point it makes are not mentioned. These facts, together with the realization that Plato must have known that there are more than three possible meanings for *logos*, make us curious as to the importance of the dream in our interpretation of the dialogue and its "negative" conclusion. Plato must have thought it important to Theaetetus' third proposal since both the dream and the third definition are stated together. My task is to make the relation between the dream and the final proposed definition of knowledge more clear.

At *Theaetetus* 152c, amid a discussion of Protagoras' "man is the measure of all things," Socrates asks Theaetetus: "Perception, then, is always of that which exists and, since it is knowledge, cannot be false?"[17] But, "what is this, we may well ask, but the definition that Socrates and Theaetetus are supposed to be hunting for? That is, knowledge is infallible apprehension of being.... This hidden definition is used again several pages later (160cd) and at 196e Socrates chides himself and Theaetetus for saying so much about knowledge when they are supposed to be ignorant of what it is."[18] This "hidden" definition is certainly consistent with the descriptions of knowledge given in other Platonic dialogues. For example, in *Republic* V Socrates says that "knowledge pertains to that which is,"[19] and in the *Parmenides* he agrees that knowledge itself, the essence of knowledge, will be knowledge of that reality itself, the essentially real."[20] And in *Republic* VI Socrates says that when the soul is "firmly fixed on the domain where truth and reality shine resplendent it apprehends and knows."[21]

There are, of course, interpretations like that of Cornford which infer from the "hidden" definition of knowledge as the infallible apprehension of being and from the very absence of any explicit references to the theory of Forms the conclusion that knowledge is apprehension of Forms. To Cornford, the "Forms are excluded in order that we may see how we can get on without them; and the negative conclusion of the whole discussion means that, as Plato had taught ever since the discovery of the Forms, without them there is no knowledge at all."[22] Cornford concludes his commentary on the dialogue by telling us that "the Platonist will draw the necessary inference."[23] There seem to me to be problems with Cornford's interpretation. First of all, as Randall points out, "Plato was not a Platonist any more than Jesus Christ was a Christian. Platonism is a disease you are likely to catch if you read Plato without much imagination. And Plato was immune."[24] So if we approach the dialogue without reading Platonism in, we might ask, "What is the non-Platonist to make of it?" Secondly, even if Plato was implying that "true knowledge has for its object things of a different order—not sensible things, but intelligible forms,"[25] *that* certainly wouldn't solve all of the problems and finally answer the question 'What is knowledge?'. After all, we would still need answers to questions like 'What is apprehension?', 'How can we be sure our apprehensions are infallible?', and 'How do we know our apprehension is really of a Form?'. Admitting that the object of knowledge is the Forms does not answer the question with which the dialogue deals. As Socrates says, "the question you were asked, Theaetetus, was not what are the objects of knowledge."[26] Besides, "the inference which Cornford attributes to Plato is not valid. If knowledge of concrete individuals cannot be defined, it does not follow that there are Forms. Perhaps knowledge is indefinable or perhaps there is no knowledge."[27]

At any rate, Socrates does seem to give a "hidden" or inconspicuous answer to the very question with which the dialogue deals and which seems to go unanswered at the close of the dialogue. And that "hidden" answer is not put through the tests that the proposed definitions of Theaetetus go through—at least not explicitly. Perhaps by examining this "hidden" answer to the question of the dialogue we can find clues as to the strategy behind the dream and the passages that follow it.

It is nothing new to us to see Plato describing knowledge as infallible. A true belief, whether about forms or about objects of sense, must be "incapable of being false if it is to count as knowledge."[28] If we can find the method by which true beliefs are transformed into beliefs that are necessarily true, incapable of being false, we should be on our way to defining knowledge. It is at this point that I find Morrow's interpretation especially impressive. As he points out, Plato does little that is in vain. It is no accident that Theaetetus is a mathematician and that Euclides praises his intellectual abilities so highly at the opening of the dialogue. For it is the mathematicians at the time of Plato whose professional occupation appears to have been just this transformation of true belief into necessarily true beliefs.[29] Clearly Socrates is impressed with Theaetetus' work toward a general definition of irrationals, and asks Theaetetus to take his answer about the roots as a model and just as he embraces all of them in one class, though they were many, he should try to designate the many forms of knowledge by one definition."[30] Thus, the mathematical method is to be the model for the search for a definition of knowledge. The mathematician frequently begins with a proposition that seems intuitively true. The goal of the inquiry is to find a proof of it. Unlike the objects of sense, the objects of mathematics and their definitions are precise and invariable.

> But there is more to mathematics than the precision of its defin-
> itions and the consequent clearness of its theorems. These theo-
> rems have the notable character of not being subject to question,
> at least not by any competent mathematician, given the entities
> with which they are concerned and the procedures by which the
> theorems have been established. They have exactly that charac-
> ter of necessity, of compelling the hearer's assent once he has
> accepted the definitions and the premises about them, which
> Plato's theory of knowledge demanded. The procedure of the
> mathematician, therefore, is an example of the kind of *logos* that
> in Plato's opinion would transform a true belief into
> knowledge.[31]

At any rate, Plato's high regard for Theaetetus, the method of mathematics, and the infallible conclusions that follow from mathematical reasoning are explicitly expressed in the dialogue. There is no doubt that Plato wanted to draw the reader's attention to mathematical reasoning.

The mathematicians of Plato's time were not only interested in extending the number of their theorems, but also in perfecting their methods and in making their procedure and results more systematic. It seems safe to infer, with Morrow, that the method of mathematicians at Plato's time was an early form of the procedure presented in Euclid's *Elements*. The method in the *Elements*, that of establishing theorems by deduction from premises previously established or assumed, is presented as the culmination of the efforts of previous mathematicians. The premises of this deductive method are either derived from more elementary premises or are themselves undemonstrated starting points. Trust in the infallibility of deductive implication, avoidance of contradiction, and a clear understanding of the terms related by implication are all features not only of mathematicians, but also of the Socratic method as it is presented in the early dialogues. But unlike the mathematicians who were attempting to establish a theorem as a necessary truth, Plato's Socrates, in the early dialogues, intends to show inconsistencies or absurdities of positions that are being tested, the result being "Socratic Wisdom," i.e., a conviction of ignorance.[32]

Many interpreters, Morrow included, see a profound change somewhere in the so-called "middle" dialogues, of which the *Theaetetus* allegedly is a part, claiming that dialectic begins at this point to be used for constructive purposes to establish propositions or beliefs. Whether this is true is difficult conclusively to establish, but it seems undeniable that Plato recognized more and more clearly the important role of premises, whether demonstrated or hypothesized, in the deductive method of reasoning. And he certainly realized that all premises were ultimately grounded in starting points, either assumed or hypothesized. An example of his use of deduction based on hypothesis is his argument for the immortality of the soul in the *Phaedo*.[33] He has Socrates tell us, "I am assuming the existence of absolute beauty and goodness and magnitude and all the rest of them. If you grant my assumption and admit that they exist, I hope with their help to explain causation to you, and to find a proof that the soul is immortal."[34] Realizing that the hypotheses themselves need some substantiation, Plato has Socrates go on, "And when you have to substantiate the hypothesis itself, you would proceed in the same way, assuming whatever more ultimate hypothesis commended itself most to you, until you reached one which was satisfactory."[35] Thus Plato knew, when he wrote the *Phaedo*, that all demonstrated conclusions ultimately rest on undemonstrated hypotheses or assumptions.

While impressed with the rigor and certainty of the mathematician's method, Plato also saw problems. Though not of particular interest to the mathematician, the problems were such that the philosopher could not ignore them. This is precisely why Plato, though clearly including mathematicians in the prestigious top half of the divided line, couldn't use mathematics as an example of the highest form of knowledge. Whereas mathematicians start from axioms and hypotheses which are taken for granted and not called into question, philosophers, placed one notch above mathematicians, earn their place because it is their business to test the truth of the hypotheses and axioms of the lower sciences.[36] Mathematicians and geometers and others in the "lower" sciences

> postulate the odd and the even and the other various figures and three kinds of angles and other things akin to these in each branch of science, regard them as known, and, treating them as absolute assumptions, do not deign to render any further account of them to themselves or others, taking it for granted that they are obvious to everybody. They take their start from these and pursuing the inquiry from this point on consistently, conclude with that for the investigation of which they set out.[37]

The philosopher, however, treats assumptions "not as absolute beginnings but literally as hypotheses, underpinnings, footings, and springboards so to speak, to enable it to rise to that which requires no assumption...."[38] Morrow, pointing out a passage from *Republic* VII, 533cd, makes Plato's criticism of the mathematical method even more obvious: "geometry and the sciences dependent on it grasp something of being; but we see that they dream about it, being unable to see it with waking eyes, so long as they use hypotheses which are unquestioned, of which they are unable to give a *logos*. For if the beginning is what one does not know, and the end and what comes between is woven from what one does not know, by what device can such consistency be converted into knowledge?"[39]

In light of all of this, it should be clear why Plato, through the mouth of Socrates, did not give a meaning of *logos* that would make Theaetetus' third proposed definition of knowledge an adequate one. The deductive proof from premises, the mathematical method, was the model, the paradigm case of giving a *logos*. But the model method, applied to a formula or definition of knowledge, carries with it a flaw. The premises, the assumptions, the hypotheses, the starting points *don't* have a *logos*; they don't ultimately rest on demonstration from premises. The mathematicians and Plato knew that deduction has to start form undemonstrated assumptions. We just couldn't keep demonstrating or proving our premises *ad infinitum*. And if, as philosophers, we had to look for more ultimate justifications for the starting points, we certainly couldn't use the method of demonstration in that search.

Socrates dream, we can now finally come to see, is simply another statement of the dilemma of reasoning from premises to conclusion. It is probably presented in a dream because, as Crombie puts it, "it is a post-Socratic theory and Plato's historical conscience is pricking him."[40] We can now quote the dream passage in full:

Socrates: I seem to have heard some people say that the "firsts," as were the elements of which we and all things consist, have no *logos*. Each of them just by itself can only be named (or asserted); nothing else can be said of it, neither that it exists (or is a fact) nor that it does not exist (or is not a fact), for we should at once be adding to it existence (truth) or non-existence (falsehood), and we ought to add nothing if we are to express just it alone. Neither "just," nor "it," nor "alone," nor "each," nor "this," ought to be added, nor any other of such terms, of which there are many. These terms circulate freely and are applied to everything, though they are different from that to which they are applied; whereas if it were possible to describe a "first" by a logos peculiar to itself, we ought to speak of it without any of these other terms. The fact is, it is impossible to describe any of the "firsts" by a *logos*; for nothing else belongs to it; it can only be named (or asserted), since a name is all that it has. As for the things composed of them [i.e., of the firsts], just as they themselves are complex, so their names when woven together produce a *logos*, for a *logos* (demonstration?) is precisely a texture of names (propositions?). Consequently the elements (*stoicheia*, letters) are without *logos* and unknowable but can be perceived, while compounds (syllables) can be known and pronounced and you can have a true belief about them. When then a man gets hold of a true belief about something without a *logos* his mind gets it right but he does not know it; for he who cannot give and receive a *logos* with regard to a thing is ignorant of it. But when he has also got hold of a *logos*, then this becomes possible for him and he is fully knowing.[41]

Confusing as the details of the dream passage may appear, the central theme seems clear enough. It is the problem of "firsts" or "elements" for which no *logos* can be given, and yet which make up the complexes for which a *logos* can be given. Both Morrow and Fowler are careful to note that the term (*stoicheia*), translated above as "elements," had several meanings in Plato's time. One use of *stoicheia* was to designate the basic premises of arithmetic and geometry. Mathematicians of the time, like Theodorous and Theaetetus, would probably understand it in this sense in the dream passage. "The dream would then naturally be taken as expounding the basic character of geometrical procedure; that is, all demonstration is a texture of propositions composed eventually of simple premises which, being simple and ultimate, cannot be demonstrated and therefore cannot be know to be true."[42] Taking *stoicheia* in this sense, the dream passage is clearly another statement of the dilemma of reasoning by demonstration from premises.

But *stoicheia* was also a general term for "element," or part of a complex and even became the common word for letter of the alphabet. Confusion over various meanings of *stoicheia* probably contribute to the difficulty in interpreting the dream passage, and may account for the differences between various views as to how to read the dream. Morrow tries to account for the various meanings of *stoicheia*, and avoids commitment to any one meaning. His point is that Plato was saying something applicable to various types of analysis. Had Plato been after specific analysts he would have identified them for us. As Morrow puts it, Plato, in the dream, has "constructed a kind of model applicable alike to all fields in which analysis is practiced. His intent may be expressed schematically as follows:[43]

ANALYSES:	PHYSICAL	LEXICAL	GRAMMATICAL	MATHEMATICAL
COMPOUNDS	THINGS	WORDS	STATEMENTS	DEMONSTRATIONS
"FIRSTS"	PARTS	LETTERS	WORDS (NAMES)	PREMISES

All four of these types of analysis have as their aim reaching the elements by which the compound under examination is to be explained. "The dream therefore is a theoretical model that exhibits the common nature of various types of analysis."[44]

The problem with any form of analysis that tries to explain compounds by means of unanalyzable elements is, according to Plato, that of understanding or knowing a compound by means of unknown and unknowable elements. As Socrates put it in the *Republic*, "if the beginning is what one does not know, and the end and what comes between is woven from what one does not know, by what device can such consistency be converted into knowledge?"[45] This same criticism is voiced in the passage immediately following the dream. The part of the theory given in the dream passage that Socrates finds "unsatisfactory" is just that which "seems to be the cleverest; the assertion that the elements are unknowable and the class of combinations is knowable."[46] The refutation given is clear. There are just two possibilities. Either the syllable (compound) is identical with its letters (elements), *or* it is an entity in itself that has arisen from the combination of letters (elements). In the first case, if we know the syllable (compound), we must also know the letters (elements) since the syllable is nothing but the letters that make it up. In the second case, the syllable, since it has a nature of its own and a "single concept,"[47] is as unknowable as the letters. Thus either the elements and compounds are both knowable or they are both unknowable. "This refutation is applicable to any form of analysis that professes to understand a complex whole by reducing it to unknowable constituent parts."[48]

At this point Morrow concludes, as I pointed out earlier, that Plato had hit upon a problem that he did not know how to solve, and thus fails in his attempt to give us a definition or formula for knowledge. Morrow finds it "remarkable how serenely indifferent Plato seems to this particular problem that has so bothered his commentators."[49] I don't find it remarkable at all. What is remarkable to me is that Morrow did not see the further implications of his own view, namely that Plato was trying to show the dilemma that any attempt at analyzing knowledge into constituent parts results in. Morrow, who so impressively accounts for every detail of the dream passage, can't account for Plato's "indifference" to this problem of any formula meant to capture knowledge. Of course Plato is indifferent. He is not frustrated over his "failure" to set forth a doctrine that once-and-for-all answers the question 'What is knowledge?' because he understands the dilemma that any attempt in setting forth such a doctrine would result in. He isn't trying to set forth a doctrine capturing knowledge and thus he can't be said to fail. What he *is* trying to do is to show us why a philosopher should avoid a dogmatic answer to the question 'What is knowledge?'. To expect Plato to set forth the answer to this question is to miss his point. The "indifference" that Morrow attributes to Plato should itself be telling. If Plato were frustrated by the problem it might suggest that he thought the answer could be conclusively given but that he himself couldn't give it. And yet Socrates is anything but frustrated at the close of the dialogue, and seems in no way unhappy or dissatisfied with concluding that at least we have the wisdom not to think we know that which we do not know.

Knowledge, for Plato, must be infallible. The method by which truths are proved to be incapable of being false is that of demonstration from premises. But if knowledge is defined as "true belief plus a demonstration," then to *know* the premises on which a demonstration is based is to be able to demonstrate them. This demonstration of premises would entail further premises in need of demonstration. Thus the demonstration would either continue *ad infinitum* or would have to have undemonstrated premises or assumptions as starting points. If the starting points are undemonstrated, then, by the definition of knowledge, they are unknown. But if they are unknown, we cannot know something complex in terms of them. And if they are known we must abandon our definition of knowledge as "true belief plus a demonstration," since they are not demonstrated. The part of the definition that guarantees infallibility, a necessary condition of knowledge for Plato, is demonstration. But demonstration, for all its rigor, rests on some undemonstrables, some hypotheses, some assumptions, some unknowns. Plato is thus trying to show us why seeking and maintaining, via the method of reductive analysis, doctrines that answer the question "What is knowledge?" is unphilosophic. Philosophers earn their higher place on the divided line just because they do not regard assumptions in a demonstration as absolute. Rather, they treat their assumptions "not as absolute beginnings, but literally as hypotheses, underpinnings, footings, and springboards...."[50]

The *Theaetetus* ends, then, with Socrates and Theaetetus agreeing that the latter is no longer "pregnant and in travail with knowledge." Everything has been brought forth with the help of Socrates midwifery and yet nothing is "worth rearing"—the final answer has not been found. But the inquiry was certainly not a waste of time. Two things were to be gained from it. First, if Theaetetus ever again conceives other thoughts, at least he will "be pregnant with better thoughts than these by reason of the present search...."[51] And the second thing to be gained is that "if you remain barren," Socrates tells Theaetetus,

> you will be less harsh and gentler to your associates, for you will have the wisdom not to think you know that which you do not know. So much and no more my art can accomplish....[52]

Plato meant to cure us of, not encourage, attempting to analyze knowledge into its constituent parts. The original question of the *Theaetetus*, "What is knowledge?", does not get a final answer in Plato. And, as Ryle tells us, "it has not got it yet."[53] If the above interpretation of the *Theaetetus* is correct, we should not have expected analysis to provide a solution to that problem, according to Plato.

～

The Ethics of Being

Albert A. Anderson

Characters:
Scott, a businessman
Oiron, a professor of philosophy

Scene:
Oiron's house

Oiron: Scott, you look tired. Are you still fighting with The Power Company over their plans to build a substation in your neighborhood?

Scott: No, they have postponed construction indefinitely.

Oiron: Then you have won. Congratulations! I'm sure your efforts were an important factor.

Scott: I don't know about that. It may just be a function of the economy. Right now it's philosophy that keeps me awake at night. The more I think about our conversation last month, Oiron, the more I'm confused and disturbed by our conclusions. I have been spending half the night reading books on ethics.

Oiron: You never cease to amaze me, Scott. I don't know how you can be so successful in business during the day the then remain awake to read philosophy at night.

Scott: It's your fault. I was sleeping just fine until our dinner conversation about the ethics of power. You have forced me to think again about my view of ethics. Those of us in the investment business confront ethical questions every day, so it's extremely important to keep a clear head about what is right and wrong. But even apart from my professional life, it is important for me personally to think clearly about such fundamental questions. In our dinner conversation with James last month, I became more sure than ever that ethical egoism is wrong. By the way, what happened to James? I brought a bottle of his favorite wine to go with dinner.

Oiron: He just called to say that he must work all evening to prepare a case that goes to court tomorrow. We can save that bottle for another occasion if you can put up with a selection from my cellar.

Scott: As usual, you know a lot more than you let on. Your taste in wines is excellent. But what I most desire is for you to help me think again about the foundations of ethics.

Oiron: Let's talk while we eat.

Scott: I wish I had taken more philosophy when I was young, because I really don't know the background of issues and concepts which keep coming up as I read. Please be patient if I ask naive questions.

Oiron: Philosophy, like red wine, gets better with age. Anyway, I am always delighted to find someone as eager as you are about philosophical matters. Ask any questions you please.

Scott: As you know, I have been attracted to Kant's ethics. But when we talked before, you raised some really troubling questions about the overall coherence of his philosophy. What I like most about Kant is his emphasis upon autonomy, but I now realize that the gulf between the realm of freedom and the world of nature presents some difficulties. You object to the gulf between his *a priori* foundations and the empirical world. It never occurred to me to question that separation. What I don't understand is where that distinction came from in the first place.

Oiron: Historians of philosophy may disagree, but I think the real culprit is Hume. Even more than Hume's preference for the life of action over idle contemplation, it was his attack upon the theologians which was especially influential in establishing this distinction in modern philosophy.

Scott: What do you mean?

Oiron: In *An Enquiry Concerning Human Understanding*, Hume says explicitly that his goal is to free us from the "abstruse questions" of metaphysics.[1] This, he said, could only be done by cultivating true metaphysics, by considering the nature of human understanding, and showing that it is simply not fitted for proving matters such as the existence of God and the immortality of souls.[2]

Scott: I recall his attack upon Descartes' ontological argument for God's existence, but I don't remember the particulars.

Oiron: To make his case, he questions Descartes' most basic assumptions and replaces them with his own. He claims that all "perceptions of the mind" can be divided into two classes; ideas and impressions. In opposition to the view that some ideas are innate, he insists that every idea "is copied from a similar impression."[3] He insists that even the idea of God can be derived from impressions.

Scott: Surely he did not think that the idea of God could come from sense experience.

Oiron: No, he thought of this as an internal rather than external impression. He argued that if we mean by God "an infinitely intelligent, wise, and good Being," we can trace that notion to the operations of our own mind "augmenting, without limit, those qualities of goodness and wisdom."[4] Ideas without impressions tell us nothing about existence or reality. Hume's theory of knowledge rests upon the distinction between the *a priori* and the *a posteriori*, between ideas that are generated simply from the law of non-contradiction and those which are derived from impressions. I think that Kant's critique of the speculative proofs of God's existence are little more than an elaboration of Hume's basic line of thinking.[5]

Scott: Kant also makes a distinction between the analytic and the synthetic. Is that not a significant addition?

Oiron: I don't think it adds much to the basic logic of the issue, though many modern thinkers have been captivated by his jargon. It was not until the middle of the present century that logicians began seriously to question the distinction between statements that are analytic and those which are synthetic. Quine is one contemporary philosopher who attacks both Hume and Kant for subscribing to "two dogmas" which, he claims, are "at root identical."[6] The first is the analytic/synthetic distinction, and the second is reductionism, the belief that all meaningful statements ultimately refer to immediate experience.[7] Quine's arguments against the analytic/synthetic distinction can be applied equally well to the separation between the *a priori* and the *a posteriori*. Once that distinction goes, the kind of positivism which began with Hume collapses.

Scott: How does he argue against those distinctions?

Oiron: The gist of his argument is that it is *logically* impossible to make the distinction. He examines a range of strategies by which a variety of logicians have sought to establish and maintain Hume's original distinction between relations of ideas and matters of fact, but every attempt fails. The reason these attempts fail is that they seek to separate language and extralinguistic fact, and that cannot be done.[8] Quine suggests that the real problem is that the empiricists have attempted to connect either individual terms (Hume) or whole statements (Frege) with immediate experience. Quine, however, contends that "the unit of empirical significance is the whole of science."[9]

Scott: So, Kant's attempt to establish ideas such as the categorical imperative as strictly *a priori* and to separate it from experience fails on logical grounds?

Oiron: That's Quine's view. I, personally, think that the real problem is ontological.

Scott: What do you mean?

Oiron: I mean that ethics must be grounded in being. Here is where I depart from Quine and a host of others who think that metaphysical questions can be avoided by concentrating on the nature of logical systems, the "Scientific method," the function of language, the structures of phenomena, the cognitive habits of subjects, expert systems, and a variety of other diversions which have been cooked up in recent years by logical positivists, ordinary and extra-ordinary language philosophers and linguists, behaviorists, pragmatists, neopragmatists, existentialists, phenomenologists, cognitive psychologists, deconstructionists, and inventors of artificial languages. Quine identified a serious modern disease by isolating the virus, but he tried to treat the symptom rather than the cause.[10] He was right in saying that the analytic/synthetic distinction lies at the root of much nonsense.[11] But, I would add to his analysis by insisting that any science worthy of the name must be grounded in being, in the nature of things.

S: Oiron, I know even less about science than I do about ethics, but I see a real danger in trying to ground values in nature. How can you generate judgments about what is good or what ought to be from what is? In trying to unite ethics and ontology, are you not making the error of trying to derive what ought to be from what is?

O: What makes you think that is an error?

S: Your critique of Kant's ethics sent me back to the library to look for alternatives. One of the most interesting books I found is G. E. Moore's *Principia Ethica*.[12] If you try to ground ethics in nature, how can you avoid what Moore called the "naturalistic fallacy"?

O: I think that Moore makes a false dichotomy.

S: Rather than a false dichotomy, it seems to me that Moore is making a clear distinction. He points out a common confusion between what is *good*, which is *not* a natural object, and any natural object. When utilitarians equate what is pleasurable, which is a natural phenomenon, with what is good, that is a common instance of *the naturalistic fallacy*.[13] If you seek to ground ethics in being, in what is, then it would seem you are guilty of that fallacy. *Good* simply cannot be defined. Good is good. It is a fallacy to equate pleasure, advantage, power, money, or self-interest with good.[14]

O: Surely you don't think that I wish to equate pleasure and goodness!

S: Oiron, I'm never sure about what you think! I know that you have great respect for Plato's philosophy. I especially remember our discussions of the *Gorgias*. That memory is partly responsible for my enthusiasm about Moore's ethical philosophy. I am convinced that the utilitarians are wrong, and Moore provides a good explanation of why. But you confuse me with your attempt to ground ethics in nature. That approach seems to play into the hands of the utilitarians and sophists like Callicles.[15]

O: Well, I don't think that a person can find happiness by scratching an itch "to his heart's content."[16]

S: I *know* that you disagree with the utilitarians and the sophists, but what I cannot understand is your attempt to link ethics and nature. It seems to me that nature is the last place we should look for what is good and right. Take a simple example. In seeking to provide a good and beautiful home for myself and my family, I must struggle against nature on a daily basis. The poison ivy which grows on my land is a constant threat to my well-being! Or, on a more serious subject, my children are increasingly threatened by the AIDS virus. AIDS is a "natural" phenomenon. If ethics is to be based upon nature, how can I reconcile what is good for me and my family with what is good for the poison ivy or the AIDS virus? Both are "natural." I contribute money to several groups that seek to save the environment. I realize that we must act quickly to restore the land, clean up the air and the water, and generally stop the massive environmental destruction which now plagues the earth. Another book I read this month, by J. Baird Callicott, seeks to establish "the land ethic." He agrees with the naturalist Aldo Leopold who says that "a thing is right when it tends to preserve the integrity, stability, and beauty of the biotic community. It is wrong when it tends otherwise."[17] I, too, wish to preserve the beauty and stability of the land, but I also wish to combat disease, avoid natural disasters, and eliminate a variety of pests and predators which are as much a part of nature as I am. So, I am skeptical about your proposal that we ground ethics in "the nature of things." Many things are, by nature, evil and corrupt. We need to oppose and correct such things, not accept and encourage them. Moore is right; it is a fallacy to confuse the good with any natural thing, whether it be the source of pleasure, the source of pain, or totally indifferent to human feelings. Ethics must be founded upon some other basis, on something like Kant's categorical imperative. If I have to choose between Kant's dualism, with its logical flaws, and Leopold's land ethic which places people on the same level as the soil and the water as part of the "biotic community," then I prefer Kant.

O: I am familiar with Leopold's "land ethic," and I share your concerns about reducing humans to the status of natural things of the sort you mention. At the same time, I think that it is high time we stop thinking of human beings as unnatural, separate from the land, or as having a special ethical status which transcends nature. The real issue is perhaps the oldest of philosophical questions: What is the nature of nature? Until we face that question head-on, we will never be able to make sense out of ethics, aesthetics, politics, or any of the other important areas of philosophy. I prefer Plato's treatment to that of any of the "moderns," because he grounds questions of value in questions of being.

S: Callicott also appeals to Plato, contending that what he calls "ethical holism"[18] is supported by Plato's moral and social philosophy.[19] But I find his use of Plato's philosophy to be quite chilling.[20] He applauds Plato's "complete indifference" to the pain and suffering of individual human beings, praising Socrates response to Adeimantus' complaint at the beginning of Book IV of *The Republic* that his proposed society ignores human happiness: He applauds Socrates' reply that it is the well-being of the community as a whole, not that of any person or special class at which his ideal community aims.[21] In light of the similarities between Plato's scheme and Leopold's, Callicott concludes that "the land ethic... is somewhat foreign to modern systems of ethical philosophy, but perfectly familiar in the broader context of classical Western ethical philosophy."[22] Oiron, if that is the model of the good life you wish to foster by turning back to the Greek world, I will take modernism as developed by Kant, Moore, and anyone else who protects the rights and values of individuals and the intrinsic value of what is good for people. If this is the choice between the "is" and the "ought," then I will take the *ought* and leave the *is* to Charles Darwin, Edwin O. Wilson, Aldo Leopold, Adolf Hitler, and all other "Latter-day totalitarians."[23]

O: Well, Scott, you *have* had a busy month. Your passionate defense of morality has always impressed me, but never more than just now. I only regret that we never had a chance to read Plato's *Republic* together, because if we had you would know that my reading of that dialogue is very different from Mr. Callicott's. Of course Plato can be read as a totalitarian. Callicott is not the first to take that discussion of the "ideal" *polis* literally and use it to justify fascism, communism, racism, and a host of other "isms" which any sane person should reject. But I do not think that is what is going on in *The Republic.*

S: Then how should one read it?

O: Very carefully!

S: I'm serious, Oiron. I'm really puzzled by your rejection of the humane moral philosophies which have given rise to modern liberal democracy and by your preference for a philosophy which is ambiguous at best and fascist at worst.

O: Don't be angry with me, Scott. I'm not being facetious. Nor do I think that Plato's philosophy is ambiguous, but his dialogues do require interpretation and careful attention to what is going on below the surface. Socrates' various proposals, and those of Plato's other characters, are artfully designed to lure us, his readers, into the discussion. He is not trying to proselytize, brainwash, persuade, or preach any specific ethical doctrine, political theory, or moral dogma. What he does in all of his dialogues is present powerful arguments for and against a variety of ethical, political, religious, aesthetic, and metaphysical views which dominated the conversation in his day and which continue to be remarkably fresh in our brave new postmodern world.

S: I am willing to be convinced, but on the basis of what I have heard so far, it is far from clear how *The Republic* could be read other than in the way that Callicott suggests.

O: Apart from a careful explication of the text, I cannot offer more than a few hints. Rather than proposing an ideal society of the sort Callicott outlines, Plato uses his characters to elaborate and then demolish that vision.[24] Rather than offering a single theory of "the good life," Plato offers several. Long before such reading became fashionable, Joseph Uemura argued that there are three separate concepts of the *polis* developed in *The Republic.*[25] The second, what Uemura calls a society of the "love of luxury and wealth,"[26] is the one Callicott confuses with Plato's positive case. But it is just the opposite, a society which Plato rejects "quite completely, and quite subtly."[27] What emerges from this way of reading *The Republic* (and Plato's other dialogues as well) is a vision of ethics which is grounded in being, one that is far superior to that of Kant, Moore, or anyone else who tries to separate ethics from ontology and then seeks to pull values out of a magic hat.

S: If he seeks to ground ethics in being, then I don't see how Plato can avoid the naturalistic fallacy.

O: There is no such fallacy. That becomes clear when Moore explains what he means in "philosophic terminology." He says that "propositions about the good are all of them synthetic and never analytic."[28] The naturalistic fallacy could exist only if we were to accept the analytic/synthetic distinction. As I argued earlier, the arguments against that distinction are fatal. Plato embraced no dualism between "is" and "ought." On the contrary, the ontology which is developed in *The Republic* (and a variety of other dialogues) soundly rejects any such bifurcation. Knowing cannot be separated either from reason or from experience. Knowing, reasoning, and experiencing are grounded in being.

S: But you do agree that people wrongly equate the good with pleasure or some other "natural" object?

O: Listen to what you are saying, Scott. It would seem that you would only be satisfied by thinking about the good as an "unnatural" object. But what, pray tell, could that mean?

S: How would *you* argue against those who equate good and pleasure?

O: The discussion of the good in Book VI of *The Republic* does that quite nicely. Socrates thinks that "the greatest of all studies concerns the idea of the good. It is the one and indispensable source of what is useful and excellent in justice and the other virtues."[29] In examining that notion, he cites the view of "the multitude" that good is pleasure, contrasting the view of those with "greater refinement" that "the good is knowledge."[30] But their reasoning is circular: "The latter, after failing to explain what kind of knowledge they mean, ultimately find themselves forced to say that it is knowledge of the good." Glaucon replies that this view is "absurd." Socrates says that it is "downright comical."[31] One group begs the question, and the other must admit that some pleasures are bad. So, they conclude that those who define the good as pleasure and those who define the good as knowledge are equally confused.

S: They are no more confused than I am. I thought you just said that for Plato goodness cannot be separated from knowing or from being. But now you refuse to unite them.

O: No, I do not refuse to unite them, I simply refuse to define goodness as one or the other, or both together.

S: Does that mean that you agree with Moore in thinking that the good is indefinable?

O: I think that Socrates regards definitions in a way quite different from modern logicians. If we eschew the analytic/synthetic distinction and reject all attempts to reduce definitions either to tautologies or to "immediate experience," then we need to think again about what sort of definition could satisfy us. Socrates constantly finds some interlocutor or other ready and willing to provide a *formula* when he requests a definition. What Socrates seeks through his special kind of dialectic is *forms*, not formulas.

S: What do you mean by "forms"?

O: Do you wish a definition?

S: Yes.

O: You remind me of Adeimantus. Just after Socrates tells him that goodness cannot be defined either as knowledge or as pleasure, he asks: "Socrates, what do you yourself think the good is? Is it knowledge, or pleasure, or something else?"[32] Socrates replies by asking whether he will be content with "opinion" in such matters. He replies that he would be content if Socrates expressed opinion and labeled it as such. But Socrates refuses, calling opinions divorced from knowledge "ugly," "crooked," and "blind."[33]

S: Then is that all there is to say? If so, I see little difference between Plato's position and that of Moore. Good is good. It is indefinable.

O: After refusing to give Glaucon mere opinion, Socrates continues the conversation by introducing the idea of the good "as a single form"[34] By using the concept of the form, "we refer to the same things as both many and one. Further, we can integrate the many into a single category and so make them one again, a unity. This unity is what we call a form, something that really is."[35]

S: But, Oiron, that does not yet tell us what a form is.

O: True. Socrates does not *tell* Glaucon what a form is, nor does he *tell* him what the good is. Instead he uses an analogy, one in which he speaks of "the child of the good, begotten in the likeness of the good. The relation of the sun to vision and its objects in the visible world is the same as the relation of the good to reason and the objects of reason in the world of intellect."[36]

S: Isn't this the famous image of the "divided line"?

O: Yes.

S: Earlier you objected to Kant's dualism, his separation between the intelligible world, which grounds the categorical imperative *a priori*, and the world of sense.[37] Now you seem to embrace just that same dualism as it is developed in *The Republic*. If that is Plato's way of thinking about being, then how does his view differ from that of Kant?

O: Plato is not a dualist.

S: Then how do you explain "the divided line?"

O: The "divided line" is an analogy, nothing more and nothing less. Socrates explicitly refused to answer Adeimantus simply by offering his opinion, so we should not be surprised if he fails to define, describe, tell, or otherwise present Glaucon with a formula. To take literally the metaphors which are developed in Books VI and VII is to replace a form with a formula. In developing his metaphor, Socrates says that the idea (or form) of the good "imbues the objects of knowledge with truth and confers upon the knower the power to know."[38] It is the "cause" of knowledge, and it is the "chief objective in the pursuit of knowledge."[39] But knowledge and truth are not identical with the good. "A still greater glory belongs to the good."[40] The metaphor which compares the good with the sun concludes with the claim that "the objects of knowledge are not only made manifest by the presence of goodness. Goodness makes them real."[41] Socrates then claims that "goodness is not in itself being. It transcends being, exceeding all else in dignity and power."[42] What are we to make of such claims, Scott?

S: It seems to contradict your central claim that ethics is grounded in being. If goodness transcends being, then that would seem to confirm Moore's demand that the good transcends nature (being), and cannot be defined in terms of any natural thing!

O: That is how this passage is often interpreted. Do you know how Glaucon responds when Socrates says this?

S: I can't remember.

O: He laughs. And then he says: "My god, hyperbole can go no farther than that."[43] In my dictionary, "hyperbole" is described as an exaggeration for effect, not meant to be taken literally. There is another reason to avoid taking this claim literally.

S: What is that?

O: It would be an ontological absurdity. To say literally that goodness is beyond being is to say that it is nothing. And that is nonsense. To say that the good "transcends" being is to say that it is not itself "being," since being is a separate form. Goodness is one form, being is another. It makes as little sense to say that goodness "is not" as it does to say literally that there is a world of sense which is "separate" from the world of forms, though that interpretation of Plato's ontology is often heard. My interpretation of Plato's metaphor is consistent with the line of analysis provided by the Stranger in *The Sophist*.

S: I have never read that dialogue.

O: In *The Sophist* we find a discussion of five forms: same, other, rest, motion, and being. The Stranger tries to explain which forms blend with one another and which do not.[44] Being is a form which blends with all others. This is Plato's way of dealing with Parmenides' puzzle about the existence of "what is not." We can apply this same logic to the relation between being and goodness. To say that goodness "transcends" being is to say that goodness is a separate form, one which has its own power and dignity. The blending of forms, all of the forms, is essential to Plato's ontology. In this way reason, experience, knowing, and all other such activities are unified in a non-dualistic ontology, one in which forms or essences are the fundamental elements of being and which either blend or do not blend with each other, depending upon their individual nature. Being, however, blends with them all.

S: Why does Plato confuse things with hyperbole rather than providing a simple, logical explanation?

O: Because he seeks forms, not formulas. This does not mean that interpretation and explanation are out of order. *The Sophist* shows that there is a way of using reason and logic to go beyond the immediate symbols of a particular dialogue. But *The Sophist* has its own symbols and metaphors, and we must be careful about taking them literally as well. Book VI concludes with a discussion of "intelligibility at the highest level," one of the most remarkable passages in all of philosophy:

This is the realm that reason masters with the power of dialectic. Assumptions are not treated as first principles, but as real hypotheses.

That is, they are not employed as beginnings, but as ladders, and springboards, used in order to reach that realm that requires no hypotheses and is therefore the true starting point for the attainment of unobstructed knowledge. When reason attains that level and becomes aware of the whole intelligible order, it descends at will to the level of conclusions, but without the aid of sense objects. It reasons only by using forms. It moves from form through forms to forms. And it completes its journey in forms.[45]

S: Oiron, this is all quite overwhelming for a mere businessman. I'll need at least another month to sort this out. ⮑

The Developmental Relationship Between Moral Reasoning and Motivation

Richard Kyte

~≫≪~

*T*hink how a child comes to grasp the concept of a lie as a moral concept. At certain times the child will be told that she "shouldn't say that"—that what she said was a "lie." She will pick up the general idea that "lying" is saying something that isn't true, but the idea will be quite general, as evidenced by her inability to distinguish, for example, lying from unintentionally saying something that isn't true. The child may nevertheless internalize the norm that prohibits "lying," even though she must often rely on adults to point out what is a "lie" and what isn't. In internalizing the norm not to "lie," she is motivated to refrain from saying whatever she considers to be a "lie," and in many cases she considers to be a "lie" whatever her parents point out to her as a "lie." At this stage, she hasn't yet internalized the norm not to *lie* because she hasn't grasped the concept of a lie. The idea that such and such is a *lie* doesn't really motivate her actions in accordance with the norm. What does motivate her actions is something like the concept "what my parents call a 'lie'." However, after a period of time in which instances of lying are repeatedly pointed out and distinguished, say, from instances of jokes or unintentional untruths, in which some forms of speech are laughed at, others ignored, and others reproved, the child learns to recognize for herself the situations in which she ought not to say such and such. She no longer needs to depend upon some other person to guide her actions in that respect, nor be provided with some motive other than the recognition that such and such is a lie. Grasping the concept of a lie thus involves the ability to recognize for oneself that certain features of a situation forbid certain types of speech, and this is also what it means to grasp the concept of a lie as a moral concept—to recognize that certain types of speech should not be uttered just because they are lies.

This brief sketch illustrates two points that will be crucial to the main argument of this paper: (1) In order to internalize norms an agent must grasp certain concepts, concepts which have a motivating influence on her actions; (2) Grasping moral concepts involves recognizing that they function to justify a range of actions. Taken together, these two propositions imply that the internalization of moral norms requires grasping moral concepts (or grasping concepts as moral) and that moral concepts serve both to justify and to motivate the ranges of behavior prescribed by the norms. If this picture is correct, the widespread assumption that the relation between cognition and motivation is static and can therefore be described independently of an account of moral development is mistaken.

Historically, there have been two broadly competing views about the relation between cognition and motivation. "Internalism" is the view that some motivation, either actual or dispositional, to act according to an obligation logically follows from thinking that one has that obligation; "externalism" is the view that denies such a relation.[1] There are many varieties of both internalism and externalism; I will restrict my discussion here to whether an individual's thinking that she has a moral obligation implies that she has some actual corresponding motivation, i.e. either a reason or a desire that is capable of moving her to act. According to some advocates of internalism (e.g. Kant, Nagel), the motivation is supplied by the moral judgment itself. In Kant's case, "*Achtung*," or "respect," which is capable of motivating the agent to act according to the moral law, arises from the agent's recognition that the law is binding on his will. According to others (e.g. Hume, Stevenson), the moral judgment just is an expression of a certain type of motivation. The difference between these types of internalism is that the latter conceives of the motivation as comprehensible independently of the moral judgment itself while the former does not. The externalist denies both versions, insisting that moral cognition and the psychological sanctions toward moral action are independent and that it is therefore possible to believe that one has a moral obligation without having any motivation to act upon it.

In the following I will argue that the internalist view that motivation is somehow "built into" moral judgments is true of early stages of morality but that continued moral development reveals how the "psychological gap"—the separation between cognition and motivation insisted upon by externalists—becomes possible. I will begin by discussing briefly how the major theories of moral development tend to lean to one side or the other of the internalist/externalist debate and will argue that those theories that attempt to explain the early stages of moral development from an externalist perspective are incoherent. In Section II I will give an internalist account of the early stages of moral development, arguing that moral reasoning and motivation are initially interdependent, that the origin of neither one can be explained on the basis of the other. Finally, in Section III I will attempt to show that such an account need not rule out externalism as a true description of a mature agent's moral psychology. Given the account offered in

Section II of how moral concepts are initially grasped, one can see how reasoning and motivation may diverge as a person matures.

I. Priority of Cognition vs. Priority of Motivation

Theories purporting to explain the growth or acquisition of morality can be divided into two types, those which give priority to cognition over motivation and those which give priority to motivation over cognition. The distinction between motivational and cognitive priority in theories of moral development does not map neatly onto the internalist/externalist distinction, but there are certain general correlations that are useful to note.[2] The theories that give priority to cognition generally assume an internalist view and consider moral development to consist in the growth or maturity of a person's point of view or *outlook*. Such theories, for the most part "cognitive" theories of moral development, attempt to explain morality on the basis of the ability to make certain types of moral judgments from which a corresponding motivation follows. According to Piaget and Kohlberg, the motivation to act according to one's moral judgments corresponds to the ability to make increasingly adequate (more equilibrated) judgments, culminating in judgments based on universalizable moral principles.[3] The other type of theory, which asserts motivational priority in moral development, presupposes either (a) an externalist perspective or (b) an internalist perspective of the sort attributed to Hume and Stevenson. I will refer to both versions as "motivational"; they generally hold that moral development proceeds through a process of "internalization" whereby an agent comes to act according to moral norms out of certain affective states. On the internalist version of this account, if you attribute morality to an agent, you are logically committed to attributing to him certain types of affective states, e.g. sympathy or compassion. On the externalist version, moral judgments come to be associated with certain affective states, but there is no logical relation between them. Both versions, however, maintain that the agent's psychological states are conceivable independently of the moral judgments with which they are associated. The development of morality is thus explained by the interaction of various non-rational motivational forces which make up a person's *character*. This type of view is typically held by both psychoanalytic and social learning theories.

The "motivational" (character oriented) theories tend to explain moral development in terms of "internalization." This is generally understood in the context of a Humean philosophy of mind in which desire and belief are independent elements which, when combined in a certain way, serve to produce morality. In a review of the psychological literature on the topic, Martin Hoffman describes moral internalization in the following way:

> Though the norms are initially external to the individual and often in conflict with his desires, the norms eventually become

part of his internal motive system and guide his behavior even in the absence of external authority. Control by others is thus replaced by self-control.[4]

The view is that norms have an action-guiding function which operates either externally or internally depending on whether certain desires of the agent are *associated* with them. According to social learning theorists, there are a variety of ways in which this association may take place, but on most accounts it comes about through punishing or rewarding the child for its behavior.[5] Hoffman again:

> The discipline encounter has much in common with many later moral encounters. In each, there is a conflict and the individual is compelled to work out a balance between behaving in accord with his desires, on the one hand, and subordinating his desires and acting in line with moral standards, on the other.[6]

The view given here by Hoffman, which is representative of "motivational" theories, operates on the implicit assumption that norms become intelligible to the child prior to the development in him of any motivation to act according to them, that acquiring the desire to act in a certain way and acquiring knowledge of how one ought to act are processes that are developmentally, but not conceptually, linked. Thus, internalization is the process of acquiring a desire to act according to some independently comprehensible rule or standard. Through this process certain affective states become "associated" with the rule or standard, and it is this association that makes "moral" judgment possible.

In contrast to the "motivational" account of moral internalization, I want to suggest an account on which acquiring the motivation to act according to a norm includes grasping the concepts that both describe and justify the norm. For although it is true that once a person knows what certain moral standards are, acting in the way they prescribe often involves weighing one's non-moral desires or interests against them, it is a mistake to think that a child typically can make such comparisons, because the ability to do so indicates that the child has already made considerable progress toward becoming a moral agent. The problem with the motivational account of internalization is that although it claims merely to describe how the child associates certain affective states with actions that are already comprehensible, it presupposes an account of the means by which the child learns what her actions are and what kinds of feelings, desires, and interests those actions can engender. By the response of adults laughing when she says one thing and reproving her when she says something else, the child not only learns that telling jokes may be pleasant and telling lies may not be, she learns what lies and jokes are, in part by discovering the range of affective states that "go along with" and help define them.

An important feature of the account offered here is the recognition that internalizing a norm requires that an agent's motivation for acting according to the norm must be explained in terms of concepts that the agent comprehends. This is more informative than the "motivationalist" account of internalization because it draws attention to the important fact that the true ascription of an internalized norm to an agent depends as much upon his cognitive state as upon his motivational state. We do not say that the child who tells the truth only because of the threat of punishment has internalized the norm that prohibits lying; we avoid attributing the internalization of this norm to him not because his motivation for acting in this way is in any sense "external" but rather because he does not grasp the concept of lying, and therefore it cannot be used to describe his motivation. It happens to be the case that the child doesn't lie, but the concept of lying doesn't figure (at least directly) in an explanation of his motivation. In order to explain the child's action it would be more accurate to say that he has internalized obedience to his parents, or perhaps that he just does whatever allows him to avoid punishment. Internalization has nothing to do with one type of motivation rather than another for the trivial reason that any kind of motivation must be "internal" if it is to explain the agent's action rather than the action of someone else.

In the view I am criticizing, evidence of the transition from a pre-moral to a moral state would be the development of the tendency, say, to feel guilt at the prospect of violating a parent's prohibitions, or to feel shame for falling short of some standard of behavior. Such a view typically presupposes that the agent's conception of the norm is acquired prior to or independently of the development of the motivation to act in accordance with it. Such a presupposition is unjustified. Guilt and shame, along with the other moral emotions, are not simply tacked on to an existing conceptual framework. Even though it is common to speak of a child "adopting" norms as internal guides to behavior, as if the norms were comprehensible to the child prior to their internalization, it is just as problematic to give an account of how a person acquires a conception of the norm as to explain how she comes to internalize it, that is, to acquire some motivation to act on it. Indeed, the explanations are interdependent. This follows from two considerations about the relation between motivation and the comprehension of moral principles.

First, certain Wittgensteinian insights about rule-following show that comprehending moral principles is dependent upon having a motivation to act in a certain way.[7] The notion that grasping a rule or principle is like having a picture in the mind that guides one's action is mistaken because any imaginative conception that one has of what actions are dictated by the rule falls far short of the indefinite number of actions the rule is supposed to cover. Grasping a rule instead consists of knowing "how to go on" that comes from participating in a "form of life."[8] Part of this "form of life" will consist of the attitudes that make moral concepts comprehensible. A person who does not share the concerns, desires, and interests of his fellows will lack access to the concepts which depend upon them. Thus, comprehension of the rule is not based on the ability to occupy some external point of view from which one "sees" how the rule is to be applied. On the contrary, seeing how the rule is to be applied is, in part, the result of the formation of concerns, desires, and interests which manifest themselves in tendencies to act in certain ways.[9]

A consequence of this is that one cannot grasp moral concepts without internalizing moral norms. That does not mean that some person who grasps the concept of a lie could not think that lying is a type of practice that one *ought* to engage in—that, as a rule, dishonesty is preferable to honesty. It does mean, however, that he couldn't *always* have thought that one ought to lie. In order initially to grasp the concept an agent must feel the restraint that the notion of something's being a lie places on his actions, and knowledge of the restraint, which can be gained only by participating in forms of life in which that restraint is operative, is necessary before he can think that the restraint should be lifted. In order for a challenge to existing practices to be intelligible, it must proceed from a knowledge of those practices. The challenger must be able to give us some reason why we should not refrain from lying, and in order to be intelligible the reason must appeal to the greater worth of some conflicting norm, or the harm that can come from lying, etc., any of which will involve familiarity with how the concept of lying functions in existing practices.

Second, it is also a mistake to think that the motivation to act according to the norm is always comprehensible independently of the norm itself. Nagel makes this point in *The Possibility of Altruism*:

> Certain ethical principles are themselves propositions of motivation theory so fundamental that they cannot be derived from or defined in terms of previously understood motivations. These principles specify how reasons for action follow from certain given conditions. Thus they *define* motivational possibilities, rather than presupposing them.[10]

It is simply not possible to make a list of all the various types of motivations that can be "associated" with ethical principles independently of any comprehension of the principles themselves. Theories that attempt to ground ethical principles on a set of independently comprehensible motivations either unacceptably restrict the range of moral behavior or else presuppose some degree of moral comprehension in the attribution of the motivations themselves.

In saying that someone "internalizes" a norm, I will not therefore mean that she has a particular type of motivation for acting in that way based on some predetermined range of "moral" feelings (e.g. guilt, sympathy, compassion), rather, I will mean that she has a tendency to act in a certain manner and that the motivation to act in that way has to be explained at least partly in terms of the agent's conception of that norm. The child internalizes the norm "Don't lie" when the concept of a lie figures in her motivation for acting according to the norm, that is, when she refrains from saying such and such because it would be a lie. A norm is "external" to the agent if she does not comprehend the concepts which figure in the description of the norm or if she has no tendency to act in accordance with it. In order to internalize a *moral* precept one must grasp certain moral concepts. Moral internalization, therefore, can be defined as grasping concepts that motivate one to act morally. If a person acts according to moral norms but does not grasp the relevant moral concepts, then although an agent's actions may be in accordance with what is recognized as moral by an outsider, her motivation for acting in that way must be described in non-moral terms, thus revealing that if she has internalized any norm at all it must be non-moral.

The result is that one cannot internalize a moral norm without grasping moral concepts, but, as we have seen, it is also the case that one cannot grasp moral concepts in the first place without internalizing moral norms. Taken together, these two considerations about the relation between motivation and the comprehension of principles suggest that neither can be construed as developmentally prior to the other. This presents a grave difficulty to any theory of moral development that attempts to explain the growth of moral cognition on the basis of motivation or moral motivation on the basis of cognition. The way out of the difficulty is to suppose that, at the early stages of morality, cognition and motivation are not distinct. Dissociation of belief from desire is possible only with mature thought and misrepresents the facts when applied to the early stages of moral development. This error is not peculiar to moral psychology; Piaget has coined the term 'adultomorphism' to denote the common misconception that the psychological structure of the child is the same as that of the mature adult.

II. The Initial Interdependence of Cognition and Motivation

From the very beginning the child takes pleasure in objects that are properly understood as external to him. But since his own pleasure is not distinct from the objects in his immediate environment, he does not seek these objects as means to his pleasure. Means-end reasoning, indeed the very ability to distinguish ends from means, is not yet available to the child. This is due to the fact that, at the earliest stages, there is no distinction between the idea of "self" and that of "other."[11] As F. H. Bradley remarks concerning the infant: "The breast of his mother, and the soft warmth and touches and tones of his nurse, are made one with the feeling of his own pleasure and pain."[12] The child doesn't "associate" these objects with pleasure, instead the "idea of the object (imagined or perceived) gives a feeling of pleasure."[13] Furthermore, the pleasantness is not separated in idea from the objective content; the child likes it for itself, not for its pleasantness. The significance of this fact for Bradley was that it showed the error of thinking that the moral sense develops through the *association* of objects with affective states. Rather, he insisted, moral development consists in the extension of interest defined in terms of the ability to take pleasure in an increasingly wide range of objects, beginning with the objects of transitory appetite (e.g. food, warmth) and progressing to the objects of interest (e.g. friendship, duty). It is coming to see that certain sorts of things are pleasurable by learning to take pleasure in them, thereby expanding both the range of objects one is able to take pleasure in and the sorts of pleasure one is capable of experiencing.

This explains how it is possible for the child to take pleasure in certain ends defined by moral concepts and how the initial motivation for acting morally is one with grasping those concepts. The type of pleasure that one takes in acting morally can only be defined in terms of what it is that one takes pleasure in. There is no independently intelligible feeling which motivates moral actions. If the child acts morally, then he does not act out of fear of punishment or desire for his parents' approval, he acts out of some motivation which can only be defined in terms of moral concepts. This is perhaps most clearly seen in the case of the moral feelings of guilt and shame—types of displeasure felt in consequence of violating what one perceives to be moral obligations or standards and not intelligible apart from the possession of moral concepts.

None of this is meant to imply that various types of association between affective states and the objects of thought—described by 'behavior modification,' 'modelling,' 'reinforcement,' etc.—do not play an important role in extending one's range of interests; it is only meant to reassert the idea that morality does not consist in such associations. Acting in certain ways because the consequences of doing so are pleasant, or because the consequences of not doing so are unpleasant, may lead one to perceive the action itself as pleasant or the denial of it as unpleasant. Making a child finish his vegetables in order to get dessert may help him learn to like vegetables, but the pleasure of eating ice cream doesn't transfer to eating broccoli. Enjoyment of broccoli is a pleasure all its own. Likewise, a child may begin by telling the truth because she seeks parental approval or desires to avoid punishment. By doing so, however, she may come to see that telling the truth is something she wants to do for no other reason than the inherent desirability of truthfulness or the undesirability of lying. As I have argued throughout, learning that lying is undesirable—that the recognition that an utterance falls under that description can itself be motivating—is part of grasping the concept of a lie as a moral concept.

What must be shown then is not how someone can acquire reasons to act morally which are given in terms of desires or ends that she already has, rather it must be shown how the agent grasps moral concepts which are themselves constitutive of the ends or desires of one who acts on the basis of them. That is, we want to know how, in grasping the concept of a lie as a moral concept, the child can regard not lying as an end that she has. In order to see how moral concepts can be motivating in this way it will be helpful to examine the use of the modal terminology by means of which norms are typically expressed, e.g. 'should' or 'ought,' 'must,' 'may,' 'shouldn't,' 'must not' and 'can't.' In certain contexts these modals serve to force or urge one to do something, to stop or prevent one from doing something, or to permit one to do something. G. E. M. Anscombe draws attention to the use of these modals in attempting to explain how one acquires the concept of a right. She asks us to think of the use of "stopping modals" in rules for playing chess, e.g. "You can't move your king:"

> Someone may want to say that the latter means "Moving your king in this situation is against the rules." So it does. But one may equally well say: "That's against the rules" is *a* special form of "you can't do that." Think how a child learns to play chess. It grasps the idea of a rule partly from this use of "you can't." After all what it 'can't' do, in another sense it perhaps plainly *can*, if you don't physically stop it. But these utterances first accompany other methods of preventing or stopping an action, and then by themselves they function to prevent or stop it. With one set of circumstances (including consequences) this business is part of the build-up of the concept of a rule; in another, of that of a piece of etiquette; in another, of that of a promise, in another of an act of sacrilege, etc.[14]

As Anscombe describes it, part of learning what the rule is involves learning what one 'can't' do in a certain situation. The idea of the rule cannot be grasped independently of seeing the necessity of not doing something. (Anscombe reminds us that this is the sense of necessity Aristotle had in mind when he said it is "that without which some good will not be attained or some evil avoided.") In saying to the child, "You can't move your king: it's against the rules," the appeal to rules gives the sense in which he *can't* move the king. It justifies the restriction on his actions, but in so doing it doesn't rest on any independent reason, because the rule itself just is a restriction on certain sorts of actions. Why can't the child move his king anyway? What kind of necessity restricts his actions? The necessity of not breaking the rules.

This passage describes how a concept can be created by appeal to one type of motivation (e.g. physical force), but once it has been created, its use is expressive of another type of motivation altogether—the motivation expressed by the concept that justifies the use of the modal. Because of this, moral concepts are not "naturally intelligible,"[15] that is, the obligation they give rise to cannot be explained in terms of any desires or ends the agent already has. In refusing to say something because it would be a lie, the child does not appeal to some end that can be achieved or promoted by not lying other than that of not lying itself. In using the concept of a lie to restrict her range of actions in a certain way she reveals a purpose that she has—that of not lying. The concept of lying, therefore, not only justifies a certain range of actions, specifiable by a norm, it also motivates those actions.

A child may, however, grasp the concept of a lie without grasping it as a moral concept. She may be able to recognize that a particular utterance in such and such a situation is a lie and yet not think that she ought not to do what she correctly recognizes as a lie. This is just to point out that what makes a concept a *moral* concept is its function as a particular kind of justification of norms. Some concepts seem to have no other function, e.g. those of a duty or a right, so that if one is to grasp the concept of a duty at all one must grasp it as a moral concept. Other concepts, like that of a lie, may or may not be grasped as moral. The result is that such concepts, if they are not themselves grasped as moral, may figure in a moral norm only if that norm is justified by some other, moral, concept. Thus, someone may consider lying to be morally wrong only in those situations where it goes against a perceived duty or where it violates someone's rights; another, who grasps the concept of a lie as a moral concept, may consider an act to be morally wrong just because it is a lie.

If the above account of how moral concepts are grasped is correct, then we need to be able to distinguish the way moral norms are internalized from the way other sorts of norms are internalized. For moral norms are internalized through the grasp of moral concepts, which involves the creation of ends not previously held by the agent. To describe this sort of internalization I shall borrow the term 'acceptance.'[16] Accepting a norm involves grasping the concepts that provide both motivating and justifying reasons for a certain range of actions. To accept a norm is thus to see it as what one ought to do while also being motivated to act according to it for that very reason. The phrase "accepting a norm" comes from Allan Gibbard. He defines it as the state that gives rise to the human syndrome of avowing and being inclined to act according to a norm.[17] A person can avow a norm with or without being inclined to act according to it, but in order to accept a norm one must both avow it and be inclined to act according to it.[18]

Acquiring a grasp of moral concepts takes place, in part, by coming to see how a particular concept can justify certain prescriptions by "making sense" of restrictions upon the range of one's possible actions. For example, if it makes sense that I ought to give blood to the Red Cross, it may do so in virtue of my conceiving it to be 'good' or 'charitable' or a 'duty.' Grasping the concepts that justify norms in this way is not independent of being moved to act according to the relevant norms. The preceding argument establishes that the concept that justifies a certain range of actions may also motivate one who grasps it to do those actions. Thus, the moral concepts, e.g. of a 'right,' or a 'duty,' or 'generosity,' or 'care,' among others, are comprehended in part by coming to accept norms in which they function as justifications. It follows that having a moral outlook requires not only that one internalize certain norms but that this is done through the acceptance of them. This is because the feature of moral norms that distinguishes them from other types of norms is that the concepts that figure in the agent's motivation for acting according to moral norms also justify those actions. The norm that prescribes giving blood to the Red Cross is justified by the consideration that it is a duty, and my acting according to that norm is explained by my desire to do my duty, or by the performance of duty being an end that I have. In short, though there are many ways in which a person can internalize a norm, a *moral* norm can only be internalized through conceiving it to be justified.[19]

III. The Divergence of Moral Reasoning and Motivation

So far I have discussed how a person's character—the part of the personality that is susceptible to motivational influences—is formed in part by the internalization of norms and, specifically, how the aspect of character especially relevant to morality is formed by the acceptance of moral norms. The acceptance of norms is what makes normative avowal possible. The capacity for normative avowal, considered independently of any motivational commitments, is what is usually meant when one speaks of moral 'outlook' or 'point of view.' The main concern of the previous section was to demonstrate that, at least in the initial stages of development, moral outlook cannot be sharply distinguished from moral character because the concept of justification is formed in conjunction with certain types of motivational influence.

A person's moral outlook, however, may eventually come to function independently of her character. In fact, it is very likely that it will, since the concepts acquired through the internalization of norms may be used to justify a range of norms extending beyond the original context in which they were acquired. As Anscombe puts it, once the linguistic practice of using modals with certain concepts is adopted, it becomes possible to separate the reason for acting from the modals which originally gave the reason its meaning. Take, for example, "You can't move your king; it's against the rules." At first the meaning of "it's against the rules" is given, in part, by this particular use of 'can't,' but later, once a person has grasped the concept of a rule from repeated use of these modals, "it's against the rules" can function as an independent reason.[20] The consequence of this is that in the early stages of development, when avowal is closely tied to acceptance, there is no actual distinction between character and moral outlook. It is only later, when moral concepts are developed in response to reflective rather than directly practical needs and on the basis of linguistic practices already established in the context of particular actions, that it becomes possible for a person intelligibly to avow norms without feeling any compulsion to act according to them. Thus, character and outlook tend to diverge as the moral agent matures. Consequently, the "psychological gap" between motivation and cognition which was not possible in the early stages of development becomes possible in the later stages.

There is no need to dwell on this since the fact of at least occasional divergence of moral reasoning from motivation in the mature moral agent is usually considered to be plainly evident. The pressing question is not whether moral reasoning and motivation diverge but how the divergence is to be understood. E.g. how are we to conceptualize occurrences of weakness of will or self-deception? That is a question to which this discussion is directly relevant but which I cannot pursue here.[21] It is sufficient for the purposes of this argument to show merely that what I have claimed about the connection between moral reasoning and motivation in the early stages of development does not preclude their divergence in the later stages.

To sum up: although the development of morality can be explained only by conceiving of character and outlook as an initial unity, as the agent matures it is possible to distinguish them as related but increasingly distinct aspects of the moral personality. In the mature agent, character is determined by the norms that hold some motivational influence over behavior. Moral outlook, on the other hand, is determined by the moral norms the agent avows. In the early stages of development this is part of character, but in the later stages outlook tends to consist of the norms the agent accepts on the basis of reflective rather than practical needs, and thus the norms the agent avows may differ from the norms he internalizes. It follows, then, that the relationship between moral reasoning and motivation is not static, and hence one cannot reach an adequate understanding of that relationship through consideration of the mature moral personality alone. The approach described here offers a way of reconciling the traditionally incompatible positions of internalism and externalism by describing the way in which the relationship between moral reasoning and motivation changes in the course of an individual's moral development . ⌒

Rachels' Defense of Active Euthanasia: A Critique

Robert N. Hull

*I*n his influential essay "Euthanasia, Killing, and Letting Die,"[1] James Rachels argues that the policy of the American Medical Association concerning euthanasia or "mercy killing" rests on an assumption that is irrational, and that this policy itself is therefore misguided. The stand that the AMA takes on euthanasia is expressed in the following policy statement, quoted in its entirety in Rachels' paper:

> The intentional termination of the life of one human being by another—mercy killing—is contrary to that for which the medical profession stands and is contrary to the policy of the American Medical Association. The cessation of the employment of extraordinary means to prolong the life of the body when there is irrefutable evidence that biological death is imminent is the decision of the patient and/or his immediate family. The advice and judgment of the physician should be freely available to the patient and/or his immediate family.[2]

By "active euthanasia" Rachels means, for example, giving a patient about to die from a painful disease a lethal injection of potassium chloride. "Passive euthanasia," on the other hand, refers to the practice of withholding medication, or other life-sustaining means, with the intention of allowing the patient to die. As he understands the AMA's policy, the AMA does not object to passive euthanasia but strongly condemns active euthanasia.

Rachels does not argue for the position that active and passive euthanasia are morally justified practices. Rather, he wants to claim that if one has no objection to passive euthanasia, then one should not object to active euthanasia either.[3] In his view the position the AMA has taken is irrational because it condemns active euthanasia while countenancing passive euthanasia. The reason why this policy is irrational is that there is no moral difference between the two forms of euthanasia. And if there is no moral difference between the two, it follows that it makes no sense to allow the one but disallow the other. Indeed, Rachels claims, if there is no such difference, the result is that "active euthanasia is very much preferable to passive euthanasia"[4] in some instances. In this paper I examine Rachels argument, and I argue that on his own consequentialist principles the AMA policy is by no means irrational, the primary reason being that a substantial moral difference does exist between the two forms of euthanasia. I would hope that it is understood, however, that I understand and have sympathy for the motivation behind Rachels' position, which I take to be a heartfelt concern for the suffering of others.

Rachels begins his case by pointing out that the assumption behind the view that, at least in some cases, some form of euthanasia is desirable, is the belief that a patient with a terminal illness who is in excruciating pain would be "literally better off dead—or at least, no worse off dead—than continuing the kind of life that is available."[5] Furthermore, Rachels would have us bear in mind that in cases such as this one "the justification for allowing the patient to die, rather than prolonging his life for a few more hopeless days, is that he is in horrible pain."[6] And given that we are disposed to consider the cessation of suffering to be an appropriate justification for hastening death by withholding life-prolonging measures in such cases, the question which presents itself is why a more efficient means for bringing an end to this suffering is considered impermissible. After all, it would seem that by merely withholding treatment rather than providing a lethal injection we are dooming the patient to more suffering than is necessary. Thus, the means we have chosen seems incompatible with the purpose of our action and with the rationale behind it. These considerations, Rachels concludes,

> provide strong reason for thinking that, once the initial decision not to prolong a patient's agony has been made, active euthanasia is actually *preferable* to passive euthanasia, rather than the reverse. To say otherwise is to endorse the option which leads to more suffering rather than less, and is contrary to the humanitarian impulse which prompts the decision not to prolong the life in the first place.[7]

Rachels believes that the reason many of us see an important moral difference between active and passive euthanasia, the former being viewed as immoral and the latter as moral because of this difference, is that we tend to think that killing someone is morally worse than letting someone die. However, Rachels himself does not share this belief. As he puts it, "the mere difference between killing and letting die does not itself make any difference to the morality of actions concerning life and death."[8]　In order to establish this claim Rachels has us consider the following example:

> (i) Smith stands to gain a large inheritance if anything should happen to his six-year-old cousin. One evening while the child is taking his bath, Smith sneaks into the bathroom and drowns the child, and then arranges things so that it will look like an accident.

> (ii) Jones also stands to gain if anything should happen to his six-year-old cousin. Like Smith, Jones sneaks in planning to drown the child in his bath. However, just as he enters the bathroom, Jones sees the child slip and hit his head, and fall face down in the water. Jones is delighted; he stands by, ready to push the child's head back under if it is necessary, but it is not necessary. With only a little thrashing about, the child drowns himself, "accidentally," as Jones watches and does nothing.[9]

Rachels points out that in this example the only difference between the behavior of Smith and Jones is that Smith killed the child while Jones let him die. But if it is reasonable to hold that there is a moral difference between killing a person and letting him die, then we ought to consider Smith's behavior more reprehensible than that of Jones. However, as Rachels observes, this is not the assessment we would make. The behavior of the two men is equally morally reprehensible. And if this is true then one cannot argue that, because of an intrinsic difference between killing and letting die, passive euthanasia is morally permissible and active euthanasia is not.

The reason Rachels believes that these considerations are relevant to the previously quoted AMA policy statement is that in it active euthanasia is characterized as "the intentional termination of the life of one human being by another.[10] Contrarily, passive euthanasia is described as "The cessation of the employment of extraordinary means to prolong the life of the body when there is irrefutable evidence that biological death is imminent...."[11]　The difference between the way the two practices are characterized leads Rachels to conclude that the AMA regards active, but not passive euthanasia, as the intentional termination of life. However, cessation of treatment *is* the intentional termination of the life of one human by another, and what is preventing the AMA from recognizing this is the mistaken view that there is a morally relevant difference between killing and letting die. By recognizing that there is no such difference, and that both practices constitute the intentional termination of human life, Rachels believes that we can move on to consider what is actually relevant: that in many cases we prolong the agony of terminal patients for no good reason.

Rachels' position in this paper is of the consequentialist variety, in that he claims that if one allows for passive euthanasia, and one admits that no moral difference exists between killing and letting die, it follows that active euthanasia merits our approval because in some instances it will bring about an outcome that we prefer. Specifically, it will bring an end to suffering that would otherwise continue if we endorsed only passive euthanasia. Thus it is the consequences of conduct—in this case the prevention of suffering—that is the basis for determining its morality or immorality.

On consequentialist grounds alone it is hard not to agree with Rachels that active euthanasia is an appropriate, morally justified action in the individual cases that he has in mind. But it does not follow from this that Rachels has succeeded in establishing the morality of active euthanasia. For consequentialist approaches to deciding tough social issues cannot limit themselves to considering the outcomes of particular cases. The proper end of reasoning about such issues is a morally sound set of rules or guidelines that can be codified in law and successfully implemented in practice. A consequentialist strategy for establishing the morality of a set of rules or guidelines for dealing with the problem of euthanasia must take into account the possible outcomes or consequences of candidate policies. After all, the point of Rachels' paper is that the AMA's *policy* is irrational; in fact, he believes that a more rational policy would be one that permits both passive and active euthanasia. By focusing on the specific outcomes of well-defined particular cases, however, he ignores the question of whether the policy he views as more rational may have intolerable consequences that cannot be anticipated given his method. That is to say, while there may be no recognizable moral difference between killing and letting die in the particular cases that he has in mind, when viewed as general practices a significant moral difference may exist. Indeed, I think that a strong case can be made for believing there is such a moral difference.

One of the cardinal reasons that some ethicists have been reluctant to endorse permitting active euthanasia is that it is uncertain what the long-term social consequences of allowing active euthanasia will be. A very disturbing possible outcome of allowing active euthanasia would be a gradual change in the general public's view of who may be legitimately chosen for a "merciful death." If active euthanasia becomes commonplace or a generally accepted practice, the psychological affect on our society—while impossible to predict with certainty—could be one of an increased toleration for and a consequent application of the view that some forms of human life are unworthy of being lived. Thus the erosion of our respect for human life that might be precipitated by a widespread acceptance of active euthanasia could lead us to include as appropriate candidates those for whom it was not originally intended—the mentally incompetent or people with severe physical disabilities, for example.[12]

Several authors have argued that the acceptance of active euthanasia in the late 1930's in Nazi Germany was a crucial move in that country's odious descent into the mass murders of the Holocaust. Leo Alexander, a psychiatrist who served as a judge at the Nuremberg trials, has written that:

> The beginnings at first were a subtle shifting in emphasis in the basic attitude of the physicians. It started with the acceptance of the attitude, basic in the euthanasia movement, that there is such a thing as life not worthy to be lived. This attitude in its early stages concerned itself merely with the severely and chronically sick. Gradually, the sphere of those to be included in this category was enlarged to encompass the socially unproductive, the ideologically unwanted, the racially unwanted and finally all non-Germans. But it is important to realize that the infinitely small wedged-in lever from which this entire trend of mind received its impetus was the attitude of the nonrehabilitable sick.[13]

Those who are inclined to reject Alexander's claims about a connection between active euthanasia and the Holocaust will point out that decades of anti-Semitism (and other forms of race hatred, bigotry and intolerance), nationalism, and a diabolically popular leader were the actual forces behind the mass murders. And, indeed, it is surely important that these ignoble features of human history be recognized as necessary conditions of the Holocaust. But as Lucy Davidowicz carefully documents in her book *The War Against The Jews 1933-1945*, the initial targets of Hitler's efforts to "purify" the German population were *lebensunwertes Leben*, or "life unworthy of life," among whom were included mental patients, deformed children, and the chronically ill. By the time that the first death camp began functioning on December 8, 1941, between 80,000 and 100,000 "racially valueless" Germans had been killed. The authorization for this killing, written on Hitler's personal stationary, read:

> Reichsleiter Buhler and Dr. Brandt, M.D., are charged with the responsibility of enlarging the authority of certain physicians to be designated by name in such a manner that persons who, according to human judgment, are incurably sick may, upon the most serious evaluation of their medical condition, be accorded a mercy death.[14]

With this ordination Hitler initiated the "euthanasia movement" that Leo Alexander claims was crucial to the onset of the Holocaust. But even if Alexander's claim is granted, in order for it to be considered relevant to the problem at hand evidence must be provided to support the view that by permitting active euthanasia today we risk repeating in the future the scenario Alexander described. Furthermore, it must be shown that this risk is limited to active euthanasia, that passive euthanasia has features unique to it that prohibit abuses active euthanasia renders possible. This is what I will try to do.

It must be admitted that we cannot claim to know what affect active euthanasia would have, in the long run, on our society's capacity to revere human life. Knowing our present and our past alone, I think, is Sisyphean labor. And yet it must be on the basis of this kind of speculation that we attempt to solve problems like the present one. My own view is that a distinct possibility exists for widespread misuse of active euthanasia in the future. While this position, like its antithesis, cannot be proven, I can offer support for it that will reveal why I consider it a credible position to hold.

I believe that the danger of abuses of active euthanasia stems less from our potential for outright malevolence than from the ethical apathy or moral complacency to which humanity is sadly predisposed. People tend to think that grievous abuses could not happen because, in the rather insular world of their mind's eye, such abuses seem at odds with their salient moral beliefs. It would never occur to them, in the relative tranquility of their lives, that the varied pressures that the vicissitudes of existence can bring to bear on those beliefs could instigate their general overthrow. But these beliefs are, generally speaking, seldom understood to the extent that they could be given an intelligent explanation, much less a stout intellectual defense. This is not to say that people do not believe the things they say they believe; as Mill wrote in a similar vein, "They do believe them, as people believe that what they have is always heard lauded and never discussed."[15] My point is that because of the tenuous hold that moral beliefs have on popular opinion we cannot assume that that opinion would remain immune to unforseen social crises, or that our respect for human life would not suffer a gradual diminution as active euthanasia became more and more commonplace. The worst possible case, of course, would be the latter two working in concert—that would be a fell alliance.[16]

That we tend to overestimate our morality and our ability to learn from experience is evidenced by a psychological study that was presented by Helge Hilding Mansson at The International Congress of Psychology in London, United Kingdom, in 1969. In this study a sample of 570 university students[17] "were asked to react to a statement to the effect that 'unfit' persons should be killed by society as a 'final solution' to the problems of overpopulation and personal misery."[18] The rather startling results of her study were that, depending on how the proposed "final solution" was described, the percentage of subjects who approved of the given proposal ranged from twenty-nine to seventy-eight percent. Perhaps most disturbing of all is that the highest percentages were recorded when the proposed victims of the final solution were described as minority groups and the emotionally and mentally unfit. The total approval for all stated conditions was fifty-seven percent. Dr. Mansson drew the following conclusion from her study:

> The overall data demonstrate that the values ordinarily associated with a commitment to, and a belief in, the sacredness or worthwhileness of human life are not unqualifiedly shared by everyone.[19]

The study, as I interpret it, reveals the weakness of its subjects' commitment to their moral beliefs, in that those beliefs could be quickly dropped when expediency intervenes. I should add here that the various proposals mentioned such contingencies as a rapidly expanding population and limited natural resources, and that it was these sorts of considerations that apparently led the survey participants who approved of the 'final solution' to do so. Again, while this certainly is not proof of what we might expect in the future, I think that the reader can understand why I consider my position plausible.

But as I mentioned earlier, the potential for abuse is morally relevant in the case at hand only if this potential can be understood as limited to active euthanasia. For if it is so limited, then on the consequentialist grounds that Rachels appears to endorse a moral difference exists between active and passive euthanasia. And it is precisely the self-limiting character of passive euthanasia that has prompted some ethicists to consider it a practice that is less susceptible to massive abuses than active euthanasia. Passive euthanasia is self-limiting in that only those who already suffer from an illness can be affected by it. Withholding treatment is not something that could threaten the lives of people who are not already sick. Because of this an inherent feature of passive euthanasia is that it will always include a specific and relevant medical dimension. Contrarily, with active euthanasia the criteria for its employment are not necessarily so restricted, and this is why the potential for grave abuses exists and this is why a moral difference exists between it and passive euthanasia, at least on consequentialist grounds. It is worth noting, finally, that similar points can be made about how the two forms of euthanasia differ regarding misdiagnoses, possible miraculous recoveries and other questions.

In conclusion, I would like to make it clear that I recognize that my paper ignores any number of pressing questions, not the least of which is whether consequentialist considerations ought to be thought hegemonical in our struggle to solve the moral problems surrounding euthanasia. One conclusion that can be drawn from all of this is that the aforementioned question will be answered, in large part, by whether a consensus can be reached concerning how we are to envisage the long-term social consequences of permitting active euthanasia. This, in turn, will hinge crucially on how confident we can be about gauging the moral maturity of our society. In this paper I have—with more than a little trepidation—offered a very modest contribution to this project. If the case I have made fails to convince, perhaps this can be viewed as a slight indication of one limitation of consequentialist thought. ⁓

Ethical Perception and Managerial Decision Making: A Conceptual and Empirical Exploration[1]

Dennis Wittmer

Preface

I would dedicate this offering to Joe Uemura, except that it is just the kind of piece that Joe would prefer to attack (in innumerable ways) than embrace. Even though it is not a typical philosophical piece, it represents the integration of several disciplines that I have studied, including philosophical roots that were nurtured by Joe. It was at Morningside College that I was "bit by worse than a viper's tooth," Joe's own special ability to spur passion for the love of wisdom.

Joe, in fact, is one of those persons I have not been able to shake. I rather vividly recall how Joe would tolerate nothing but reasoned argument and truth. Indeed, the preface to my (empirical) dissertation begins with acknowledgement of Joe, in spite of the fact that the work was not in philosophy. Joe's kind of uncompromising demand for quality and reason, I fear, may be the vestige of the past, given the current emphasis to please and entertain students "as customers."

Yet, there was also a gentle, calm quality that I recall about Joe. He had time for students! He had the patience to help them move along at their own pace. He even had the time for a special trip (without compensation) to perform our wedding ceremony. Even there he demanded some explanation of our commitment. Now, from the other side of the academic table, I can appreciate the giving nature of his commitment as teacher (and friend). Joe is quite simply a remarkable man whom I was privileged to have affect my life.

Introduction

The well-being of organizations, their members, and society are affected by the ethical decisions made by those charged with leading and guiding these organizations. This proposition provides the basis both for the importance of understanding ethical decision making behavior and for developing management strategies and policies to promote ethically sound decision making in organizations.

The public depends on business executives and public administrators making wise and ethically sound decisions. The public may be cynical about power driven politicians, rigid and rule bound government bureaucrats and greedy businessmen. At the same time, demands and expectations for responsible decision making appear to be growing as the public increasingly perceives its well-being threatened by the practices and policies of various public and private organizations. This is perhaps seen most clearly in the current S&L scandals, a threat to fiscal well-being, and in the growing social movement to protect the environment, a threat to physical well-being (e.g. the Exxon Valdez incident). These problem areas also represent the common interplay of public and private sector managers and the shared responsibility for the problems.

Assuming that ethical behavior is desired and demanded of managers, there is need to increase our knowledge about organization and management ethics. One important approach is to define and explore normative or prescriptive theory, providing frameworks to guide managers in fulfilling their ethical and moral responsibilities (e.g. Rohr, 1989; Denhardt, 1988; Burke, 1986; Cooper, 1986; Brady, 1990). Beyond identifying the legal obligations of managers and administrators, normative frameworks may provide rational decision models, an understanding of fundamental ethical values to guide decisions, or explications of virtues that characterize the ethical administrator.

Another important approach to the study of organization and management ethics is to develop a better behavioral understanding of ethical behavior and decision making in organizations (e.g. Ferrell and Fraedrich, 1991). Such knowledge has implications for the selection and training of managers, organizational design, reward systems, and the creation of internal and external control mechanisms. The purpose of the research reported here is to contribute to our knowledge about ethical decision making behavior among managers and administrators. This is not a rejection of normative theory, but a call to complement the normative with the behavioral and scientifically based understanding of management ethics. While a growing field of research in the last decade, behavioral theory and empirical studies are still quite limited, especially in the area of organizational and management ethics.

The objectives of this paper are: (1) to propose a theoretical model of ethical decision making that includes ethical perception or sensitivity, (2) to present an instrument developed to measure ethical sensitivity in managerial contexts, and (3) to relate the results of testing this instrument in a decision making experiment.

The discussion shall proceed by first briefly discussing a conceptual model that includes ethical perception as an important element. The concept of ethical perception will then be developed. The methods and empirical measures used in the decision making exercise will then be discussed briefly, and this will be followed by a presentation of the results of the empirical analysis. Finally, a set of conclusions and caveats will be discussed, especially as they relate to management practice and future research.

Conceptual Framework and Behavioral Models

While numerous factors may influence the decisions of managers in situations with ethical dimensions, one important variable is the degree to which the situation is perceived, interpreted or seen as "ethical" (Jones, 1991; Hebert, Meslin, Dunn, Byrne, & Reid, 1990; Ferrell, Gresham, & Fraedrich, 1989; Rest, 1986). Decisions and behavior will, in part, depend on the manager's sensitivity to the ethical aspects of the situation. It is not reasonable to expect someone to engage in ethical deliberation, let alone act ethically, if the situation is not even viewed as ethical. In short, ethical *deliberation* implies or requires ethical *detection.*

In his popular best seller on organization and management, leadership, and personal development, Stephen Covey's theory of personal development is predicated on the view that we must understand "how perceptions are formed, how they govern the way we see, and how the way we see governs how we behave" (Covey, 1989, p. 17). Problems confronting decision makers may be seen by the relative emphasis on the point of view adopted (e.g. self-interested, organizational, legal or ethical). The particular framework or schema adopted is then expected to have an influence on the alternatives considered and the decision outcomes.

Behavioral Models

The proposed model builds on several recent efforts to develop a behavioral theory of ethical decision making. Linda Trevino (1986) has proposed a "person-situation interactionist model" to explain ethical decision making behavior in organizations. Trevino's model posits individual moral development as a critical independent variable in explaining ethical/unethical decision making, with various individual or personal variables (e.g. locus of control and ego strength) and situational variables (e.g. organizational culture and job context variables) as moderators.

A group of researchers from Clarkson University views ethical behavior as a function of individual characteristics and environmental influences, but as mediated through an individual's decision-making process (Bommer, Gratto, Granvander and Tuttle; 1987). Their model expands external influences to include various "environments" (work environment, government/legal environment, social environment, professional environment, and personal environment). Internally, the theory is expanded to include individual decision process factors (information acquisition and processing, perceptions of rewards and losses, and cognitive processes). The Clarkson model is important by making explicit the importance of perception to the decision process and outcomes. Information of either the nature of the situation or the character of the environment is seen as selectively filtered by the manager or decision maker and as having an effect on decision outcomes.

Another important contribution to the development of the model proposed here is the work of James Rest (1986), who has proposed a four-component model for understanding moral psychology, the first component of the model being interpretation or perception of a situation. Rest's approach to the complexity of moral behavior is to ask the following question: "When a person is behaving morally, what must we suppose has happened psychologically to produce that behavior?" (Rest, 1986, p. 3) His answer is a theory that individuals work through four psychological processes to produce the ethical behavior. These components include: ethical *interpretation* or *perception* of situations in terms of alternative courses of actions and the effects on the welfare of those involved or affected; ethical *judgment* or *formulation* of what would be the morally right course of action (that is, reasoning to some conclusion about the ethically right action); *selection* or actual *choosing* of the moral values and actions; and finally *implementation* or *executing* the moral course of action, which the behavioral follow-through or "doing" of what is determined to be morally right.

Drawing upon these recent conceptual models, the model proposed here conceives of ethical decision making behavior among managers as a function of an individual's *cognitive decision process* (to include the components conceived of by Rest), various *individual attributes* (e.g. self-esteem, age or gender) and various *environmental factors* (e.g. organizational reinforcements, organizational culture or professional standards). Thus, in the most general form the ethical decision making model adopted is:

Ethical decision making = f (ethical decision process, individual attributes, environmental factors)

This model (see Figure 1) incorporates aspects of each of the models discussed above, placing cognitive processes (e.g. moral perception and moral reasoning) at the center of the theory, such that behavior is understood as determined by how one perceives the situation and reasons to some conclusion about what to do in a particular situation. But the model also provides for the influence of individual and environmental factors that may influence the reasoning processes and managerial behavior.

To illustrate, consider a manager who is presented with a copy of a competitor's proposal and whether or not to use this information to improve one's own proposal. Applying the proposed model, the decision will depend on how sensitive the manager is to how the information was obtained and the consequences on the competitor of using the information. The decision will also depend on the moral reasoning employed, perhaps for example, that since this is an instance of stealing, the information ought not be used. Yet, environmental factors might influence the final decision, such as the organizational pressure on the manager to generate resources for his or her unit. At the same time, other individual factors may influence a final decision, such as self-esteem or ego integrity of the individual. The decision then is a product of cognitive decision processes as well as individual attributes and environmental forces.

Ethical Perception

This study is one of the few efforts to measure individual differences in ethical perception, and it appears to be the first to do so among management students. Ethical perception or moral sensitivity is conceptualized as the recognition or awareness of the ethical aspects of situations.

Ethical Situations

What is an ethical situation? By most accounts, it involves, as a necessary condition, that decisions or contemplated behavior will have a significant impact on the welfare of oneself and other persons (Velasquez,1988; Barry, 1986); although some have extended the scope of interests to be considered to include animals (e.g. Singer, 1975; Regan, 1983) and the environment (e.g. Commoner, 1971; Rolston, 1988). An ethical situation can also be thought of as one in which the ethical norms, standards, practices and values of a society or group *deserve consideration* in determining a decision or course of action.

What makes (managerial) situations ethical? What are ethical dimensions? Classical ethical theory may useful in illuminating these concepts. Aristotle understood that ethics was fundamentally about choice (decisions) and the pursuit of the good (happiness). Moral virtue (arete) was viewed by Aristotle as making choices (concerning appetites and passions) in accordance with a principle of choosing the "mean." Moreover, the good life for Aristotle and the Greeks (more generally) was to be achieved only in a political and social environment (city state). Thus, moral virtue for Aristotle can be understood as behaviors, decisions and choices (in accordance with principles) that would foster cooperative living, including appropriate choices where conflicts are involved.

Some of this Aristotelian theory may help to illuminate the "ethical" dimensions of decision situations. Consistent with this Aristotelian focus on principles of conduct that promote individual happiness and social life, most contemporary accounts maintain that an ethical situation involves, as a necessary condition, that decisions or contemplated behavior will have a significant impact on the welfare of oneself and other humans (e.g. Velasquez, 1988; Barry, 1986); although some have extended that which should be considered to include animals (Singer, 1975; Regan, 1983) and even the physical environment (Commoner, 1971; Frankena, 1979; Blackstone, 1980).

Typical of researchers in ethical decision making, Jones (1991) adopts a broad conception of an ethical or moral situation, stating that "...the action or decision must have consequences for others and must involve choice, or volition...." (p. 367). But such a broad conception is insufficient to delimit ethical decision situations from nonethical decisions. Indeed, all everyday management decisions affect others and involve choice. Some (e.g. Norton, 1987) have argued that since all decisions fit this criteria, there are *no* morally neutral acts. For example, an apparent nonethical decision to order pencils for the office will have *some* consequences for others. Perhaps one employee mildly prefers the feel of a different brand of pencils. However, this fact would not be sufficient to warrant calling this an ethical decision. Every choice will affect others in some way, but this fact by itself does not define an ethical situation, since this would have the consequence of trivializing ethical considerations and not distinguishing ethical decisions from any other decisions.

Such examples indicate why ethical situations or decisions are thought to involve "*significant*" impact on others. Thus, in the pencil ordering decision, perhaps a pencil manufacturer will close from lack of sales, resulting in a plant closure and layoffs. Because of such significant impact, the decision might then be considered an ethical one. Yet, even these circumstances stretch our sense of what one might think of as an ethical decision. While one might regard this situation in ethical terms, there appear to be no particular norms or standards that require or deserve consideration in the described circumstances. Moreover, the single order of pencils will not have a significant impact (by itself), so it does not seem to be "ethical" because the particular decision would lack any "significant" impact on the welfare of others.

Yet, these criteria (*significant* impact on the welfare of others and choice) do seem to exclude some decision situations from being "ethical." How one understands and defines "significant" and "welfare of others" are critical and debatable. However, situations involving choice of etiquette (e.g. whether to have the staff dress in formal or semi-formal attire) would not ordinarily be considered "ethical," since at least on the face of it such decisions would not significantly affect the welfare of those involved. Or an aesthetic choice about the architecture for a new office building, by itself, would not be "ethical." Both of these cases involve "values," to be sure, but in themselves they do not involve "ethical values."

It may be useful to further define ethical situations beyond affecting (or even significantly affecting) human welfare, in part because of the difficulty in defining "significant" and "human welfare." What also defines an ethical situation are the particular norms, standards or principles relevant in guiding decisions. Moral standards and principles would include fairness, honesty, justice, human dignity, and integrity, among others. Such values and principles, then, could be seen as constituting the "ethical" dimensions of situations, and a situation could be thought of as "ethical" to the extent that these values and principles are *relevant and deserve consideration* in a particular situation. Buchholz (1992) defines an ethical decision as "...a decision where questions of justice and rights are serious and relevant moral considerations" (p. 47). Such a definition is consistent with the above analysis, but unless all of morality reduces to justice and rights, it may be more useful to include the range of other norms, standards and principles (e.g. honesty, truthfulness, generosity, integrity, among others).

One might respond that these (ethical) values *always* deserve consideration. This is, no doubt, true and makes a fundamental point about moral principles. They are, in an important respect, the first principles of social organization and control. Organizational values or dimensions of situations may also be relevant and may be guided by principle (e.g. "control the external environment in order to preserve organizational resources"), but ethical principles are generally thought of as overriding when conflicts occur. Recognizing and adhering to basic ethical standards and principles is fundamental to cooperative social life. Thus, "...moralities are best understood as special forms of social control...." (Baier, 1965, p. v).

Yet, in many situations ethical standards are not at issue or in jeopardy of being compromised. Accordingly, we would not consider such situations to be "ethical." While adherence to ethical standards and principles is always expected (and in that sense *all situations are ethical*), unless a situation more directly and explicitly requires or involves considerations of ethical standards and principles, we would not describe the situation as an "ethical" one.

The above analysis indicates the importance of various elements in understanding "ethical decision situations": choice; right and wrong; cooperative social life; having significant impact on others; and justice, rights, and other particular standards and principles. For purposes of this study, an "ethical situation" is taken to be essentially one in which *"ethical dimensions" are relevant and deserve consideration in making some choice that will have significant impact on others.* "Ethical dimensions" are those norms and principles that "provide the basic guidelines for determining how conflicts in human interests are to be settled and for optimizing mutual benefit of people living together in groups" (Rest, 1986, p. 1).

Points of View

Perceiving a situation ethically involves adopting an ethical point of view, which requires, at least in part, being able to see situations from the point of view of others and being aware of ethical norms and standards that apply to the situation.

There are various points of view that may be adopted when individuals confront decisions. For example, when deciding whether to increase the price of a product (e.g. the price of an Aids drug), one may consider the decision from the point of view of the company, the manager himself, the consumer, or the general public. Different interests are involved and weighted according to the priorities assigned by the decision maker. Moreover, decisions and decision makers are relatively self-interested or disinterested, depending on their priorities. In theory at least, managers, in their capacity as managers, generally tend to weight the good of the organization more heavily in making decisions, and may generally then adopt an organizational point of view, that is, thinking primarily in terms of what is good for the organization. Compared to a strictly self-interested point of view, an organizational perspective can be thought of as more disinterested by taking into account a larger number of interests. However, while expanding the interests taken into account, the point of view may exclude the interests of many affected by their decisions.

An *ethical* point of view is another disinterested point of view that expands further the interests considered when confronting a decision situation. In his classic analysis of "the moral point of view," Baier (1965) argues that because the moral point of view functions as an "arbitration for conflicts of interests," it cannot therefore be the same as adopting the point of view of any particular individual or group. Moreover, Baier maintains that adopting a moral point of view is characterized by greater universality, such that it involves adopting rules that are "meant for everyone" and at the same time are "for the good of everyone alike." The interests of everyone affected are, in effect, taken into account when adopting an ethical point of view. This, of course, is not to say that an ethical point of view is the only point of view that should be adopted or the point of view that should always guide managers in decision making. However, the contention here is simply that decision makers and mangers will, in fact, adopt different points of view and hence have different perceptions of situations, which will in turn have an impact on decision outcomes.

A Perceptual Scheme for Managerial Decision Making

In terms of managerial decision making, one way of conceptualizing the perceptual scheme or the point of view adopted, when confronting decision situations, is along the following dimensions: personal, organizational, legal, and ethical. A manager might perceive a situation primarily from a personal point of view, that is viewing the alternative courses of action, for instance, in terms of career advancement or job security. This would be adopting a self-interested or strictly personal point of view. On the other hand, a decision maker might see the situation more in terms of the organization, emphasizing the resources or image of the organization. Yet another typical perspectives might be a legal point of view, seeing the situation in terms of compliance with the law or following rules and regulations. Finally, an ethical point of view might be adopted, seeing things in terms of ethical norms or principles such as honesty, fairness or harm to others. In the research reported here, these four perspectives or points of view were measured for a group of subjects engaged in a managerial decision making exercise. Differences were observed and related to decision outcomes and other key variables in the general model of ethical decision making.

Methods and Measures

Design

To measure ethical perception and explore its relation to decisions, an experimental design was deemed appropriate. A laboratory experiment provides a way of submerging an ethical case in a larger managerial decision making framework. This is useful for constructing a more representative environment of problems confronted in daily decision making, where ethical situations arise both in the context of a busy daily agenda and without anyone necessarily drawing attention to the situation as "ethical." Ethical sensitivity research to date has tended to cue subjects by having them identify the "ethical" features of vignettes (Hebert, Meslin, Dunn, Byrne, and Reid; 1990) or by studying their ethical sensitivity as part of an educational experience in professional "ethics" (Bebeau, Rest and Yamoor, 1985; Volker, 1984). In the fast pace of daily managerial decision making, there is often little time for careful analysis and reflection. An experimental design allows for the study of management decisions in an environment that simulates day-to-day task pressures, while not cuing subjects as to the ethical character of particular situations.

Subjects

Subjects were students from Syracuse University and from the State University of New York's (SUNY) College of Science and Technology. Since the study was, in part, comparative in nature, subjects were drawn from several colleges and programs of study.

Public Administration. One group of subjects were students in a Master of Public Administration (MPA) program in the Maxwell School of Citizenship and Public Affairs at Syracuse University. While most were pre-career students, a small number of the sample were mid-career students. Subjects were solicited from 86

Business Administration. Another group of subjects were students in the School of Management at Syracuse University. While most of the students were matriculated in the Master of Business Administration (MBA) program, a few of the students were upper division undergraduates. Students were solicited from classes in organizational behavior and one small group (13) from a class in business ethics. Another group of business management students was drawn from the State University of New York's (SUNY) College of Science and Technology. Subjects were drawn from a business policy class, which was the final and integrating course to complete an undergraduate degree in management.

The Decision Making Exercise

The experiment consisted of a three-part paper and pencil exercise. Each part was contained in a separate folder and administered as a single experimental packet. The first folder consisted of general instructions for the experiment, an inventory of demographic and personal data, and tests for several personality characteristics. The third folder contained only the Rest Defining Issues Test (DIT), a test of moral development. This part of the exercise was placed last to avoid sensitizing or cuing subjects as to the ethical character of the study. The second folder contained the actual decision making exercise.

Decision Making Exercise. A decision making exercise was constructed in which subjects assumed a managerial role making decisions about a variety of tasks and problems that managers might typically find in their in-basket upon arriving at work. Subjects were asked to sort through the tasks, recommend a course of action for each item, and record their recommendations on a log sheet (in the sequence chosen by the subject). The tasks included phone messages, internal memos, and external correspondence. The items consisted of one ethical case and eight "fillers" (items whose content and response were not relevant to the ethical experiment). Upon completion of the log sheet, subjects were instructed to complete two other forms in an attempt to "better understand their decision making processes." These responses provided the data for measuring ethical sensitivity.

The "Ethical" Case. An "ethical" situation was embedded in the set of in-basket materials. Several faculty with differing areas of expertise were consulted in developing an appropriate case. This group included individuals trained in moral philosophy, moral psychology, political science, and management. The ethical case involved the unfair and dishonest use of the information to undercut a competitor's proposal. Having acquired a copy of a competitor's proposal from one of their ex-employees, a staff member (in a memo) requests guidance in pursuing proposed revisions that would undercut the competitor. A tradeoff is proposed that would reduce the margin of profit but improve the chances of being awarded the contract. The context is further complicated by impending layoffs unless the unit generates new revenues. The situation is considered an "ethical" one, principally, because it involves potential harm to others as well as norms or standards of honesty and fairness.

Measurement of Key Variables

Ethical Perception/ Moral Sensitivity. Two instruments were used to capture differences in ethical perception. Because of the exploratory nature of the inquiry, both an open-ended question and a more structured instrument were used. As discussed, the different points of view or perceptions were conceived of as individual or personal, organization, legal, and ethical.

One measure is The Perception Test (EPT). Patterned after Rest's Defining Issues Test (DIT), the EPT is a structured instrument that includes twelve items constructed to capture four points of view (organizational, personal, legal, and ethical). The organizational items included organizational resources, employee jobs, and image and reputation of the organization. Personal or self-interested items included personal reputation, career advancement, and personal job security. Legal items included compliance with the law, following regulations, and legal liability. Ethical items included honesty with clients, community harm, and fairness.

The second measure was an open-ended question as to why the subjects recommended the course of action in relation to the ethical decision item. This instrument preceded the structured measure. The open-ended measure was intended to function both a reliability check on responses to the structured measure and as a way of gathering information about other perceptual categories beyond the twelve included in the structured list.

Decision Outcome / Ethical Behavior

The decision, choice or ethical behavior exhibited was the subject's recommended action to the ethical decision item, i.e. whether to approve a plan to undercut a competitor's proposal based on information "unethically" acquired. The situation is considered an "ethical" one, principally because it involves potential harm to others as well as the relevance of principles of honesty and fairness in organizational transactions.

In this case the most ethically right action was considered to be not using information from the competitor's proposal or rejecting the recommendation to revise the firm's proposal based on information contained in the competitor's proposal. Such a decision might also be the most prudent thing to do, if one is concerned about the possibility of such behavior being discovered. The ethical decision item was coded in nine separate categories, later collapsing the responses into one of three categories (adopting the proposal, rejecting the proposal, or a noncommittal category typically recommending further analysis and meetings). The basic coding scheme adopted was a three level ordinal scale:

Ethical behavior: rejecting the recommendation (to undercut the competitor)
Uncommitted: recommending meetings or further analysis; noncommittal
Unethical behavior: adopting the recommendation (to undercut the competitor)

Results

Ethical Perception

Rating. The primary instrument for measuring ethical perception was the Ethical Perception Test (EPT), consisting of both rating and ranking elements. The results of the item ratings for the "ethical case" are reported in Table 1. Based on group mean scores, public management students (PA) saw image of the organization as most important (4.10), followed by honesty in relations with clients (4.08) and revenues for the organization (3.97). Business management students (BA) saw revenues and image of the organization as most important, followed by honesty and fairness. Analyzing group differences showed that the only items yielding statistically significant differences were on perceptions of honesty and compliance with the law, and in both instances PA students rated the items higher.

Since the twelve items were constructed around four dimensions, the item scores were aggregated to create a dimension score. As seen in Table 1, both groups of managerial students rated the organizational dimension highest, followed by ethical, legal and personal. On these dimension scores no significant differences were found between sectors.

Ranking. The relative importance of the items, and thereby the perceptual orientation of the subjects, was further assessed from the rankings assigned by the subjects. Subjects were asked to rank the top three and bottom three items from the list rated. Table 2 shows the relative percentages of items perceived as most important to subjects. Consistent with the rating responses, subjects saw the situation primarily from an organizational point of view, with over 60% of subjects from both groups selecting an organizational item as most important. The item selected most commonly was organizational resources and revenues (37.3 % and 39.7%), indicating that even though only an experimental situation, subjects saw protecting the resources of the organization as most critical. While the organizational resources and revenues item was rated and ranked first for business students, the resources item was rated third but ranked first by PA students.

While subjects saw the case primarily from an organizational point of view, ethical factors were rated and ranked as the second most important dimension for both groups. Nearly 20% of public management students selected honesty to clients as the most important factor in the situation and their decision. The percentage of business management students selecting honesty was only half (10.3%) that of the public management students, and a larger percentage of business students saw the case primarily in legal or personal terms, as seen in Table 2.

Thus, what emerges is a rather consistent pattern, whether rating or ranking, of individuals perceiving the case or situation primarily in organizational terms, while secondarily perceiving the ethical dimensions of the situation as important.

Ethper. As a final measure of ethical sensitivity, the top three ranked items were combined on the basis of whether an ethical item was selected. While a subject might not select an ethical item as *most important*, a subject could still be relatively sensitive to ethical factors. As a measure that would be sensitive to such situations, the top three ranked items were aggregated, based on whether an ethical item was selected, with values for ethical perception (ETHPER) ranging from 0 to 3. As seen in Table 3, the distribution of scores shows the majority of subjects in both groups selecting an ethical factor among the top three ranked items, with 62.5% of the public management students and 52.3% of business management students selecting at least one ethical item. On the other hand, this leaves a substantial number of subjects who *did not see any ethical factor* as one of the top three factors in the "ethical" case.

Ethical Decision or Behavior

If it is possible to capture individual differences in ethical perception or sensitivity, it is important to determine the relation of such sensitivity to decision outcomes and behavior. Decisions were the open-ended responses to "ethical case." Two individuals coded the decision item, achieving an interrater reliability of .89.

The distribution for the decision item is seen in Table 4. Approximately one-third of the subjects chose the most ethical course of action, while approximately 40% of the subjects chose the most unethical action. A Chi-square test indicated that educational group (PA and BA) was independent of decision. It is also interesting to note that four individuals (3 PA and 1 BA) actually recommended to notify the competition about receiving a copy of their proposal. This decision demonstrated a high level of ethical (and perhaps prudent) behavior, usually accompanied with a recommendation to admonish the responsible parties.

Perception and Decision

What then was the relation of ethical perception and the recommended decision? Table 5 presents a crosstabulation of ethical perception and ethical decision. A Chi-square test confirms that it is highly unlikely (p < .01) that decision is independent of ethical perception. Moreover, strength of the association was found to be .30. As seen in Table 5, those choosing the most unethical course of action were also more likely to perceive the fewest ethical factors as important in the situation, whereas those recommending the most ethical course of action were more likely to perceive ethical items as important in the situation.

Finally, in order to test features of the more general model and control for alternative explanatory variables, an analysis of covariance (ANCOVA) for unbalanced samples was employed to test a more fully specified model with decision outcome as the dependent variable. Other independent variables (besides ethical perception) included AGE, EDUCATIONAL GROUP, LEVEL OF MORAL DEVELOPMENT, LOCUS OF CONTROL, AND STAGE OF MASLOW'S HIERARCHY OF NEEDS. However, while the model was statistically significant (p=.005, F-Value=3.55), yielding and Adjusted R-Square of .114, ethical perception (ETHPER) was the only statistically significant independent variable (p=.001)

Conclusions and Caveats

This paper has been an exploratory analysis of ethical perception or sensitivity in managerial decision making. It has shown how the concept can be included in recent behavioral models of ethical decision making. It has also presented the results of an exploratory effort to develop a measure of ethical sensitivity and test it in a decision making exercise.

Several conclusions might be drawn from the experiment and the use of the measures of ethical sensitivity. First, not surprisingly, subjects adopted primarily an organizational point of view, being most sensitive to organizational goods such as resources and image. Indeed, nearly 40% of subjects viewed organizational revenues and resources as the single most important factor in the "ethical case." A good manager, no doubt, must consider several points of view, legal, ethical and organizational. Yet in terms of relative importance, the priority of an organizational point of view is clearly evidenced.

A second conclusion might be that subjects were generally sensitive to the ethical features of the "ethical case," with individual and some group differences observed in relative ethical sensitivity. Approximately 57% of subjects identified at least one ethical good (e.g. fairness or honesty) in the three most important features of the situation. However, *perception* or *interpretation* of this "fact" may be like viewing the glass as half-full or half-empty. That is, from another point of view this means that over 40% of subjects did not identify *any* ethical features of the situation in the top three of importance. Yet this item was prepared as an "ethical" case.

Very little comparative (public-private) research has been done in the area of managerial ethics, with Bowman's (1976) work on attitudes as an exception. Results reported here indicate that public management students were more sensitive to the ethical issues, in particular to the importance of honesty. In terms of the decision, there were no significant differences observed between the educational groups.

A final conclusion might be that ethical perception is clearly related to ethical behavior. While the relationship is relatively modest, the more ethically sensitive subjects were more likely to recommend the most ethical course of action. However, some individuals who scored low on ethical perception recommended the ethical action. This likely indicates a prudent perspective without seeing the importance of ethical considerations. On the other hand, some individuals scored relatively high on perception but chose the least ethical course of action. These individuals, while recognizing the ethical features, may have adopted a more short-term perspective, opting for using the information to protect resources of the organization.

However, a variety of caveats and questions are raised by this rather exploratory research. For example, was the measure of ethical perception capturing a general trait of individuals, or was it simply measuring relative differences specific to the case or context? How useful is this kind of instrument as a general measure of ethical perception? Moreover, individuals may have been responding to the amount and order of the information present. For example, little information was provided concerning how a decision might impact on the subject's personal good in the organization, thus perhaps accounting for the relatively lower importance given to self-interested factors in the decision. Such questions raise numerous issues concerning the reliability and validity of the measurement of ethical perception.

Finally, how might these results be useful and what are the next steps of research? First, perception of situations will vary and this is expected to have an impact on managerial decision making. Thus, assessment and education tools could be created to increase the sensitivity of managers to the ethical aspects of situations. This is currently being used in the dental profession (Bebeau, Rest and Yamoor, 1985). Such assessment and training tools could be extended to the field of management. Besides refining and improving the assessment instrument (EPT), another task for future research could be the collection of cases from the field. These could be used as more realistic cases for training managers and sensitizing them to ethical aspects of situations in particular areas of management.

Normative ethical analysis is important in the area of managerial ethics, precisely because one does not always know what is the "right" thing to do. Normative ethics can provide understanding that may help managers confronted with dilemmas. On the other hand, we also need a better behavioral understanding the factors that facilitate or inhibit individuals acting in accordance with accepted norms. The differences in how individuals perceive situations should not be overlooked as an important factor in why individuals behave (ethically) as they do. ➤

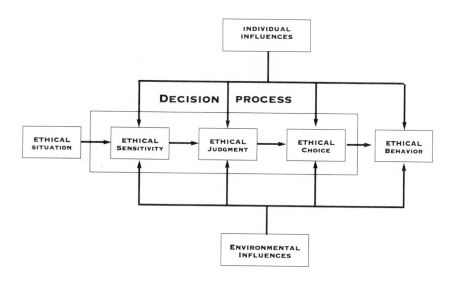

Figure 1. General Behavioral Model for Ethical Decision Making

Table 1

Ethical Perception Test
Mean Rating Score
By Sector and Perceptual Items / Dimension

Item	PA	BA	p=
Image	4.10	4.00	ns
Revenues	3.97	4.03	ns
Job	3.69	3.58	ns
ORGANIZATION	11.73	11.61	ns
Honesty	4.08	3.61	.01
Fairness	3.75	3.68	ns
Harm	2.46	2.49	ns
ETHICAL	10.29	9.78	ns
Compliance	3.20	2.75	.07
Regulations	3.22	3.11	ns
Liability	2.90	2.84	ns
LEGAL	9.33	8.71	ns
Reputation	3.18	3.10	ns
Career	2.39	2.44	ns
Security	2.41	2.49	ns
PERSONAL	8.16	8.25	ns

Table 2

Ethical Perception
Item / Dimension Ranked Most Important
Percentage by Sector

Item	PA	BA
IMAGE	15.7	10.3
REVENUES	37.3	39.7
JOBS	9.6	10.4
	——	——
ORGANIZATIONAL	62.6%	60.4%
HONESTY	19.6	10.3
FAIRNESS	5.9	4.4
HARM	2.0	1.5
	——	——
ETHICAL	27.5%	16.2%
COMPLIANCE	5.9	7.4
REGULATIONS	0	0
LIABILITY	0	4.4
	——	——
LEGAL	5.9%	11.8%
REPUTATION	2.0	2.9
CAREER	2.0	5.9
SECURITY	0	2.9
	——	——
PERSONAL	4.0%	11.7%

Group comparisons using T-Test and Wilcoxon Rank Sum Tests
ns = not statistically significant (p > .10)

Table 3

Ethical Perception Score
By Sector

ETHPER	PA (n=48)		BA (n=65)	
	#	(%)	#	(%)
0 (least)	18	(37.5)	31	(47.7)
1	16	(33.3)	20	(30.8)
2	14	(29.2)	13	(20.0)
3 (most)	0		1	(1.5)

Chi-Square (2df) = 1.367   p= .505

Table 4

Ethical Decision
By Sector

Decision	Total (n=120)		PA (n=52)		BA (n=68)	
	#	(%)	#	(%)	#	(%)
Ethical	40	(33.3)	18	(34.6)	22	(32.3)
Uncommitted	33	(27.5)	15	(28.8)	18	(26.5)
Unethical	47	(39.2)	19	(36.6)	28	(41.2)

Chi-Square (2df) = .268   p= .875

Table 5

Ethical Perception and Decision
(Number of Individuals)

Ethical Perception (ETHPER)
(ranked least =0 to most=3)

Decision	0	1	2	3
Unethical	28	9	8	0
Uncommitted	12	12	5	1
Ethical	9	14	16	0

Chi-Square (6df) = 18.87   p=.004
Kendall's Tau-b = .30

References

Aristotle. *Nichomachean Ethics.* In R. McKeon (Ed. & Trans.), *The Basic Works of Aristotle.* New York: Random House, 1941.

Baier, K. *The Moral Point of View.* New York: Random House, 1965.

Barry, V. *Moral Issues in Business.* Belmont, C.A.: Wadsworth, 1986.

Bebeau, M. J., Rest, J. R., and Yamoor, C. M. "Measuring Dental Students' Ethical Sensitivity." *Journal of Dental Education,* 1985, 49 (4), 225-235.

Bommer, M., Gratto, C., Gravander, J., and Tuttle, M. "A Behavioral Model of Ethical and Unethical Decision Making." *Journal of Business Ethics,* 1987, 6, 265-280.

Bowman, J. S. "Managerial Ethics in Business and Management." *Business Horizons,* 1976, 19, 48-54.

Brady, F. N. *Ethical Managing: Rules and Results.* New York: Macmillan, 1990.

Buchholz, R. A. *Business environment and public policy.* (4th ed.). Englewood Cliffs, NJ: Prentice-Hall,1992.

Burke, J. P. *Bureaucratic Responsibility.* Baltimore, MD: Johns Hopkins, 1986.

Commoner, B. *The Closing Circle.* New York: Alfred Knopf, 1971.

Cooper, T. L. *The Responsible Administrator: An Approach to Ethics for the Administrative Role.* Port Washington, NY: Kennikat Press, 1982.

Covey, S. R. *Seven Habits of Highly Effective People.* New York: Simon and Schuster, 1989.

Denhardt, K. G. *The Ethics of Public Service.* Westport, CT: Greenwood Press, 1988.

Ferrell, O. C. and Fraedrich, J. *Business Ethics: Ethical Decision Making and Cases.* Boston: Houghton Mifflin, 1991.

Ferrell, O. C., Gresham, L. G., & Fraedrich, J. "A synthesis of ethical decision models for marketing." *Journal of Macromarketing,* 1989, 9, 5-16.

Herbert, P., Meslin, E. M., Dunn, E. V., Byrne, N., and Reid, S. R. "Evaluating Ethical Sensitivity in Medical Students: Using Vignettes As An Instrument." *Journal of Medical Ethics,* 1990, 16, 141-145.

Jones, T. M. "Ethical decision making by individuals in organizations: An issue-contingent model." *Academy of Management Review,* 1991, 16, 366-395.

Norton, D. L. *Moral minimalism and the development of moral character.* Unpublished doctoral dissertation, University of Delaware, 1987.

Regan, T. *The Case for Animal Rights.* Berkeley, CA: University of California Press, 1983.

Rest, J. R. *Moral Development: Advances in Research and Theory.* Westport, CT: Praeger, 1986.

Rohr, J. A. *Ethics For Bureaucrats: An Essay on Law and Values.* New York: Marcel Dekker, 1989.

Rolston, H. *Environmental Ethics.* Philadelphia: Temple University Press, 1988.

Singer, P. *Animal Liberation.* New York, NY: New York Review Books, 1975.

Trevino, L. K. "Ethical Decision Making in Organizations: A Person-Situation Interactionist Model." *Academy of Management Review,* 1986, 11, 601-617.

Velasquez, M. *Business Ethics: Cases and Concepts.* Englewood Cliffs, NJ: Prentice-Hall, 1988.

Volker, J. M. "Counseling Experience, Moral Judgment, Awareness of Consequences, and Moral Sensitivity." Doctoral Dissertation. Minneapolis, MN: University of Minnesota, 1984.

Retention and Advising: Paternalism, Agency and Contract[1]

❧

Christopher Dreisbach

We may accept as given the perception, if not the demonstration, that faculty advising can play an important role in a college's retention efforts and programs.[2]

What we are not so ready to agree upon is the nature of the advisor-advisee relationship that is most conducive to retention. This lack of agreement may derive from the variety of institutions, each with its own mission, goals, and clientele (Daigle 40; Brophy 42; Lenning, et al. 5); and the variety of characteristics and what is expected of advisors and advisees (Bean 710; Brophy 9,10; Crockett 247; Heard 12). But we can allow for such variety and still make some general and useful observations concerning possible types of advisor-advisee relationships and the value of each type *vis-a-vis* retention efforts.

This paper borrows the basic models of the professional-client relationship from professional ethics: paternalism, agency, and contract. It applies these to the relationship in question: the one between advisor and advisee. And the paper argues for the general superiority of the contract model while nevertheless recognizing its limits.

"Advising" and "Retention"

Since the terms "advising" and "retention" are broad, some working definitions might be useful.

First, our discussion focusses on *faculty* advising as set apart from, e.g., psychological/personal counseling,[3] mere course scheduling (Kazazes 13), admissions and financial aid orientation/advising, professional advising (Crockett 250), and peer advising (Crockett 250, Daigle 41).

With Dressel we may distinguish the faculty advisor as being an assigned faculty member who (1) assists students in the selection of courses and fulfillment of degree requirements, (2) monitors academic performance, (3) responds to students' concerns or questions about electives, major, preparation for exams, study habits, academic deficiencies, career development, and personal problems (158).[4]

With Lenning, et al., we make take "student retention" to refer to student *persistence* to the (1) completion of a degree or certificate, (2) completion of a chosen program, but short of a degree or certificate, (3) completion of a chosen term or course, or (4) attainment of a personal goal, but short of a degree or certificate (2). This permits us to distinguish persisters from stop-outs (students who leave but come back), attainers (people who leave having achieved a personal goal but not a degree or certificate), and drop-outs (the opposite of persisters) (Heard 17). We should also note that dropping out may occur for positive reasons, e.g. a good job offer, or may be more beneficial than staying in school (Lenning, et al. 9).

Thus an ideal retention program aims at retaining students who can benefit from staying in college and only for the amount of time the student requires to reap the benefits he seeks or deserves. In other words, e.g., a college has not failed to retain a student who has taken the computer courses she needs to upgrade her job skills and then left the college without pursuing further studies. Nor has a college failed to retain a student when the student's dropping out was in the best interest of the student.

It is worth adding that a well-developed program helps not only the student who can benefit from such help, but also the institution by maintaining and increasing the caliber of its students and by contributing to its financial viability.

———

The academic advisor's main interest is the welfare of the advisee, even if that welfare entails the advisee's leaving the college. As a representative and employee of the college, the advisee also plays a role and has an interest in the retention efforts of the college. The academic advisor fulfills his responsibilities by giving the students worth retaining the best advising service possible relative to the mission and goals of the college and the needs of the advisee.

If advising aids retention, it follows that whatever enhances advising enhances retention. The literature offers many suggestions for enhancing advising ranging from *training* for advisors to institutional inducements for good advising (e.g. Atkins 23; Crockett 254; Forrest 69,74; Gordon 130; Hollander 10; Lenning, et al. 17; Kazazes 1). But the element of effective advising on which we wish to focus is the appropriate quantity and quality of advisor-advisee interaction.

Much has been made about the value of interaction and some discussion has taken place which attempts to identify elements of that interaction (Cahn 35, 36; Daigle 41; Finney 7-9; Gordon 127; Hollander 4-5). But we need to get a clearer idea of what such interaction might entail and here we shall find useful consideration of the professional-client relationship.

Paternalism, Agency, and Contract

In *Professional Ethics*, Michael Bayles articulates three basic models of the professional-client relationship: paternalism, agency, and contract. Each model differs from the others according to the allocation of responsibility and authority for decision-making (70-79).[5]

(1) In the *paternalism* model the professional assumes most of the responsibility and authority for decision-making. At times the professional may find it necessary to act or fail to act on behalf of the client without the client's voluntary and informed consent. According to this model, an advisor could be justified in drafting advisees' class schedules, e.g., without consulting the students or encouraging them to draft their own.

This model is defensible to the extent that the professional usually has knowledge superior to the client's in the matter for which the professional has been hired: the client cannot give full and informed consent and must trust the professional to exercise expert judgment. However, when the client is intelligent enough to make informed decisions, the professional should be able to provide clear and sufficient information for the client to participate in the decision making. On the face of it, therefore, the paternalism model seems inadequate when the client is capable of making decisions.

Closely related to the paternalism model is the *fiduciary* model which recognizes the professional's superior knowledge but allows for the client's consent to a decision. While this improves on the paternalism model per se, allowing the client a measure of authority and responsibility, it does not give the adult, intelligent client enough of the responsibility which the client might wish or should assume. Advisees are responsible at least to some extent for the consequences of their scheduling, so that even if they accept an advisor's draft of a schedule, their acceptance is a decision to go with the schedule and not mere consent to the advisor's authority.

(2) The *agency* model gives most of the responsibility and authority for decision-making to the client, with the professional acting on behalf of and under the direction of the client. An advisor assuming an agent's role might insist that the students draft their own schedules and assume responsibility for any mistakes in planning for meeting requirements.

This model holds a certain appeal for those who do not like to put control of their lives in the hands of others, even if those others have professional abilities, which the client needs but lacks. But it fails to recognize the ethical freedom and responsibility of the professional and takes from him his independence of judgment. Furthermore, it fails to take into account the professional's responsibility to third parties.

(3) The *contract* model puts the client and the professional on equal footing, recognizing "the freedom of two equals to determine the condition of their relationship" (Bayles 72). In this vein the advisor and the advisee might make their respective suggestions and then come to a mutually satisfying decision concerning the advisee's schedule.

In a culture such as ours, where freedom and equality of opportunity are so highly prized, this model has strong appeal. However, Bayles notes, the professional and client may not be relevantly equal. One would hope, for example, that the professional's knowledge exceeds the client's. Further, the client usually has a more personal stake in the situation for which the professional is being paid. And the professional has more freedom to enter into the relationship.

A particular sort of contractual relationship is one based on *friendship* "a close relationship of mutual trust and cooperation: a mutual venture, a partnership" (Bayles 73). An advantage to this model is the degree of the professional's interest in the client's welfare: the intent goes beyond getting paid for the job or doing the job well. However, the facts that the professional is being paid and that, professionally, the professional and client are unequal, suggest the hazards of trying to force a friendship onto a professional relationship.[6]

I believe that of these three models the contractual one lends itself best to the advisor-advisee relationship. Of course this model has its shortcomings and either of the other two models might be more appropriate in certain situations. Nevertheless, the general superiority of the contractual over the paternalistic and agency models can be argued from the very concept of advising and from the experiences and perceptions of advisors and advisees.

Let us return to our working definition of advising. The emphasis is on helping students develop their academic selves and on contributing to their self-confidence (Lenning, et al. 17). Toward this end the advisor *assists* students in scheduling courses and programs; *monitors* students' performances; and *responds* to students' questions concerning their academic, personal, social, and professional lives, with such response coming sometimes in the form of simply listening and sometimes in a more active forms such as the encouragement to clarify life and career goals (Crockett 244-48).

In the light of this definition one argument we can offer in defense of the contract model involves arguing against the paternalism and the agency models. The paternalism model is the *in loco parentis* model, one which has disappeared from most colleges. Colleges today do or should treat their students as adults who must assume much of the responsibility for their own education (cf. Finney 9, 10). Indeed, where younger students are concerned, one of the benefits of a college education is the opportunity to mature with guidance. Of course, students vary considerably in their readiness for decision-making (Crockett 248), their levels of maturation (Tinto 91-93), and their learning styles (Heard 12). But all of these differences are or should be seen as existing within the context of adulthood burgeoning or well-advanced. Thus the paternal model of an advisor-advisee relationship is less appropriate than the models which recognize the responsibility of the students for their own learning.

The fiduciary model—a moderate form of the paternalism model—has an attraction not seen in the more general category of paternalism: it recognizes the authority and expertise of the advisor, while giving the advisees the opportunity to consent to the advisor's decision. The crucial point here is that the model calls for the advisees' *consent*, not their *decision*. But as Crockett notes,

> Advising is a decision-making process by which students realize their maximum educational potential through communication and information exchanges with an advisor: it is ongoing and multifaceted, and the responsibility of both student and advisor. (248)

The advisor should not be given the authority to or the responsibility for making decisions alone where the advisee is also responsible for the consequences of the decision. And advisees that cannot assume such responsibility do not belong in college.

The agency model, on the other hand, places too much of the responsibility and authority for decision-making on the student. Certainly students new to college life need guidance from an advisor that places a responsibility on the advisor beyond that of an agent. And even students who are well into their college careers but who can benefit from seeing an advisor are seeking the advice of one they expect to be knowledgeable and authoritative. Indeed, if advisors are agents at all, they are agents of the college, not of the advisees. To apply the agency model to the advisor-advisee relationship, therefore, would be a disservice to all concerned.

In one sense, then, the contract model wins by default: the other two are simply untenable. But the contract model is not immune to criticism. For one thing, advisees often appear to expect the advisors to make the decisions and to assume responsibility for the consequences of those decisions. Many of us who have served as academic advisors have been confronted by angry students who will fail to graduate because of an earlier scheduling mistake. Surely, the advisees yell, this is the fault of the advisor![7] Also the college is often faced by angry parents who expected the college to serve *in loco parentis*, an expectation that is allegedly justified by the parents' paying of the tuition. And many advisors put themselves in a paternal position, sometimes out of expediency and sometimes out of a patronizing sense of their relationship to their advisees.

In the other extreme, students, parents, and/or advisors may expect the student to assume sole responsibility for their decisions. Students are, we have admitted, adults and the advisor's primary function is to teach, not to rear, nurture, or scold. Of course to those embracing this extreme we might ask what purpose the advisor serves beyond keeper of the rubber stamp. And if there is no other purpose, then use of faculty as advisors would be a gross waste of time.

So we must defend the contract model on more positive grounds. This paper has offered suggestions in this direction: the emphasis on interaction, the acknowledgement of both the expertise of the advisor and the responsibility of the advisee, the role of the advisor as guide, not parent, etc. And several references to the literature have indicated support for this model (e.g. Cahn 36; Brophy 7; Crockett 248). But it may be appropriate to interject a more personal observation.

At Villa Julie College, I have been advising for ten years. All relevant indicators point toward the superiority of the contractual model over the others. Villa Julie is a private, independent four-year liberal arts college, with a variety of students and programs. Faculty advising plays a major role in the college's retention program (along with admissions and financial aid counseling, psychological counseling, peer advising, extracurricular activities, and remedial programs). Freshmen and sophomores must see their advisors for midterm grades and for schedule approval; juniors and seniors have the option of seeing their advisors for these. All students are encouraged to think of their advisors as performing the functions discussed above and are encouraged to take full advantage of the advising services.

In a survey distributed to students during the final week of the Spring 1990 semester, students were asked to state how important availability of an advisor is to them and how they perceive the nature of the advisor-advisee relationship.[8] Of the 495 students surveyed (out of a student body of 1099 FTE), 133 claimed that the availability of the advisor was significant to their decision to stay at Villa Julie College; 7 saw the paternalism model as best, 128 saw the agency model as best, and 352 saw the contract model as best. Comments further supported the students' preference for the contract model.

In my own experience and the experience of other advisors with whom I have discussed this paper, students are more receptive to advising when they are put on equal footing in decision-making and when they are treated as adults, if not peers, rather than as children or inferiors.

The evidence so far, then, suggests the superiority of the contract model.

The nature of advising, the literature, and the experiences of advisors and advisees point this superiority. Our discussion has been a cursory, if not preliminary, one which begs for critique and elaboration. It is the modest aim of this paper to stimulate such study. ∽

Works Cited

Atkins, Karen B. *The Effect of an Orientation-Advising Program on Attrition Rates of the Allied Health Division at Spartanburg Technical College.* Practicum. Nova U, 20 April 1978. (ERIC Reproduction Services - ED 174 272).

Bayles, Michael D. *Professional Ethics.* 2nd ed. Belmont, CA: Wadsworth, 1989.

Cahn, Steven M. *Saints and Scamps: Ethics in Academia.* Totowa, NJ: Rowman, 1986.

Beal, Philip E. and Lee Noel. *What Works in Student Retention: The Report of the Joint Project of the American College Testing Program and the National Center for Higher Education Management Systems.* Iowa City, IA: ACT, 1980. (ERIC Reproduction Services - ED 197 635).

Brophy, Donald A. *The Relationship Between Student Participation in Student Development Activities and Rate of Retention in a Rural Community College.* May 1984. (ERIC Reproduction Services - ED 277 419).

Crockett, David S. "Academic Advising." *Increasing Student Retention.* Ed. Lee Noel, et al., San Francisco: Jossey-Bass, 1987. 244-263.

Daigle, Stephen L. *Attrition and Retention in the California State University and Colleges.* Long Beach, CA: California State University, Oct. 1979. (ERIC Reproduction Services - ED 262 679).

Dressel, Paul L. *Handbook of Academic Evaluation.* San Francisco: Jossey-Bass, 1976.

Finney, John M. *Student Evaluations of Academic Advisors.* American Association of Collegiate Registrars and Admissions Officers Monograph #40. DC: The Association, 1987?

Forrest, Aubrey. "Creating Conditions for Student and Institutional Success." *Increasing Student Retention.* Ed. Lee Noel, et al., San Francisco: Jossey-Bass, 1987. 62-77.

Gordon, Virginia N. "Students with Uncertain Academic Goals. "*Increasing Student Retention.* Ed. Lee Noel, et al., San Francisco: Jossey-Bass, 1987. 116-37.

Heard, Frank B. *The Development of a Retention Plan to Mitigate Low Enrollments at Shelby State Community College.* Practicum. Nova U, May

1988. (ERIC Reproduction Services - ED 296 751).

Hollander, Patricia A., et al. *A Practical Guide to Legal Issues Affecting College Teachers.* Asheville, NC: College Administration Publications, 1985.

Holm, Shirley M. *Retention of Adult Learners in an Individualized Baccalaureate Degree Program.* Dissertation. U of MN, April 1988. (ERIC Reproduction Services - ED 298 250).

Kazazes, Barbara A. *Academic Advising for Retention Purposes.* Jamestown, NC: Guilford Technical Community College, [1982]. (ERIC Reproduction Services - ED 284 612).

Lenning, Oscar T., et al. *Student Retention Strategies.* AAHE-ERIC/Higher Education Research Report #8. DC: American Association for Higher Education, 1980. (ERIC Reproduction Services - ED 200 118).

Tinto, Vincent. *Leaving College: Rethinking the Causes and Cures of Student Attrition.* Chicago: U of Chicago P, 1987.

Walsh, E. M. "Revitalizing Academic Advisement." *Personnel and Guidance* 57 (1979): 446-449.

Dewey's Theory of
Aesthetics and Art

Thomas A. Wilson

*T*his essay is my interpretation of John Dewey's philosophy of aesthetics and art. Its purpose is to distill the essence of his thought on this topic from the wealth of insights and examples he furnishes. This interpretation may not be in full accord with that of Joseph Uemura, whom we honor in this festschrift. As Professor Uemura has had occasion to remark, however, teachers are not to be blamed for the mistakes of their students.

Although Dewey's theory of aesthetics is, like its subject-matter, too rich and diverse to admit of reduction to a formal deductive model, there are nevertheless four basic elements to his work in this field which, when elaborated, result in a complete theory. These four elements are experience, emotion, the relation between form and substance, and rhythm-symmetry.[1]

Experience is not separated from nature. Because it is in and of nature, experience is empty of content even as a concept if considered apart from nature. As Dewey says:

> Things interacting in certain ways *are* experience; they are what is experienced. Linked in certain ways with another natural object—the human organism—they are *how* things are experienced as well.[2]

The essential conditions of life determine the nature of experience. The reason for this is that since the human being, although different from other animals, has many needs and functions in common with them, even the brain and other organs by which human life is maintained have been brought about by "the grace of struggles and achievements of a long line of animal ancestry."[3]

In summarizing Dewey's essay "The Need for a Recovery of Philosophy," Lewis E. Hahn points out that in the traditions of both British empiricism and continental European rationalism, experience is primarily a matter of knowledge and is regarded as a private event internal to the experiencing organism. For Dewey, on the other hand, experience is the interaction between the living organism and its social and physical environment.[4]

Aesthetic experience is the most characteristically human type of experience because in it consciousness, the type of experience unique among all the animals to human beings, is most completely manifested. This is evident by examining what Dewey means by "consciousness" and by seeing how he draws his distinction between the aesthetic and the artistic in experience.

"Consciousness" is a short-hand term for "conscious experience." Its distinguishing feature is that meanings which are signs of and clues to further experience, instrumental meanings, and meanings which are immediately enjoyed, suffered, and possessed, final meanings, are simultaneously present and, though distinguishable, unified. "And all of these things are preeminently true of art."[5]

Meanings, in turn, are qualities of interactions among organisms and of interactions between organism and environment when mind makes its appearance upon the stage of evolution. This requires some explanation.

Animals are sentient beings; that is, they interact with their environment by means of sense-organs. When means of locomotion develop in the organism, receptors of events at a distance from the organism also evolve. Response by the organism to these events at a distance are eventually differentiated into preparatory, anticipatory, fulfilling and/or consummatory activities or states. These activities and states become suffused with the tones of sex, food, or security to which they contribute. The activities and states thus suffused are feelings. As organisms become more complex, feelings become ever more various in quality and intensity.[6]

The form of interaction between and among organisms by which feelings are communicated is language, and the property of the organism which engages in the process of communication of feelings is mind.[7]

One might conclude from the foregoing that consciousness is a wider, more inclusive term than mind, but this is not the case. Dewey asserts that on the psycho-physical level consciousness refers to feelings but that at the level of mind consciousness refers to ideas. Mind, he says, refers to the entire network of meanings as embodied in organic life, while consciousness refers to the perception or awareness of particular meanings or sets of meanings. It follows, then, that mind is a wider term than consciousness. To summarize this point, it is best to let Dewey speak for himself:

Mind is contextual and persistent; consciousness is focal and transitive. Mind is, so to speak, structural, substantial, a constant background and foreground; perceptive consciousness is process, a series of heres and nows. Mind is a constant luminosity; consciousness intermittent, a series of flashes of varying intensities. Consciousness is, as it were, the occasional interception of messages continually transmitted, as a mechanical receiving device selects a few of the vibrations with which the air is filled and renders them audible.[8]

The difficulty with this analysis (which I think is essentially correct) is that, at least on this planet, the organism which provides the lion's share of the background babble and the organism which acts as the interpretive receiving set are one and the same: the human being. On the other hand, Dewey's notion of the relation between mind and consciousness allows for at least the possibility of the operation of unconscious and subconscious mind. Also, if and when biologists settle the question of whether some behaviors of non-human species, such as the gestures of the higher apes, the noises of dolphins, and the honey-locating dance of bees, constitute language systems, these behaviors, if they are determined to be linguistic in some sense, could be cited as examples of mind without necessitating that they also be designated acts of consciousness. The importance of this distinction is that acts of consciousness seem to be properties of persons, and I for one would balk at calling a bee a person.

With an account of what Dewey means by "consciousness" having been set forth, the distinction between aesthetic and artistic experience may now be examined. In *The Quest for Certainty*, Dewey maintains that aesthetic perception is concerned with particulars as such, without regard to the external uses to which they might be put.[9] An example of aesthetic perception or experience, given in *Experience and Nature*, is the delight that attends vision and hearing, "an enhancement of the receptive appreciation and assimilation of objects irrespective of participation in the operations of production."[10]

The aesthetic, qualitative character of experience is what allows the human being to have *an* experience; that is, to discriminate particular experiences from the stream of experience. An experience is aesthetic when it possesses a quality which, in spite of the variation of the constituent parts of the experience, unifies and pervades the experience.[11] In an experience of thinking, for example, the experience is finished or consummated when a conclusion is reached. Only after the conclusion is reached, however, can the premises which led to that particular conclusion be distinguished. From this Dewey concludes that an experience of thinking has an aesthetic quality. The material of an intellectual conclusion consists of signs or symbols which have no intrinsic quality but which refer to entities and events which in another experience are capable of being qualitatively apprehended.

Even though the signs and symbols which constitute the material of an experience of thinking do not possess any intrinsic quality, the experience itself is qualitative because there is present in it the internal integration and fulfillment reached through organized and ordered movement. Since, without this quality, thinking would be inconclusive, it follows that no experience of thinking is *an* experience unless it is aesthetic.[12]

All particular human experiences are aesthetic, but not all *of* human experience is aesthetic. To illustrate this it should first be observed that not all aesthetic experience is desirable or beneficial. The experiences suffered by those armies and peoples attacked by Caesar and Napoleon, for instance, were tragic and grisly, but no less aesthetic for all that.[13] Secondly, where habit, convention, and inattention determine activity, there is no unity, no means of distinguishing one experience from another, merely successive states or occurrences, and these from the standpoint of the observer and not the doer or sufferer. Such experience is anaesthetic.[14]

The aesthetic quality of an experience is produced in the human being by the experience and in the experience by the human being. Art involves action by the human being which deals with energies and materials by manipulating, combining, refining, and assembling them in order to bring about a state of satisfaction—a type of aesthetic experience involving a positive appraisal of the integral unity of whole and part. This satisfaction is not to be had from the materials and energies left unaltered. This process operates on what are traditionally called the fine and useful arts in the same fashion.[15]

To say, as Dewey says, that artistic experience is of even greater importance than is aesthetic experience is to say that creation is superior to taste. On this assumption, he holds, science is art, art is practice, and the most relevant distinction to be drawn is between intelligent modes of practice—modes in which enjoyed meanings are present—and nonintelligent modes.

> When this perception dawns, it will be a commonplace that art—the mode of activity that is charged with meanings capable of immediately enjoyed possession—is the complete culmination of nature, and that "science" is properly a handmaiden that conducts natural events to this happy issue.[16]

Emotion, the relation of substance and form, and rhythm-symmetry, the three remaining major elements in Dewey's theory of aesthetics, serve to characterize the nature of art and to distinguish the fine arts from the useful arts. By means of interactions and continuities of experience, perceptual feelings, as S. Morris Eames points out, become refined and differentiated.

> Some of these perceptual feelings emerge into sensations, some into concepts, some into desires, and some into emotions.

Sensory and conceptual feelings are basic to knowledge; desires are basic to morals; and emotions are basic to art.[17]

Dewey says that the aesthetic quality which unifies and renders an experience complete is emotional. He does not mean that emotions are merely comprised of the traditional list including joy, hope, fear, anger, etc., but in addition that emotions ar qualities of an experience as it occurs in time. This temporal aspect of emotions obliges one to think of them as qualifications of a drama, changing as the drama progresses.

As aesthetic qualities of experience, emotions belong completely neither to the experiencing self nor to the experienced objects and events but rather to both in particular interactions. Dewey's examples of this are the jump prompted by fear and the blush prompted by shame. In order for these activities to be characterized as emotional, they must be parts of a situation persisting over a discernible length of time and they must be concerned with or directed toward specifiable objects, events, and issues or results. Fear becomes emotional, then, when it is fear of something, someone, or some event. Shame becomes emotional when it is thought or felt by the self to be the disapproval by the self or others of some particular action or set of actions.[18]

By unifying the parts of an experience which otherwise would not be parts of the same experience, emotion fulfills its aesthetic function. When this unity is not merely felt or perceived but produced in a given series of the materials and energies of nature (media), the function of emotion becomes not merely aesthetic but artistic as well. The means by which emotion unifies art is the act or process of expression.

An expression of emotion is the interaction of emotion with the raw material for the art product, the medium. The result of this interaction is the art product itself. This expression or interaction takes place over time. In this connection Dewey observes wryly that even God took six days to create the universe and that a less sketchy account than is given in Genesis would show that it was only at the end of that period that God was fully aware of what He had set out to do with the chaotic medium which confronted Him. Dewey would seem to prefer the version of creation given in the *Timaeus* to that recounted in Genesis, since he remarks that only a subjective emasculated metaphysics would have God create the universe out of nothing rather than out of unformed matter.[19]

When the emotional quality suffusing and unifying a given subject-matter reaches a sufficient level of intensity, it stirs up or activates meanings and attitudes derived from prior experience. The meanings and attitudes so activated become emotionalized images, conscious thoughts and discrete emotions. Dewey employs the metaphor of the forge of the blacksmith or silversmith and asserts that to be inspired is to be set on fire by a thought or scene.

This inspiration, or kindled thought or scene, either burns itself cut to no purpose, often resulting in the tortuous and unhappy emotional unbalance of the individual, or, with luck, converts the crude metal of the thought or scene into an expressed and refined artistic product. In the happier outcome, the elements in the self proceeding from prior experience are thrust into action in the form of fresh images, impulsions, and desires. These elements emerge from the subconscious and are "fused in the fire of internal commotion."[20]

Because fresh images, impulsions, and desires have their immediate source in the subconscious (though their ultimate origin is in the interaction of the individual with his or her environment; that is, in experience), inspiration is traditionally attributed to sources external to the self, usually divine.[21]

Dewey believes that most incorrect notions of the nature of the act of expression stem from the view that any given emotion is completely formed in the psyche of the individual and that the expressive object or product apparent to the observer is the result of this fully formed emotion hurling itself upon external material. In contrast to this view, Dewey holds that emotion is directional; that is, it is to or from or about something objective and particular, though in all likelihood vague, in fact or idea.

As applied to art, if emotion really were completely formed before it suffused a given medium of artistic expression, individual works of art would be rendered superfluous. The reason for this is that emotions are not particulars but rather are generic types of feeling. This, at any rate, is what I interpret Dewey as meaning when he says that fear is fear, elation is elation, etc., each type of emotion being differentiated internally only by differences of intensity.[22] This view is similar to the Aristotelian notion that matter is the principle of individuation—the matter in this case being the medium—while form is the home and source of generality or universality. The difference is that, although for Aristotle form is only manifested in informed matter, nevertheless his forms are static while Dewey's "forms," the aesthetic, emotional qualities of experience, have histories, developments, careers, and are located in specific places at specific times. Thus Dewey's account is evolutionary while Aristotle's is merely taxonomic.

Art is selective because of the role of emotion in any act of expression. A given emotional quality will exclude all those elements in the medium of artistic expression which are uncongenial with the mood which unifies a given work of art. Indeed, the presence in an art product of elements in the medium not so excluded is a sure sign of bad art, for in such a case the unity of part and whole is incomplete; there are loose ends.

In the more positive rendition of the notion of the selectivity of art, Dewey, in one of his more famous turns of phrase, says that emotion "reaches out tentacles for that which is cognate, for things which feed it and carry it to completion."[23] Emotion reaches out for appropriate material to work into the medium. The appropriateness of the material is determined by the experienced emotional affinity between the individual and the given material, an affinity generated by the already ongoing qualitative interaction between the individual and the already chosen elements of the medium. Dewey points out here that although emotion is necessary for the act of artistic expression, it is not the significant content of a work of art. Weeping at the sight of a long lost friend, for example, is an emotional outburst or discharge but is not a work of art. If the mood generated by the sight of the long lost friend prompts one to write a poem, however, the poem itself becomes the matter and content of the emotion.[24]

Dewey, then, does not subscribe to a representative theory of art. The aesthetic experience gained in contemplating the *Mona Lisa*, for instance, occurs between the observer and the portrait hanging in the Louvre rather than among the observer, the portrait, and the long deceased model who sat for Leonardo.

P.G. Whitehouse divides the commentators on Dewey's aesthetics, especially on *Art as Experience*, into two camps. One camp holds that this work is a treatise by a pragmatist in the well-demarcated field of aesthetics. Into this group he puts Stephen C. Pepper, Eliseo Vivas, and B.A. Shearer. The opposing camp maintains that *Art as Experience* is an extension into aesthetics of an equally well-demarcated theory of experience by a pragmatist. The solitary soldier bivouacked here by Whitehouse is Philip M. Zeltner.[25] In addition to Zeltner, I would place S. Morris Eames and Bertram Morris in this camp.[26]

Whitehouse agrees with the second group of authors and argues *inter alia* that the difficulty in coming to terms with Dewey's view of the role of emotion in aesthetics is in understanding how it is that emotion is not only in the act of artistic expression, but also in the art product and in the observer's perception of the art product. The difficulty arises because of Dewey's insistence, alluded to above, that emotion is not the significant content of a work of art.[27] The problem, then, is to explain how emotion enters into both the art product and the observer's perception of it. The answer, Whitehouse thinks, is a careful understanding of what Dewey means by "in" when he says that emotion is in the work of art and in the appreciator's perception of that work.

The key to this understanding is the delineation of the different contexts of the word "in." When one says that cookies are in the jar, the word "in" is embedded in a spatial context, but other uses of "in" illustrate other contexts. "John is in the club" illustrates a social context; "He died in 1969" illustrates a temporal context; and "There are two twos in four" illustrates a quantitative context.[28]

Whitehouse maintains that "He showed courage in everything he did" illustrates the context Dewey had in mind in his discussion of emotion.

> We mean that whatever the actions were that he took, each one was marked by the same psychological state. In short, it was his courage that marked, attended, and informed everything he did. When we consider what he did (whatever it actually was) we

conclude that it was a result of his incipient courage. We infer that courage gave particular meaning to the act; courage was in every aspect of the act. Indeed, the act might have been quite different had not his courage been its motivating and guiding force.[29]

If "emotion" is substituted for "courage" and if the act mentioned is an act of artistic expression, the result is what Dewey means in asserting that emotion is present in the art product and in the observer's appreciation of that product. Since emotion is the cause of what the artist *qua* artist does, it is in every artistic act. It marks the result of the act. The result of the act, the art product or expressive object, embodies the emotional quality which brought it into being by unifying those tangible elements, the medium, out of which the art product was composed. When the observer interacts with the art product, he or she, being a live human creature of the same species as the artist, will have an emotional, aesthetic experience. The expressive object is the conclusion of the aesthetic experience of the artist, but the object is the stimulus for the aesthetic experience of the observer.[30]

Whitehouse's analysis is, I think, fundamentally correct, but it would have been better to say that the art object is the occasion rather than the stimulus of the observer's aesthetic experience. The reason for this preference is that, thanks especially to Pavlov, Watson, and Skinner, "stimulus" now generally implies a "response" which is in some, though perhaps only attenuated, sense automatic, and an aesthetic experience is not automatic.

Perception of an art object is indeed aesthetic, qualitative, and therefore suffused with emotion. The observer may, however, arrest the perception by stopping the process of interaction in its preliminary stages. When this happens, recognition rather than full perception occurs. In the act or process of recognition, some detail or set of details functions as a cue for bare identification. The result of recognition is that the observer labels or classifies the object and does not fully perceive it. Dewey's example of recognition is recognizing a person on the street for the purpose either of greeting or of avoiding him or her rather than for the sake of seeing what is there.[31] Thus the exhausted tourist plodding wearily through the corridors of the Louvre toward a waiting bus or taxi does not have an aesthetic experience of the magnificent works of art displayed there even though they are encountered in his or her field of vision.

The processes by which emotion enters into the art product an the observer are set forth in Dewey's accounts of the relation between form and substance and the nature of rhythm-symmetry. Since objects of art are expressive, each art form is a language. Each artistic medium (painting, sculpture, music and so on) expresses meanings in a unique way. The unique character of each medium constitutes the idiomatic aspect of art. As all language, regardless of its idiom generally or medium in the case of art, encompasses what is said and how meanings are communicated, the distinction between substance and form arises.[32]

Substance is the material out of which a work of art is composed. It belongs to the public, observable world rather than to the self. Self-expression is still an element in the work of art, however, because the self, the artist, takes this material and gives it back to the public world in such a way—the form—that there is a new object in the world, the art product. The material of the work of art must be public, for if it were merely idiosyncratic there would be no expression of meanings but only what Dewey calls "the state of the madhouse." The manner of what is expressed in the work of art, though, is both individual and unique. Thus, to recur to the example of the *Mona Lisa*, the original painting now in France is a work of fine art but each lithographic reproduction of it is an example of craftsmanship which, though valuable in its own right, must be classified as at best useful rather than fine art.[33]

Dewey by no means disparages useful art, however. On the contrary, he attacks those aesthetic theories which maintain a rigid distinction between fine and useful art in order to develop an esoteric notion of art; that is, a notion based not on the idea of the qualitative character pervading and defining each discrete human experience but rather on the idea that among the qualities and relations encountered in experience there is a mysterious quality (such as "beauty") which inheres in works of fine art but not in works of useful art. The customary distinction between a work of useful art and a work of fine art is that a work of useful art serves some purpose extrinsic to its coming to be and to its existence. Dewey, though, argues that the mere extrinsic use of objects such as bowls, rugs, garments, and so on, is a matter of indifference as to whether the artists who made them had the satisfaction in the process of making them and the enjoyment in the perception of the finished products which distinguishes the fine from the merely useful. One example is the aesthetic satisfaction experienced by the angler in casting and playing out the fishing line—a satisfaction by no means diminished by the fact that the catch is eaten. The notion that there is an unbridgeable gulf between fine and useful arts is, Dewey thinks, one of the lamentable features of modern industrial civilization.[34]

Just as substance involves what is done by the artist and what is presented to the observer, so form involves both how the artist fashions the medium and how the observer experiences the particular art product. The distinction between substance and form is in the reflection of the artist and of the observer rather than in the work of art itself, for the work of art is matter as formed into an aesthetic substance.[35]

A work of art is only properly so called when it lives in an individualized experience. Pieces of canvas, hunks of marble, and sheets of paper are not in themselves works of painting, sculpture, and literature. Only when these media are formed in determinate ways and when a human being experiences what is so formed is a work of art in being. Form, says Dewey, thus involves a way of presenting, feeling, and envisaging experienced matter in order to convert it most effectively and readily into material for an enhanced aesthetic experience on the part of observers not possessed of the skill and imagination of the artist. The symphonies of Beethoven, for example, are not strictly speaking the lines and dots on paper but are rather the sounds produced by symphony orchestras playing these great works.[36]

Although the distinction between substance and form is in reflection upon nature rather than in nature itself, since the discrete elements of nature experienced by the human being are always instances of formed matter, nevertheless a generic account of form is necessary in order to discern more easily how the concept of form enters into the work of art.[37] Originally, Dewey thinks, form was identified with physical shape or figure. The geometrical and spatial properties perceived through vision were the probable models for this belief, but Dewey points out that words and sentences as heard have shapes. His example of this is the view that a misplaced accent inhibits the recognition of a word or sentence more than does any other type of mispronunciation.

In addition to the geometrical and spatial properties it possesses, shape also has a function as it is related to recognition. As so related, lines, volumes, edges, and colors are perceived as being adaptations to ends. A spoon, for instance, has the shape it has in order to carry liquids to the mouth. Thus far the notions of shape and form coincide in aesthetic theory. There is more to form than shape, however, for as Dewey says:

> In some cases fitness is indeed so exquisite as to constitute visible grace independent of the thought of any utility.[38]

Dewey thinks that what happened to the notion of form in the history of philosophy is that when it was discovered how useful this notion could be in the definition and classification of objects, a metaphysical theory was elaborated which totally neglected the relation of form to shape. The form of a thing was now held to be intrinsic to that thing because of the metaphysical structure of the universe. Since the form was, in the theory, that component of a thing by which it is discriminated from other things (chairs from tables from trees, for instance), it was thought that the form makes that thing what it is. The intrinsic character of forms follows from this view. What also follows from this view is the belief that the form is the intelligible eternal element in an object, while the matter of the object is fluctuating and chaotic.

The term "design" is significant in Dewey's position on the relation of substance and form in aesthetic experience. "Design" signifies both purpose and arrangement or mode of composition. The examples of these two meanings of "design" are the design of a house, the plan on which it is constructed for the purposes of those who live in it, and the design of a painting or novel, the arrangement of its elements by which, in direct perception, it becomes an expressive unity. Design, considered as encompassing both of its meanings, is external to the material composition of the artistic medium. The example given by Dewey of this externality is that of privates in an army engaged in battle. Privates in such a situation have only a passive share in the general's design or battle-plan.[39]

> Only when the constituent parts of a whole have the unique end of contributing to the consummation of a conscious experience, do design and shape lose superimposed character and become form. They cannot do this so long as they serve a specialized purpose; while they can serve the inclusive purpose of having *an* experience only when they do not stand out by themselves but are fused with all other properties of the work of art.[40]

Substance and form, then, are interfused and unified in a work of art in such a manner that it is the work of art as a whole which is experienced in aesthetic (qualitative) perception rather than matter plus shape plus design. This unity and interfusion of substance and form in the work of art is accomplished by means of the bringing about and occurrence in the art product of rhythm and symmetry, which are in turn the modes in which the energies of the artist enter into the art product itself.

Dewey maintains that previous aesthetic theories, in spite of the fact that some of them have stressed the notion that aesthetic experience is an affair of immediacy of perception, have made a grave error in identifying rhythm solely with regularity of recurrence amid changing elements. The error involved in this identification is the failure to realize that aesthetic rhythm itself is a matter of perception and so includes a contribution by the observer in the act of perceiving as well as the artist in the act of production.

One consequence of this error is the conclusion that since, if one discounts weathering, paintings and statues remain in a relatively fixed state over time, there are two kinds of fine art, the spatial and the temporal, and that only spatial art can possess symmetry and only temporal art can possess rhythm. The denial of rhythm to paintings, architecture, and statues inhibits the clear perception of qualities vital to the complete aesthetic perception of these works.[41]

Recurrence is necessary for rhythm, but recurrence is not, in aesthetics, merely literal mechanical repetition either of material units or of exact temporal intervals. Rather, aesthetic recurrence is the recurrence of relationships which define and delimit the parts of a work of art on the one hand, giving them an individuality of their own, but which connect and relate all the parts in the construction of an expanded and complete work of art on the other.[42]

It is, therefore, appropriate to say that rhythm, conceived as aesthetic recurrence, applies to the visual arts. Once the relation between rhythm and symmetry is understood, it will become equally clear that symmetry applies to temporal arts, such as music and the dance.

Dewey says that rhythm and symmetry are the same thing, but with a difference of attentive interest on the part of the perceiver. Symmetry, the measuring of one thing in relation to another, is the quality discerned by the perceiver who pays attention to aspects and traits of the work of art in which completed organization is displayed. Relative fulfillment and rest are the hallmarks of symmetry. In rhythm, movement is the focus of interest. Symmetry, because it is an equilibrium of counteracting energies, involves rhythm. Rhythm, since it is a pulsating set or series of energies, requires that there be positions of rest between pulsations and therefore involves measure, symmetry.[43]

The general outline of Dewey's theory of aesthetics and art is now clear. Experience is the interaction of organism and environment. Aesthetic experience is the conscious perception by the human being of the integrated unity of whole and part. As such, aesthetic experience is the process and principle by which discrete human experiences occur.

Art is the deliberate transfer by the live human creature of the aesthetic emotional qualities of his or her experience into materials and energies external to the self in order that those, both the artist and others, who perceive these altered materials and energies may undergo aesthetic experiences which are more vivid and intense than if the art product were never brought into existence. As such, art is both expressive and creative. The transfer of aesthetic qualities from the artist to the art product to the observer is accomplished by the organization of materials into formed matter, distinguishable after the fact in human reflection into substance and form, and by the organization of energies into the modes of rhythm and symmetry.

Mood or emotion is the principle by means of which some materials and energies are included in the work of art and others are excluded. The work of art itself includes the aesthetic emotional qualities transferred to the art product by the artist, the art object produced by the artist, and the aesthetic experience obtained in the perception of the art product by the interested observer.

An account of the nature and function of artistic criticism will round out this examination of Dewey's theory of aesthetics and art. Dewey asserts that criticism, both etymologically and ideally, is judgment. Before elaborating his own view, however, he points out two defects inherent in previous theories of criticism.

One defect is what Dewey calls "judicial" criticism. A judge in the legal sense occupies a position of social authority. He or she determines the fate of persons and causes and, by so doing, determines the legitimacy of future courses of action. The natural human desire for respect and authority combined with distrust of novelty lead to the judicial attitude in aesthetic criticism.[44] Judicial decisions are formed on the basis of general rules thought to be applicable to all particular cases. The difficulty in applying this procedure to aesthetic criticism is that, unlike in law where rule-making procedures are well established and consist of prior court rulings and legislative enactments, the only source for aesthetic "rules" consists of prior works of art. As a result,

> Representatives of the school of judicial criticism do not seem to be sure whether the masters are great because they observe certain rules or whether the rules now to be observed are derived from the practice of great men.[45]

Dewey thinks that the real source of the rules cited by the judicial critics is admiration for the works of the outstanding artistic personalities of the past, but admiration which has become servile with the passage of time. The results of this servility are largely egregious blunders. As an example of this, Dewey mentions the resurrection of the critical judgments of the painter Renoir in 1933, fifty years after they were first enunciated. In those judgments, the critics of the day accused the artist of a random mixing of the most violent colors, resulting in paintings which were the products of a diseased mind, and which could only produce nausea similar to sea-sickness on the part of the observer.[46] It is appropriate to add here that in the thirties, the works of Dali and Picasso were criticized in some quarters for their failure to live up to the purity of those of Renoir. Even the best of the judicial critics, according to Dewey, fail to realize that in any art the very meaning of an important new movement is its expression of a new mode of interaction between the live human creature and his or her environment and that art is therefore crippled by automatic identification with familiar antecedent techniques.[47]

The excesses of judicial criticism produced what might be termed the "mirror-image" excesses of impressionist criticism, which is the second defect in theories of aesthetic criticism prior to that of Dewey. The impressionist critic believes that the artist merely records the impression he or she receives from the world at a certain hour and that all the critic can do is to record his or her own impressions of the art product at a given moment. Dewey does not deny that the aesthetic experience of the observer occurs as the observer interacts with the art product, but he strenuously opposes the inference from this view that the validity and import of the experience are affairs of the passing moment. To accept such an inference would be to reduce all aesthetic experience to "a shifting kaleidoscope of meaningless incidents."[48]

Dewey thinks that the fundamental error of the impressionist school of criticism is the failure of its members to realize that in the work of art the artist is constrained by the medium—a medium which is objective material in the publicly observable world. If the critic is to report faithfully to the public the aesthetic experience involved in a particular work of art, he or she must be sensitive to the same constraints as to what is expressed and how it is expressed.

The chief reason for the rise of the school of impressionist criticism was the justifiable reaction against the false notion of objective aesthetic standards held by the judicial school. The false notion is that a standard, properly so called, can apply to a work of art. A standard possesses three characteristics. First of all, it is a particular physical thing existing under specified physical conditions. The British imperial gallon, for example, was defined by an act of parliament in 1825 as a container holding ten pounds avoirdupois of distilled water, weighed in air with the barometer at thirty inches, and with the thermometer at sixty-two degrees Fahrenheit. Secondly, a standard measures a particular thing, such as a length, a weight, or a volume. Finally, a standard defines things with respect to quantity and is physically applied. A yard-stick, for instance, is physically laid down on that which it measures in order to determine length.[49]

A standard, then, both is and measures a fact. Works of art, however, exist not merely as facts (such as, in painting, rectangular solids of canvas of certain dimensions, one surface of each being coated with pigments of varying color, thickness, and texture, etc.) but preeminently as values—expressions of meaning. The attempted application of a standard to a work of art thus is bound to fail.

To say that no standards apply to a work of art is not to say that there are no criteria for aesthetic criticism, however. Dewey's criteria for the critical judgment of a work of art are contained in his theory of the nature and function of criticism which, now that his objections to other theories have been stated, will be examined here.

Generally, artistic criticism is a search for the properties of a work of art which justify—in the sense of explain—the direct reaction of the observer to it. When the observer says that a play is fine or rotten, for example, this reaction is not criticism. Criticism is a detailed account of the elements which result in either the fineness or the rottenness of the play. As such, it is a survey which serves the same function for the appreciator of the work of art as does the map or guidebook for the tourist in a foreign country.[50] Just as the guidebook or map is an instrumentality for making the features of a foreign country more vivid and pertinent to the tourist, so criticism makes the work of art more vivid and pertinent to the art appreciator. To the extent that criticism succeeds, it enhances artistic experience just as binoculars enhance the visual experience of objects at a distance.

Specifically, artistic criticism is the enunciation of synthetic and analytic judgements about the work of art. These judgments are obtained by the interaction between the critic and the art product. Analytic and synthetic judgments can be distinguished from each other but not separated—isolated from each other—in any work of criticism because the discrimination of parts, the function of analytic judgments, is only significant when the whole of which the parts are components is clearly understood.[51]

Dewey observes that since there is no art form in which there is only a single tradition, it is important that the critic become familiar with as many traditions in the art form considered and with as many works of art by the artist whose particular work is under consideration as possible. Such familiarity will prevent distortion in judgment by the critic and will provide the means by which the critic can detect the intent of the artist and the adequacy of the execution of that intent.[52]

The unifying as distinct from the discriminating phase of judgment is synthesis. Synthetic judgments are those elements of a work of criticism which make it an art form itself at its best and a blue-print produced mechanically at its worst. The synthesis in a work of criticism is the elaboration by the critic of a unifying pattern or strand which connects all the elements in the work of art and results in an integral whole.

Works of art usually do not possess merely one unifying principle, however, and the prior life experiences of each critic are as divergent in principle from those of his or her colleagues as are those of any human being from any other. Dewey believes, therefore, that one mode of unification selected in a work of criticism is as good as another, provided that two conditions are fulfilled. The first condition is that the unifying theme selected by the critic must be genuinely present in the work of art. The second condition, following from the first, is that the critic must be able to demonstrate that the theme selected permeates all parts of the work of art so that there are no loose ends. The test of the success of any work of criticism is whether, after the reader has read and understood it, he or she has a new guide and clue to his or her own experience of the work of art.[53]

There are two pitfalls, loosely called "fallacies" by Dewey, which the sincere and wary critic should avoid. The first of these is the explanation of works of art in terms of factors which are only incidentally inside them. In this mode of explanation, factors which may have entered—and perhaps even did enter-into the making of a work of art are introduced and discussed as though they accounted for the aesthetic content of the work. The psychoanalytic explanation of *Whistler's Mother* in terms of an Oedipus complex or the sociological explanation of Thoreau's *Walden* in terms of the influence of New England Quakerism are two examples of this pitfall. Dewey does not deny that knowledge of such factors, if this knowledge turns out to be correct, adds to human knowledge, but the bodies of knowledge added to are psychology and sociology (in these examples) and not aesthetic experience.

The second pitfall is what Dewey calls the "confusion of categories." In this mode of explanation, the critic assumes that the artist begins with material which already possesses a recognized status, be it religious, historical, philosophic, or whatever, and then flings it at the public with "emotional seasoning and imaginative dressing." This point of view mistakenly treats works of art as though they were merely transmissions of other forms of experience rather than, as is the case, new forms of experience in themselves. Russian, Byzantine, Gothic, and early Italian paintings, for instance, are equally religious, yet their aesthetic qualities are different. Far more significant aesthetically than their common Christian subject-matter, Dewey thinks, is the influence of mosaic form on each school.[54]

In the art appreciator who does not presume to write critical essays, the counterpart to confusion of categories is confusion of values, the former confusion being merely the articulation of the latter. Both of these confusions stem from neglect of the fundamental significance of the medium. Dewey remarks that every art, including science, philosophy, and what are called the fine arts, involves use of particular media transformed in certain ways in accordance with principles arising from the purposes of each art. Science, for instance, uses media adapted to the purposes of prediction, control, and increase of power over nature through the understanding of its processes. The experiences of scientists may also be aesthetic, but what makes them so is the enhancement of perceptual experience which is the characteristic of aesthetic experience. What follows from this is that when a given experience possesses more than one value, which is often the case, critical analysis must not confuse values by confusing categories. To conclude this example, then, scientific analysis and aesthetic analysis must remain distinct in order to obtain a clear understanding of both science and aesthetics.[55]

Dewey's theory of criticism follows from and complements his theory of aesthetics and art. Just as aesthetic experience is the intensification of perceptual experience and art is the enhancement of aesthetic experience, so criticism is the enhancement of artistic experience by its entry into reflection and articulation.

The significance of art for human life is for the most part beyond the scope of an expository essay such as this one. It should be noted, nevertheless, that according to Dewey imagination is the chief instrument of the good, for morality rests on the ability of each human being to place himself or herself imaginatively in the place of others.

> The first intimations of wide and large redirections of desire and purpose are of necessity imaginative. Art is a mode of prediction not found in charts and statistics, and it insinuates possibilities of human relations not to be found in rule and precept, admonition and administration.[56] ❧

James and Reid:
Meliorism vs Metaphysics

Ronald E. Beanblossom

William James is remembered for, among other things, his distinction between the tough-minded and the tender-minded, i.e., between empiricism and rationalism.[1] Having marked this distinction, James assumes for pragmatism the role of mediating between the tough-minded and tender-minded views. "I have all along been offering it [i.e., pragmatism] as a mediator between tough-mindedness and tender-mindedness."[2] Thus far, James' claim for the role of pragmatism appears to share a direction taken by Kant because Kant, too, seems to mediate between rationalism and empiricism. Agreeing with empiricism, Kant claims that all of our knowledge begins with experience. And, agreeing with rationalism, Kant claims that not all of our knowledge arises out of experience.[3] Moreover, like Kant, James' pragmatic views, with certain restrictions, permit a person to believe what they want. This freedom to believe has melioristic implications in both cases. Melioristic implications are revealed in Kant's claim "I have therefore found it necessary to deny *knowledge* in order to make room for *faith*."[4] Similarly, James' meliorism emerges in his famous thesis:

> Our passional nature not only lawfully may, but must, decide an option between propositions, whenever it is a genuine option that cannot by its nature be decided on intellectual grounds; for to say, under such circumstances, "Do not decide, but leave the question open," is itself a passional decision - just like deciding yes or no - and is attended with the same risk of losing the truth.[5]

However, the meliorism resulting from James' attempt to mediate between rationalism and empiricism presents a different challenge than Kant's to Reid's claim that there is metaphysical knowledge. In what follows I will examine James' view of pragmatism and consider how Reid would reply to it. Thus, I will consider James' and Reid's views on the relation of epistemology and metaphysics, the role of first principles, and meliorism. This examination is important for two reasons. In the first place it is important because pragmatism is credited with having helped displace Reid's common sense philosophy which was the dominant philosophy in "...American universities during the greater part of the nineteenth century...."[6] Moreover, this examination is important because Reid has been credited with having influenced pragmatism.[7]

I

In his 1906 and 1907 lectures for the Lowell Institute and Columbia University William James initially seems to support the priority of metaphysics. He speaks supportively of the view that "...the most practical and important thing about a man is still his view of the universe.... We think the question is not whether the theory of the cosmos affects matters, but whether in the long run anything else affects them."[8] To be sure, James considers pragmatism to be the means of resolving metaphysical questions.

> The pragmatic method is primarily a method of settling metaphysical disputes that otherwise might be inter- minable.... The pragmatic method in such cases is to try to interpret each notion by tracing its respective practical consequences.... If no practical difference whatever can be traced, then the alternatives mean practically the same thing, and all dispute is idle. Whenever a dispute is serious, we ought to be able to show some practical difference that must follow from our side or the other's being right.[9]

However, it is clear that for James the priority lies not with metaphysics but with pragmatism as an epistemological method. Pragmatism "...does not stand for any special results. It is a method only."[10] For James, as for Kant, epistemology is prior to metaphysics in the sense that he attempts to determine how we know before deciding what we know. Only after this epistemological matter is settled can we determine what, if any, metaphysical knowledge is possible.

An important difference between James and Kant is that James, unlike Kant, contends it is possible to settle metaphysical disputes, i.e., James contends that metaphysical "knowledge" is possible. For Kant, the examination of reason or how we know, results in the conclusion that knowledge is limited to possible experience. By its very nature, this characterization of knowledge precludes metaphysical knowledge. "For we are brought to the conclusion that we can never transcend the limits of possible experience, though that is precisely what this science [i.e., metaphysics] is concerned, above all else, to achieve."[11]

For James, pragmatism is an epistemological method which is not limited by the strictures of experience as viewed by Kant and by positivism. For Kant, and for positivism, experience refers to phenomena. James views experience more broadly as the "practical." Thus, "It cannot be said that the question, Is this a moral world? is a meaningless and unverifiable question because it deals with something non-phenomenal. Any question is full of meaning to which, as here, contrary answers lead to contrary behavior."[12] Not only are metaphysical questions meaningful but, as noted above, they can be settled. Thus, James' characterization of pragmatism as an epistemological method makes possible metaphysical "knowledge."

Reid and James are in agreement that metaphysical disputes are legitimate disputes and that these disputes can be resolved. However, for Reid, metaphysical disputes can be resolved, not because we enter the dispute armed only with a method of inquiry; rather metaphysical disputes can be resolved because of our fundamental metaphysical commitments. Thus, when metaphysicians attempt to persuade us that there is no motion, or no difference between right and wrong, or that there is no such thing as a mind, "Sensible men, who never will be skeptics in matters of common life, are apt to treat with sovereign contempt everything that hath been said, or is to be said upon this subject. It is metaphysic, say they: who minds it?"[13]

Should we, therefore, pay no attention to metaphysics? Reid recognizes that one might, as Hume did and Kant was to do, condemn metaphysics as impossible. "If, therefore, a man find himself entangled in these metaphysical toils, and can find no other way to escape, let him bravely cut the knot which he cannot loose, curse metaphysic, and dissuade every man from meddling with it...."[14] However, Reid is not persuaded that metaphysical quagmires are due to an inherent defect of metaphysics, a defect which makes the resolution of metaphysical disputes, as well as metaphysical knowledge, impossible. Rather, the fault lies with the metaphysical skeptic who requires the same type of proof or justification for fundamental metaphysical beliefs as for any other belief.

> But is it absolutely certain that this fair lady [i.e., metaphysics] is of the party? Is it not possible she may have been misrepresented?... Ought she then to be condemned without any further hearing? This would be unreasonable. I have found her in all other matters an agreeable companion, a faithful counsellor, a friend to common sense, and to the happiness of mankind. This justly entitles her to my correspondence and confidence 'till I find infallible proofs of her infidelity.[15]

Not only is metaphysics as a science to be judged innocent until proven guilty, but as evidenced by their inclusion in Reid's list of necessary first principles, so are fundamental metaphysical beliefs to be judged innocent until proven guilty.[16] It is because of these beliefs that metaphysics as a science becomes possible; we are able to resolve metaphysical disputes by reference to what we already know about the necessary truths of metaphysics.

Having said that pragmatism "...at the outset, at least, stands for no particular results," having said that pragmatism has "...no dogmas and no doctrines save its method," and having characterized the pragmatic method as one of looking away from "supposed necessities,"[17] how, finally, would James reply to Reid? In the first place, pragmatism, James reminds us, refers not merely to an epistemological method but to a theory of truth.[18] According to pragmatism, truth is man-made.

> In our cognitive as well as in our active life we are creative. We add both to the subject and to the predicate part of reality. The world stands really malleable, waiting to receive its final touches at our hands. Like the kingdom of heaven, it suffers human violence willingly. Man engenders truth upon it.[19]

Whereas for rationalism Being is one, for empiricism in general and pragmatism in particular, Being is many.

> The import of the difference between pragmatism and rationalism is now in sight throughout its whole extent. The essential contrast is that for rationalism reality is ready-made and complete from all eternity, while for pragmatism it is still in the making, and awaits part of its complexion from the future.[20]

However, with this distinction between, on the one hand, rationalism, with its first principles and "supposed necessities," and, on the other hand, pragmatism as a methodology and a theory of truth, it appears that epistemology does not precede metaphysics; it would seem that pragmatism does begin with a metaphysical dogma. Hence, James says that pragmatism, torn by the question of whether Being is one or many, casts her lot with the metaphysical claim that Being is many. "*The alternative between pragmatism and rationalism, in the shape in which we now have it before us, is no longer a question in the theory of knowledge, it concerns the structure of the universe itself.*"[21]

However, it could be argued that such a commitment is not inconsistent with James' characterization of pragmatism. James claims only that pragmatism does not *begin* with, i.e., presuppose, any dogmas - save its method and theory of truth. To see that some metaphysical commitments must be first principles and are not merely consequences of employing the pragmatic method, James' views on first principles must be examined.

II

I noted previously the apparent agreement between James and Kant that with certain limits we are free to believe what we want. However, this apparent agreement that under certain circumstances we are free to believe what we want and the attendant meliorism result from quite different views on the status of categories and first principles. For Kant, the categories are necessary ways of thinking which cannot be known to apply to that which transcends experience.

> This deduction of our power of knowing a priori... has a consequence which is startling, and which has the appearance of being highly prejudicial to the whole purpose of metaphysics.... For we are brought to the conclusion that we can never transcend the limits of possible experience, though that is precisely what this science is concerned, above all else, to achieve.[22]

Hence, Kant makes way for faith or belief in matters for which knowledge is precluded, to wit, that which transcends experience.

James, on the other hand, denies that there are such necessary ways of thinking. "Cosmic space and cosmic time, so far from being the intuitions that Kant said they were, are constructions as patently artificial as any that science can show. The great majority of the human race never use these notions but live in plural times and places...."[23] As artificial constructions similar to those we find in science, metaphysical concepts are hypothetical in nature and are capable of being tested according to the same criterion of truth as is used to test all hypotheses, to wit, the pragmatic criterion of truth. "*If these theories work satisfactorily they will be true....* On the one hand there will stand reality, on the other an account of it which it proves impossible to better or to alter. If the impossibility prove(s) permanent, the truth of the account will be absolute."[24] Thus, for James, the denial of necessary ways of thinking reopens the door - a door closed by Kant's efforts - to the possibility of resolving metaphysical disputes.

Reid and Kant agree that there are "first" principles. They disagree about how we come to know these principles and about the limits of their application. For Kant, the problem with a commitment to *first* principles is not their unchanging nature or universal application. Rather, the problem with a commitment to first principles is their perceived immunity from the need for justification. Thus, Kant's categories perform the function of first principles in establishing the existence of necessary and universal concepts, e.g., cause and effect. Moreover, categories have the advantage of being justified as to their necessity. What is lost, however, is the range of applicability of these concepts. As a result of the justification for them which Kant provides, these necessary principles of thought apply only to appearances. Reid, however, contends that these principles of thought are truly *first* principles, i.e., principles which neither require nor are capable of the sort of justification which Kant seems to demand. Moreover, Reid contends, these first principles apply not just to the way things appear but to the way things really are.[25]

James characterizes the pragmatic method as "*the attitude of looking away from first things, principles, 'categories,' supposed necessities; and of looking towards last things, fruits, consequences, facts.*"[26] To appreciate the difference between James' and Reid's views, to determine whether, as James claims, all metaphysical beliefs are consequences rather than first principles, and to determine whether, as James contends, epistemology precedes metaphysics, the nature of Being will be briefly examined.

In the discussion of whether Being is one or many, James notes that *in the abstract* empiricism in general and pragmatism in particular find appealing the view that Being is one; indeed, the view might be judged a matter of philosophic common sense.

> A certain abstract monism, a certain emotional response to the character of oneness, as if it were a feature of the world not co-ordinate with its manyness, but vastly more excellent and eminent, is so prevalent in educated circles that we might almost call it a part of philosophic common sense. Of course the world is One, we say. How else could it be a world at all? Empiricists as a rule, are as stout monists of this abstract kind as rationalists are.[27]

Yet, pragmatism ought not to be dazzled by the initial attractiveness of this monistic view of nature, for pragmatism presupposes no dogma. The pragmatic question, then, must be asked.

> Thus the pragmatic question 'What is the oneness known as? What practical difference will it make?' saves us from all feverish excitement over it as a principle of sublimity and carries us forward into the stream of experience with a cool head. The stream may indeed reveal far more connexion (sic) and union than are now suspect, but we are not entitled on pragmatic principles to claim absolute oneness in any respect in advance.[28]

James' claim that we cannot, on pragmatic grounds, commit ourselves in advance to either monism or pluralism is radically at odds with Reid's views. As James notes, the concept of substance has been used by monists as the unifying concept. "...Universal substance [is that] which alone has being in and from itself, and of which all the particulars of experience are but forms to which it gives support."[29] Among Reid's first principles of necessary truths is the belief in substance. According to Reid, we find it necessary to distinguish between sensible qualities and substances to which they belong; we find it necessary to distinguish between thought and minds to which they belong. This distinction is evident in *how* we express ourselves, i.e., it is evident in the structure of language which reflects the beliefs of mankind. Thus, languages employing subjects and predicates convey our belief in the distinction between substance and the qualities which belong to those substances. Moreover, our belief in this distinction is often implied by *what* we say.[30] Reid does not give examples of what he means. However, it would seem that when someone holds you responsible for your actions, it is *you* to whom they refer is a unity or substance, some one thing who really is responsible rather than a plurality or congeries of perceptions put together for the sake of the perceiver's convenience. It is *you* who are judged responsible despite any accidental changes you may have undergone in the interim.

One of the troubling aspects of James' position emerges from the pragmatic question "What practical difference will it make?" in deciding whether reality is one or many. Having concluded that there is little or no practical difference resulting from either hypothesis, James should not opt for one position or the other—as he himself admits. "With her criterion of the practical differences that theories make, we see that she must equally abjure absolute monism and absolute pluralism."[31] Yet, James contradicts his claim that pragmatism carries with it no dogma, that epistemology precedes metaphysics. "Pragmatism, pending the final empirical ascertainment of just what the balance of union and discussion among things may be, must obviously range herself upon the pluralistic side."[32] No less troubling than this apparent contradiction are the claims that there can be an "*empirical* ascertainment" of an admittedly *metaphysical* question and that an *empirical* ascertainment can be "final." As Reid notes, metaphysical claims are claims about what is necessary, e.g., every event *must* have a cause.

> ...the proposition to be proved is not a contingent but a necessary proposition. It is not that things which began to exist commonly have a cause, or even that they always in fact have a cause; but that they must have a cause....
>
> Propositions of this kind from their nature, are incapable of proof by induction. Experience informs us only of what is or has been, not of what must be....[33]

Furthermore, the metaphysical commitment which rejects absolute monism determines what and how we can know. That is to say, pragmatism, as a methodology and theory of truth would seem to necessitate a rejection of absolute monism and, thus, not be predisposed to discover the unity claimed by absolute monism. It is only by virtue of the metaphysical assumption of a pluralistic universe, i.e., a universe in which Being is not absolutely one, that it would seem to make sense to speak of reality and truth as malleable.[34] Even if one concludes that the ultimate nature of reality is change, we cannot change or alter the nature of that reality or truth. Yet, unlike other empirical methodologies which also presuppose pluralism, pragmatism, according to James, *can* entertain the hypothesis of absolute monism. "Some day, she admits, even total union, with one knower, one origin, and a universe consolidated in every conceivable way, may turn out to be the most acceptable of all hypotheses."[35] The dimension of pragmatism and the practical which James uses to entertain the hypothesis of absolute monism despite its commitment to pluralism is meliorism. Likewise, it is meliorism that enables pragmatism to mediate between empiricism and rationalism. It is the rejection of metaphysics in favor of meliorism that also separates James and Reid. Thus, in what follows I will examine this crucial aspect of James' concept of the practical.

III

In the second of the series of lectures delivered at the Lowell Institute and Columbia University James claims that pragmatism shares the positivistic "...disdain for verbal solutions, useless questions and metaphysical abstractions."[36] Indeed, if anything, according to James, pragmatism represents a more radical though less objectionable form of empiricism than positivism or other forms of empiricism. "That means the empiricist temper regnant and the rationalist temper sincerely given up."[37] Despite this affirmation of empiricism and denial of rationalism, James in subsequent lectures at the Lowell Institute and Columbia University (in 1906 and 1907) views pragmatism as a mediator between the tough-minded (empiricism) and tender-minded (rationalism).

> I have all along been offering it [i.e., pragmatism]expressly as a mediator between tough-mindedness andtender-mindedness. If the notion of a world ante rem, whether taken abstractly like the word winter, or concretely as the hypothesis of an Absolute, can be shown to have any consequences whatever for our life it has meaning. If the meaning works, it will have some truth that ought to be held to through all possible reformulations, for pragmatism.

> The absolutistic hypothesis, that perfection is eternal, aboriginal, and most real, has a perfectly definite meaning, and it works religiously.[38]

This deviation from positivistism is evident in metaphysical questions other than those dealing with the nature of Being. In each of these issues meliorism accounts for the deviation. For example, positivism would dismiss as meaningless the question of whether this is a moral universe. However, this is a significant question for pragmatism.

> It is only in the lonely emergencies of life that our creed is tested: then routine maxims fail, and we fall back on our gods. It cannot be said that the question, Is this a moral world? is a meaningless and unverifiable question because it deals with something non-phenomenal. Any question is full of meaning to which, as here, contrary answers lead to contrary behavior.[39]

Having previously claimed that pragmatism has no dogma, no metaphysical starting point, James begins his metaphysical examination of the nature of obligation and the good with the metaphysical claim that there is no moral order which exists apart from sentient beings.[40] In James' view of the universe there is no good except as created by sentient beings. So far as a sentient being "...feels anything to be good, he *makes* it good."[41] Likewise only sentient beings determine obligation.

> ...the moment we take a steady look at the question, we see not only that without a claim actually made by some concrete person, there can be no obligation, but that there is some obligation wherever there is a claim.... Our ordinary attitude of regarding ourselves as subject to an overarching system of moral relations, true "in themselves," is therefore either an out-and-out superstition, or else it must be treated as a merely provisional abstraction from that real thinker in whose actual demand upon us to think as he does our obligation must be ultimately based.[42]

Thus, on James' account of the good and obligation we are left either with a moral relativism (subjectivism) based on the feelings of individual thinkers or a moral absolutism achieved by relativising good and obligation to the feeling of a solitary thinker.

Meliorism permits James on practical grounds to embrace absolutism, despite his commitment to subjectivism. James offers essentially two practical arguments. The first is a "slippery slope" argument. If there is absolutely nothing which is intrinsically good and which we have an obligation to perform despite our feelings to the contrary, the practical result is what James calls a "nerveless" sentimentality or unlimited sensualism. Subjectivism, left unchecked, "...exhausts itself in every sort of spiritual, moral, and practical license. Its optimism turns to an ethical indifference...."[43] There may be a *feeling* that ethical indifference and moral license are intolerable. Thus, meliorism permits James to reject on practical grounds that subjectivism to which his metaphysical analysis of the good and obligation committed him at the outset.

The second argument in which James' meliorism permits him to embrace absolutism, despite his commitment to subjectivism, is based upon the antinomian or romantic result of subjectivism. A world in which morals are subjective "...appears to us potentially as what.... Carlyle once called it, a vast, gloomy, solitary Golgotha and mill of death."[44] There is no theoretical escape from these unacceptable results of subjectivism. There is only a practical escape. James' meliorism makes it permissible to regard the good and obligation as

> ...something else than our feeling as our limit, our master, and our law; be willing to live and die in its service—and, at a stroke, we have passed from the subjective into the objective philosophy of things, much as one awakens from some feverish dream, full of bad lights and noises, to find one's self bathed in the sacred coolness and quiet of the air of the night.[45]

Thus, in the case of ethics a prior metaphysical commitment, to wit, to the claim that there is no moral order independent of sentient beings, commits James to subjectivism. Given the presupposition of subjectivism, there is no *theoretical* escape from its consequences. However, meliorism can justify, on *practical* grounds, opting for a belief in objectivism. If we *make* the truth in ethics, then subjective satisfaction can justify the belief that there is objectivity in morals. This objectivity can be achieved by believing in an ultimate sentient being.

Similarly, in considering the metaphysical question of whether the thesis of determinism or indeterminism is true, James claims that "...from any strict theoretical point of view, the question is insolvable."[46] However, there is the possibility of a practical resolution, a resolution justified by meliorism.

> The arguments I am about to urge all proceed on two suppositions: first when we make theories about the world and discuss them with one another, we do so in order to attain a conception which shall give us subjective satisfaction; and second, if there be two conceptions, and the one seems to us, on the whole, more rational than the other, we are entitled to suppose that the more rational one is the truer of the two.[47]

What does James mean by rationality? By rationality James seems to mean consistency *with* our demands for subjective satisfaction as well as *among* the beliefs that provide subjective satisfaction.

If a certain formula for expressing the nature of the world violates my moral demand, I shall feel as free to throw it overboard, or at least to doubt it, as if it disappointed my demand for uniformity of sequence, for example; the one demand being, so far as I can see, quite as subjective and emotional as the other is.[48]

Moral subjectivism fosters a sort of fatalism or pessimism. What happens doesn't make any difference since what one individual wants to believe is no better or worse than what another individual wants to believe. There is, thus, no basis for moral condemnation if all moral beliefs are equally good. Likewise, determinism fosters fatalism or pessimism. We cannot do anything about what happens. Why have regret over the occurrence of an event if things could not have been otherwise? "I cannot understand the willingness to act, no matter how we feel, without the belief that acts are really good and bad. I cannot understand the belief that an act is bad, without regret at its happening. I cannot understand regret without the admission of real, genuine possibilities in the world."[49] Thus, for James, not only does belief in indeterminism give him subjective satisfaction but the belief in indeterminism is consistent with his moral demands, demands likewise justified by subjective satisfaction. The belief in indeterminism is, therefore, more rational for James. "For my own part, though, whatever difficulties may beset the philosophy of objective right and wrong, and the indeterminism it seems to imply, determinism, with its alternative of pessimism or romanticism, contains difficulties that are greater still."[50]

IV

Reid's emphasis upon the practical concerns of life and the use of those concerns in resolving philosophical disputes may give rise to the mistaken notion that he has more in common with pragmatism in general, and James' meliorism in particular, than is in fact the case. Reid's arguments relating to the belief in personal freedom might seem to support this mistaken view. Thus, it is important to examine these aspects of Reid's philosophy to show that though the practical plays an important role in both the philosophy of Reid and James, it is used in quite different ways and for different purposes. Indeed, the differences between Reid and James concerning the nature and role of the practical are the keys to understanding their respective views on metaphysics.

For Reid, common sense beliefs are not a fund of basic beliefs which are altered over time as practical needs may require. For example, when conflicts within our system of beliefs are generated, common sense beliefs are not altered in order to resolve the conflict and thereby enable us to accommodate new beliefs. Instead, new beliefs must be accommodated, i.e., be consistent with our fund of common sense beliefs or else be rejected. Thus, when a philosophy attempts to alter or omit a common sense belief in order to resolve conflicts of belief, the effort is doomed. When philosophy calls "...to her bar the dictates of common sense.... These decline this jurisdiction; they disdain the trial of reasoning, and disown its authority; they neither claim its aid, nor dread its attacks."[51] Reid is *not* claiming that common sense beliefs are immune from all examination. Rather, he must mean that our attempts to accommodate non-commonsensical beliefs cannot come at the expense of common sense beliefs; personal expediency or subjective satisfaction is not a virtue. This interpretation of the above quotation is supported by Reid's later comments on disputes about common sense beliefs. Reid acknowledges that common sense beliefs are not immune from examination. Disputes may even arise about whether a belief is a common sense belief, i.e., first principle. Reid provides a list of criteria for resolving such disputes.[52] However, common sense beliefs or first principles are immune from alteration and deletion arising from other philosophical or practical agendas.

The practical is used by Reid as one test of common sense beliefs. However, the consideration is not whether such beliefs provide subjective satisfaction. Rather, the consideration is whether we find it practically *necessary* to accept these beliefs. Though appearance does not always coincide with reality, Reid seems to believe that a "metaphysic" which has no relation to experience is suspect. Thus, one of the tests of common sense beliefs is "practical," i.e., our practices. "When an opinion is so necessary in the conduct of life, that without the belief of it, a man must be led into a thousand absurdities in practice, such an opinion, when we can give no other reason for it, may safely be taken for a first principle."[53] You cannot prove that you should trust your senses. However, the belief that the senses are a reliable source of knowledge is a first principle as attested to by the practical *necessity* of believing them. "But what is the consequence? I resolve not to believe my senses. I break my nose against a post...; I step into a dirty kennel; and after twenty such wise rational actions, I am taken up and clapped into a madhouse."[54] This sense of the practical, however, is one which James is also forced to acknowledge, despite his claim that truth is "created." "The future movements of the stars or the facts of past history are determined now once for all, whether I like them or not. They are given irrespective of my wishes, and in all that concerns truths like these *subjective preference* should have no part"[55] (emphasis mine). According to Reid, it is not just the stars which are fixed and to which our beliefs must conform. Metaphysical truths are fixed and our beliefs and knowledge must conform to them or we risk both philosophical and practical absurdity.

For Reid there is a theoretical resolution to metaphysical problems. The practical necessity of observing common sense beliefs, i.e., first principles, does not imply a practical resolution to metaphysical problems but a theoretical resolution. The necessity of observing first principles is due to the nature of reality. Thus, some philosophical disputes can be theoretically resolved by reference to what we know to be true of the nature of things.

> Zeno endeavored to demonstrate the impossibility of motion;
> Hobbes, that there was no difference between right and wrong;
> and this author [i.e., Hume], that no credit is to be given to our
> senses, to our memory, or even to demonstration. Such philoso-
> phy is justly ridiculous, even to those who cannot detect the fal-
> lacy of it. It can have no other tendency, than to shew (sic) the
> acuteness of the sophist, at the expense of disgracing reason and
> human nature, and making mankind Yahoos.[56]

For Reid our common sense beliefs about the nature of things, e.g.,
human freedom, are to be treated as innocent until proven guilty. James' practical
arguments for indeterminism, as outlined above, appear to be similar to Reid's
arguments for moral liberty. James finds it difficult to understand a willingness to
act without the belief in good and bad; he cannot understand regret over our failure to do good without the belief in indeterminism. The belief in determinism is
subjectively distasteful to James. Reid argues that we are *all* under a practical
necessity of believing in personal freedom as evidenced by our efforts at deliberat-
ing, making choices and promises, and by the fact that we hold ourselves and others accountable for the actions we and they perform.

> *We have, by our constitution a natural conviction or belief, that we
> act freely*—a conviction so early, so universal, and so necessary in
> most of our rational operations, that it must be the result of our
> constitution, and the work of Him that made us.

> Some of the most strenuous advocates for the doctrine of neces-
> sity acknowledge... that we have a natural sense or conviction
> that we act freely; but that this is a fallacious sense....

> If any one of our natural faculties be fallacious, there can be no
> reason to trust any of them; for He that made one made all....[57]

Thus, not only is the necessity of belief in the first principle of moral liberty universal, it is reflective of the real nature of man.

Moreover, Reid offers more than a practical justification for the claim
that the belief in personal freedom is a first principle reflecting the real nature of
mankind. Our natural faculties are on an equal footing; they stand or fall together
unless some reason can be given to show that they are individually defective.

The evidence of sense, the evidence of memory, and the evidence of the necessary relations of things, are all distinct and original kinds of evidence, equally grounded on our constitutions: none of them depends upon, or can be resolved into another. To reason against any of these kinds of evidence is absurd; nay to reason for them is absurd. They are first principles; and such fall not within the province of reason[ing], but of common sense.[58]

Those who use reasoning to persuade us that we ought not to trust reasoning refute themselves. Thus, "He must either be a fool, or want to make a fool of me, that would reason me out of my reason[ing] or senses."[59] If our natural faculties are on an equal footing, then all of them are to be regarded as reliable or as innocent as reason itself until proven otherwise. Likewise, the beliefs resulting from these natural faculties are innocent until proven guilty. Such beliefs can be and have been put on trial and, thus, are not beyond dispute. However, we should not delude ourselves into thinking that we do or can proceed with no beliefs or dogmas and that these beliefs or dogmas have no connection with the real nature of things of which man is a part. Indeed, the latter delusion is itself a metaphysical belief.

Whereas Reid finds theoretical solutions to metaphysical questions, James finds only practical solutions based upon the demands of subjective satisfaction, i.e., meliorism. Whereas Reid claims truth is objective, James claims it is subjective. James claims truth is subjective in part or in total because, he says, there is no test of what is really true that has ever been agreed upon. Thus, "...practically one's conviction that the evidence one goes by is of the real objective brand, is only one more subjective opinion added to the lot. For what a contradictory array of opinions have objective evidence and absolute certitude been claimed!"[60] In this same passage James claims that Reid uses "common sense" as the test of what is true. However, the claim is misleading because it oversimplifies the significance of Reid's use of "common sense". As noted earlier, James is concerned with practical outcomes or consequences rather than with beginning principles. For Reid, as shown in the discussion of moral liberty, common sense or first principles pertain to metaphysical truths. This is where the law against infinite regress seems to end for Reid. The justification for what we claim to know must ultimately lead to our fundamental beliefs about the nature of reality. That is to say, the first principles or common sense beliefs with which we must commence the quest to determine how we know and what we know are metaphysical first principles. In this sense, for Reid, practice presupposes a metaphysical theory, a theory which in turn is tested by such things as universal practice and consistency among our metaphysical beliefs.

James' practical beliefs, on the other hand, are not grounded, or so he would have us believe, in metaphysics. As a result James must rely on meliorism. His views on religion conform to this emphasis upon subjective satisfaction.

> You see now why I have been so individualistic throughout these
> lectures, and why I have seemed so bent on rehabilitating the
> element of feeling in religion and subordinating its intellectual
> part. Individuality is founded in feeling; and the recesses of feel-
> ing ... are the only places in the world in which we catch real
> fact in the making, and directly perceive how events happen,
> and how work is actually done.[61]

More importantly, as James himself seems to realize, in choosing meliorism over
metaphysics as determinant of one's epistemology James has transformed philosophy into a form of religion. "You see that pragmatism can be called religious, if
you allow that religion can be pluralistic or merely melioristic in type."[62]
Moreover, James is forced to concede to Reid that melioristic subjectivism and pluralism are at odds with philosophy which, insofar as it pursues the truth, poses an
objective truth as its end.

> Multiply the thinkers into a pluralism, and we find realized for
> us in the ethical sphere something like that world which the
> antique skeptics conceived of—in which individual minds are
> the measures of all things, and in which no one "objective" truth
> but only a multitude of "subjective" opinions can be found.

> But this is the kind of world with which the philosopher, so
> long as he holds to the hope of a philosophy, will not put up.[63]

To this Reid need only reply, "precisely." And, the way to avoid the skeptical or
subjective consequences of meliorism is to recognize the priority of metaphysics
and the primacy of metaphysical first principles. In doing so philosophy will be in
accord with the fundamental practices and common sense beliefs of mankind. ᵞ

Seeing a Donkey's Jaw, Drinking Green Tea: Self and Ordinariness in Ecophilosophy

Deane Curtin

"...to see mountains and rivers is to see Buddha-nature. To see Buddha-nature is to see a donkey's jaw or a horse's mouth."

"'This' is Buddha-nature . . . . We can find this in everyday life, eating a meal or drinking green tea."

—Dogen

I

*E*cofeminists share the conviction with deep ecologists that a transformative ecophilosophy must radically reformulate—not simply reform—the concept of self. They agree that the Cartesian understanding of self as an autonomous individual that exists apart from nature is a root cause of environmental degradation. Yet, there has been little agreement on the positive task of how to formulate the new ecological self.

Deep ecologists contend (in Arne Naess's terms) that the Cartesian self can be expanded to include identification with the whole of nature as Self, thus eliminating the sense of alienation from nature. Some ecofeminists have argued, however, that the deep ecological expansion of self to Self (part to whole) is the product of a hierarchical, masculine conception of morality, and, consequently, that deep ecology is not as deep as it claims to be.[1]

I contend that holist, hierarchical formulations[2] of the deep ecological Self either fail to fully express, or are inconsistent with, commitments to nonanthropocentrism and nondualism. As an alternative that does honor these commitments, I argue that the awakening of an ecological self occurs within what I shall call contexts of ordinariness. These are contexts about which women tend to have expert knowledge. Therefore, no non-feminist account of the ecological self can be complete. If deep ecology is fundamentally committed to nonanthropocentrism and nondualism, therefore, there is no reason, in principal, why its central project concerning Self-realization should not be reformulated to take advantage of ecofeminist perspectives.

In exploring the role of ordinariness in the awakening of an ecological self I draw heavily on the Japanese philosopher Dogen (1200-1253).[3] Dogen, along with Spinoza and the poet Robinson Jeffers, is cited by deep ecologists as one of the progenitors of deep ecology. In Devall's and Sessions' *Deep Ecology*, the distinguished Soto Zen roshi, Robert Aitkin, writes about "Gandhi, Dogen and Deep Ecology." Devall and Sessions themselves quote from Dogen liberally in explaining deep ecology. Arne Naess has argued for the unity, though not the identity, of Spinoza's philosophy, Mahayana Buddhism, and deep ecology. Warwick Fox approvingly quotes Dogen at the conclusion of his recent book *Toward a Transpersonal Ecology*. Indeed, many deep ecologists have been influenced by Buddhist philosophy, often by Dogen in particular. These include Devall, Naess, Aitkin, Fox, Carla Deicke, Joan Halifax, Dolores LaChapelle, Gary Snyder, John Seed, Jeremy Hayward and Andrew McLaughlin.[4]

I depend on Dogen, however, not as an appeal to deep ecological authority (as if deep ecologists should agree with me because Dogen said it), but because I believe Dogen is an important philosopher whose work merits careful consideration. Starting from nondualist and nonanthropocentric premises that are consistent with the theoretical commitments of deep ecology, Dogen turns out to be saying something fundamentally different about the ecological self than Spinoza, Jeffers, Naess, or Fox.

I shall confine my interest in Dogen's philosophy to two areas, first, his idea of Buddha-nature as the impermanence of all beings, not just sentient beings. Dogen thus provides a nondualistic, nonanthropocentric grounding common to *all* beings (sentient and nonsentient) that reveals their interconnectedness. Second, I am concerned with Dogen's understanding of the relational self as it is shaped by his concept of Buddha-nature.[5]

II

Buddha-nature. Early in his masterpiece, the *Shobogenzo* (Treasury of the True Dharma Eye), Dogen takes up the question of Buddha-nature (*Bussho*) in a fascicle of the same name. Dogen's strategy is to begin with classical formulations of Buddha-nature that were well-known to his audience. Then, while partially endorsing Buddhist tradition, he also transforms their meanings. As Norman

Waddell and Abe Masao have noted, Dogen often sacrifices grammatical correctness in his translations from Chinese to Japanese for the illumination of an important and original philosophical point.[6]

He begins by quoting from the *Nirvana Sutra*, the principal Mahayana sutra on Buddha-nature. The passage, in a traditional translation, reads, "All sentient beings without exception have the Buddha-nature..." By quoting the *Sutra*, he acknowledges tradition.[7] However, he also knew that this formulation is open to the charge of dualism. Saying that all sentient beings *have* Buddha-nature distinguishes Buddha-nature from the beings that have it, treating it as a potential quality of sentient beings.

The traditional formulation also implies a distinction between daily practice and the actualization of enlightenment. Meditation and ordinary, daily practice would be maintained, accordingly, not as ends in themselves, but only for the sake of achieving a future end, an end that exists now only as a potentiality.

To remove these hints of dualism, Dogen twists the expression "All sentient beings without exception *have* the Buddha-nature...," to read, "All sentient beings without exception *are* Buddha-nature."[8] Buddha-nature, for Dogen, is not a quality that sentient beings can *have* (or lack); rather, all sentient beings *are* Buddha-nature. Buddha-nature is fundamental reality.

Another important issue is the scope of Buddha-nature. Buddhist tradition often restricted it to those beings that have the potential for enlightenment, either in this life (humans) or in a future life (other sentient beings that can be reborn as human beings). Nonsentient entities such as rivers and mountains are excluded. But Dogen refuses to accept the sentient/nonsentient distinction as fundamental. He says emphatically, "Impermanence is in itself Buddha-nature.... Therefore, the very impermanency of grass and tree, thicket and forest, is the Buddha-nature. Nations and lands, mountains and rivers, are impermanent because they are Buddha-nature. Supreme and complete enlightenment, because it is the Buddha-nature, is impermanent. Great Nirvana, because it is impermanent, is the Buddha-nature"[9] Dogen is both radical and traditional. To be non-dualist, Buddhist philosophy must commit to the fundamental reality of *all* beings as Buddha-nature, not just sentient beings. This is explained, however, by reference to the most traditional of Buddhist commitments: the impermanence of all being.

These ideas are expressed most strikingly and poetically in the "Mountains and Waters Sutra" (*Sansui-kyo*). Dogen challenges his audience to understand mountains and rivers themselves as sutras, as expressions of the Buddha. He quotes a Chinese source, "The green mountains are always walking; a stone woman gives birth to a child at night," and comments:

> Mountains do not lack the qualities of mountains. Therefore
> they always abide in ease and always walk. You should examine
> in detail this quality of the mountains' walking.

> Mountains' walking is just like human walking. Accordingly, do
> not doubt mountains' walking even though it does not look the
> same as human walking. The buddha ancestors' words point to
> walking. This is fundamental understanding. You should pene-
> trate these words.[10]

Taken out of context, these lines may be read as an anthropomorphic projection:
"Mountains' walking is *just like* human walking." But instead of implying that the
mountain's being should be understood in terms of human being, the metaphor of
walking points to a dehomocentric understanding of *all* being. Fundamentally,
mountains and humans abide in their impermanence.

Abe puts this dehomocentric reversal succinctly:

> When Dogen emphasizes "all beings" in connection with the
> Buddha-nature, he definitely implies that man's *samsara*, i.e.,
> recurring cycle of birth and death, can be properly and com-
> pletely emancipated not in the 'living' dimension, but in the
> 'being' dimension. In other words, it is not by overcoming gen-
> eration-extinction common to all living beings, but only by
> doing away with appearance-disappearance, common to all
> things, that man's birth-death problem can be completely
> solved. Dogen finds the basis for man's liberation in a thorough-
> ly cosmological dimension. *Here Dogen reveals a most radical
> Buddhist dehomocentrism.*[11]

This is an insight with profound implications for the issue of anthropocentrism.
We fail to understand life and death, the fundamental *human* problem, if we deal
with it only in human terms. We fail, as well, if we deal with it in terms of all sentient beings. The life-and-death of human beings is subsumed by the generation-
and-extinction (impermanence) of all sentient beings, and the generation-and-
extinction of all sentient beings is subsumed by what Abe calls the appearance-and-
disappearance of all beings. There will be no release from human suffering until
human beings experience themselves in the "cosmological dimension" of all beings,
both mountains and persons.

    The Self. Dogen was particularly concerned to reject two possible misun-
derstandings of self. The self is not an organic entity, like a seed, out of which
other things grow. On this metaphor, Buddha-nature stands in a dualistic relation
to its "fruit." Dogen therefore rejects a teleological explanation of self in the style of
Aristotle. Self does not become real at the end of a long process. Rather, for Dogen,
Buddha-nature is completely actual at each moment.

    He also rejects an ancient view called the Senika heresy according to
which there is a permanent self that is detached from change in the phenomenal

world. Of those who espouse this view he says, "...they have not encountered their true self."[12] His charge is phenomenological: such people have not yet had a certain experience, they have not "encountered" their true self as multiple, interpenetrating other beings.

Dogen contends that the introspective search for an enduring, autonomous self is futile. To understand the self is to "forget" the Cartesian self. A famous passage from the *Genjokoan* of Dogen states this precisely:

> To study the Buddha way is to study the self. To study the self is
> to forget the self. To forget the self is to be actualized by myriad
> things. When actualized by myriad things, your body and mind
> as well as the bodies and minds of others drop away. No trace of
> realization remains, and this no-trace continues endlessly.[13]

To "forget" the self is to penetrate the delusion of the Cartesian self. It is to "Know that there are innumerable beings in yourself"[14] and thereby to realize one's true self in the cosmological dimension. Dogen can be seen as making a Humean point: careful phenomenological examination does not reveal a "singular" Cartesian self, but "innumerable beings" present to multiple spheres in which beings exist in relation to other beings.[15]

To meet this true self, Dogen's advice is "just sit"; practice seated meditation (*zazen*). Zazen is a practice that reveals Buddha-nature through "undivided activity" (*zenki*), activity concentrated right here and right now. It brings one into the "presence of things as they are" (*genjokoan*). One of Dogen's most revealing descriptions of this state of direct presence reads:

> When you ride in a boat, your body and mind and the environs
> together are the undivided activity of the boat. The entire earth
> and the entire sky are both the undivided activity of the boat.[16]

What exists at that moment is the undivided activity of "the boat." Body, mind, boat, and environs are not separate, neither are they absolutely identical: "although not one, not different; although not different, not the same; although not the same, not many."[17]

This passage shows that there *is* a self for Dogen; the self does not disappear or merge into the cosmos. He never denies that there are multiple, provisional, contextually defined borders that shape the sense of self. Self is not simply reducible to nature, nor is it reducible to any of the other beings that are related to the self. He maintains difference. Self is always experienced *in relation* to other beings, however, and those relations define what it means to be a self. Indeed, each person's set of defining relations at a given moment will be unique. For Dogen, self-realization is non-hierarchical, non-dualistic and dehomocentric.

The realized person, then, is neither a Cartesian unchanging self, nor an Aristotelian potentiality. A true self is one that practices undivided activity in the present moment, a practice that reveals the interpenetration (Buddha-nature) of all beings. In each moment there is full and complete realization, unlike the Aristotelian self, and, unlike the Cartesian self, there is direct experience of the non-substantiality of the self. Thomas Kasulis calls this "person as presence."[18]

We are now in a position to connect Dogen's earlier dogged insistence on the impermanence of Buddha nature with his account of the self. To begin with the distinction between sentience and non-sentience, rather than with the impermanence of all beings, is to encourage a delusory understanding of the self in relation to other beings. It moves toward a self that stands apart from "nature," an ideal Cartesian observer that judges rather than participates. It moves away from the ordinary, impermanent self that interpenetrates ordinary beings in daily life. The Senika heresy provides a hierarchical, dualistic picture of self in relation to nature. For Dogen, this hierarchy is a stairway to delusion, the delusion that permanence is fundamental reality.

Buddha-nature, self and ordinariness. While Dogen often focuses on seated meditation, and about co-enlightenment with mountains and waters, these are never separated from the practice of ordinary, daily life. It has often been noted that a meeting with a Chinese temple cook was instrumental in Dogen's view that practice and realization are one. In *Dogen's Formative Years in China*, Takashi James Kodera relates that during a three month period during which Dogen was confined aboard ship before being allowed to enter China, he had a conversation with a Chinese temple cook from A-yu-wang mountain. The monk was sixty-one years old and had traveled a great distance to purchase Japanese mushrooms to make gruel. Kodera writes:

> Dogen was deeply impressed with the devotion of the old monk and asked him to stay the night on the ship. The chief cook declined the offer for fear that it might interfere with the normal procedures at his monastery the following day. Dogen wondered why someone else could not prepare the meal in his place. He asked why a monk as senior as this one remained as chief cook and did not instead engage in sitting in meditation is pursuit of the Way. The old monk laughed loudly and said to Dogen: 'My good man from a foreign land, you still do not comprehend discipline; you still do not know the words.'"[19]

Dogen, then a headstrong, young intellectual, misunderstood the old monk because he thought daily chores were in conflict with formal pursuit of enlightenment through seated meditation. Through his experience in China, however, especially through later meetings with this and other chief cooks, he came to see that his immature view was mistaken.

The Mahayana claim that nirvana and samsara (birth and rebirth) are the same is brashly expressed by Dogen through the identity of ordinary, everyday activities with nirvana. Nirvana is not reached suddenly at the end of a process that leaves daily life behind; it is realized in mindful, everyday action.[20] The fact that vegetarianism has been an important daily commitment in Buddhist philosophy, whereas it has usually been neglected in hierarchical, abstractionist philosophies, is hardly an accident. It reflects a deep difference in the kinds of practices that are regarded as philosophically informative.

Several of Dogen's most engaging writings concern a reorientation of life toward the ordinariness, the dailiness, of life, through mindfulness about food, personal hygiene, and care for others. In *Fushuku-hampo* (Mealtime Regulations) he quotes the *Vimalakirti Sutra*: "When one is identified with the food one eats one is identified with the whole universe; when we are one with the whole universe we are one with the food we eat." He goes on to comment on this passage, "If the whole universe is the Dharma then food is also the Dharma: if the universe is Truth then food is Truth: if one is illusion then the other is illusion: if the whole universe is Buddha then food is also Buddha."[21] The experience of co-enlightenment which is expressed paradoxically in talk of "mountains' walking" is here expressed plainly and intuitively. Proper relationship to Buddha-nature—mindful practice of the truth of impermanence—is right before us all the time in ordinary life.

Undivided activity is an "everyday activity" (*Kajo*) for Dogen. In remarks reminiscent of the co-enlightenment of persons and mountains he says:

> In the domain of buddha ancestors, drinking tea and eating rice is everyday activity. This having tea and rice has been transmitted over many years and is present right now. Thus the buddha ancestors' vital activity of having tea and rice comes to us....
>
> From this you should clearly understand that the thoughts and words of buddha ancestors are their everyday tea and rice. Ordinary coarse tea and plain rice are buddha's thoughts—ancestors' words. Because buddha ancestors prepare tea and rice, tea and rice maintain buddha ancestors. Accordingly, they need no powers other than this tea and rice, and they have no need to use powers as buddha ancestors.[22]

Mindful practice of daily relations with food counteracts the abstractionist tendencies of people (particularly philosophers) to think that only the permanent and abstract are fully real. Food is the dharma because direct presence to the impermanence of food reveals the arbitrariness of borders we construct when abstracting from immediate experience. Since food becomes the self, and then becomes not-self again (as sayings posted near toilets in Zen monasteries recall), this demands that the self be reconstructed as impermanent and relational.

IV

Dogen and deep ecology. Arne Naess and Warwick Fox have argued that the core of deep ecology is the expansion of the Cartesian self to the broader, inclusive, cosmological Self that identifies with all of nature. We have seen that Dogen speaks of a relational sense of self that experiences interpenetration with nature in contexts of ordinariness. The question I wish to address now is whether the fully realized deep ecological Self is the same as Dogen's self.

Deep ecologists, Spinoza, Jeffers and Dogen all aspire to a nondualistic, nonanthropocentric orientation that makes their work interesting and important to environmental philosophers. However, the connections between Dogen and deep ecology as they have been made to this point are simply too broad to be useful. They conceal Dogen's most distinctive contribution to the philosophy of self, the centrality of ordinariness in formulating an ecological self that is non-dualistic, non-hierarchical and dehomocentric.

Consider what Naess says in his classic article "Identification as a Source of Deep Ecological Attitudes":

> There is a process of ever-widening identification and ever-narrowing alienation which widens the self. The self is as comprehensive as the totality of our identifications. Or, more succinctly, our Self is that with which we identify.

> Identification is a spontaneous, non-rational, but not irrational, process through which the interest or interests of another being are reacted to as our own interest or interests.

He says clearly that by identification he does not mean identity. Identification, according to Naess, preserves diversity; we identify with the interests of "another being."

Having acknowledged diversity, however, he amplifies his position in puzzling ways, puzzling because the holist, hierarchical language seems to deny what he has just asserted:

> Through identification, higher level unit is experienced: from identifying with 'one's nearest,' higher unities are created through circles of friends, local communities, tribes, compatriots, races, humanity, life, and ultimately, as articulated by religious and philosophic leaders, unity with the supreme whole,

the 'world' in a broader and deeper sense than the usual. I prefer
a terminology such that the largest units are not said to comprise
life and 'the not living.' One may broaden the sense of living
'living' so that any natural whole, however large, is a living
whole.

There is a hierarchy in Naess's construction of the process of identification that
moves from parts to "unity with the supreme whole." (The very distinction
between self and Self by means of capitalization indicates this.) While he grants
that there are multiple ways in which "oneness" can be experienced, including the
political means of Gandhi, he also says, "This way of thinking and feeling at its
maximum corresponds to that of the enlightened, or yogi, who sees 'the same,' the
atman, and who is not alienated from anything."[23]

In these passages, Naess commits exactly the error Dogen warned against
in *Bussho*. He warned against the Senika heresy according to which the Self is a permanent entity that stands above the manifold changes of nature. Yet, for similar
reasons, Dogen was emphatically rejecting the Indian idea of *atman*, the Hindu
permanent self. The Buddhist philosopher David Kalupahana has written,

> The self (*atman*)... is the permanent and eternal reality
> unsmeared by all the change and fluctuations that take place in
> the world of experience. In fact, it is the basis of the unity of
> empirical experience of variety and multiplicity, of change and
> mutability, of past, present and future. The real self and the
> unreal or mutable self, the transcendental apperception and
> empirical consciousness are graphically presented with the para-
> ble of the "two birds" perched on one branch, the one simply
> watching and the other enjoying the fruit.[24]

The distinction between real self and unreal self, Kalupahana points out, becomes
normatively charged when connected to *brahman* and the caste system. The distinction between real and unreal self is, then, both ontological and ethical. The
ontological distinction rests on a conceptual hierarchy that is remarkably familiar to
Western philosophers, a hierarchy that places the permanent and the eternal above
change and mutability, unity above variety and multiplicity. The Self as *atman* is
better (higher) because it experiences the world as, in Naess's terms, "oneness."

Naess has often distinguished between the philosophical and popular uses
of terms. There is no doubt that he has often been misinterpreted because of his
critics' failure to appreciate this. But it is doubtful whether the distinction will help
Naess here. It is one thing to choose a term because it carries helpful popular associations; it is another to choose a term whose precise meaning *contradicts* what he
says about the recognition of diversity. Naess's explanation of the ultimate realiza-

tion of Self in terms of *atman* is, therefore, deeply confusing regardless of whether it is intended to be popular or philosophical.

These troubling connections between the deep ecological self and an eternal self are worsened when other deep ecologists follow Naess in adopting the part/whole model to explain the expansion of self to Self. Freya Mathews is typical of many in distinguishing between atomistic (Cartesian) and holistic (deep ecological) ways of understanding the self. Both understand the relationship of as one of "part and whole." However, in contrast to regarding persons as distinct atoms, the holistic view, endorsed by Mathews, understands that "each element, being logically constituted by its relations with the other elements, is conditioned by the whole."[25]

In spite of casting the two models of self as *distinct* alternatives, it is significant that in Mathews' own words they are made to depend on the *same* hierarchical model of part to whole. If they are fundamentally the same in respect to their model of explanation, where is their difference? This leads to the suspicion that Self is the Cartesian ego writ large. It would appear that *this* version of the deep ecological Self is still conceptually tied, possibly against its will, to the old hierarchical project whose goal is to find an entity that is whole, "permanent," "unsmeared by change."

The influence of Spinoza weighs heavily here, and like the Hindu *atman*, moves deep ecology in the direction of a hierarchical, nonrelational Self. Spinoza, Descartes' best critic, clearly saw that Descartes' claim for human minds—that they are independent substances—must fail. This is because, unlike God, human minds are neither epistemically or ontologically independent. They require a rational explanation in terms of an external "cause," and they are not self-existent.

Descartes' mistake taught Spinoza that only "the whole" can be truly independent in both senses, so only God, or nature, can qualify as substance. Substances are nonrelational for Spinoza because, by definition, there is nothing else to which they *can* relate. Similarly, Naess and others are in danger of defining the Self nonrelationally. The whole *cannot* relate to anything else just because it is the whole.

I grant that there are many passages in the deep ecology literature that are at odds with this reading. Naess himself has said in an unpublished essay, "In my outline of a philosophy (Ecosophy T) 'Self-realization!' is the logically (derivationally) supreme norm, but it is not an eternal or permanent Self that is postulated. When the formulation is made more precise it is seen that the Self in question is a symbol of identification with an absolute maximum range of beings." With Buddhist philosophy in mind Bill Devall has written, "...all is impermanent. All is changing." Some of his essays can be read as moving in the direction of a recognition of ordinariness as the context in which the ecoself is awakened. Gary Snyder's writings on Dogen often display an acute sense of the impermanence that pervades everyday life.[26]

The problem is that the deep ecology literature has endorsed *both* a holist and nonholist, a nonrelational and relational, understanding of Self. There has not been clear, unequivocal recognition that there are (despite Mathews) *three* competing models of self: the Cartesian atomic self, the Spinozist, holist Self expanded to the supreme whole, and   Dogen's relational self that is awakened in contexts of ordinariness. Unlike the Cartesian and Spinozist selves, the relational self cannot be expressed in terms of parts and wholes.

It would be a fundamental misreading of Dogen's Buddha-nature to say that it is the supreme whole of all impermanent beings, and that the "myriad things" are parts. There is no sense of ascending to higher and "higher unities" that lead to a "supreme whole" in Dogen . Abe Masao puts this point succinctly by contrasting Spinoza's understanding of nature with Dogen's:

> In Spinoza the One God has, in so far as we know, two "attributes" thought (cogitatio) and extension (extensio); particular and finite things are modifications, being called the "modes" of God, which depend on, and are conditioned by, the divine and infinite being.

But Dogen's "myriad things" cannot be understood as *modes* of Buddha-nature. They are, rather, fully real as simple (relational) beings. Abe says,

> A pine tree, for instance, is not a mode of God as Substance, but a mode of "what", namely a mode without a modifier. Therefore, a pine tree is really a pine tree in itself, no more and no less.[27]

Dogen's Buddha-nature is not a code word for metaphysical unity. Dogen issues an invitation to cultivate a kind of experience—direct presence to the interpenetration of all things—that is neglected precisely because we are seduced by the abstraction that only "the whole" is ultimately real.

Dogen's fundamental reality can give expression to both unity and diversity without resorting to hierarchical abstractions. The phenomenological description he gives of direct presence speaks as much of diversity as of unity: "...although not one, not different; although not different, not the same; although not the same, not many."[28] When Dogen says "not one" this marks the fact that the direct experience of the ordinariness of life is the experience of interpenetration without ultimate, metaphysical unity. An ecological consciousness for Dogen is not, as for Jeffers or Naess, an experience of "wholeness." It is an experience of interpenetration with a "...concrete existence—a 'this'." "Thus Buddha-nature is a 'what,' a concrete, real being."[29]

Warwick Fox and identification with nature. In *Toward a Transpersonal*

Ecology, Fox advances Naess's work by distinguishing three bases of identification: personal, ontological, and cosmological. Roughly, these coincide with the ecofeminist approach, Zennist or Heideggerian approaches, and the deep ecological approach. We are in a position to see that Fox misrepresents both ecofeminism and the Zen of Dogen. In both cases his hierarchical thinking does not allow him to appreciate the role of ordinariness in the awakening of an ecological self.

Dogen would challenge Fox's distinction between the personal and the ontological. It distinguishes indistinguishables and is implicitly dualistic. There is a ontological phenomenology in Dogen. Through mindfulness about everyday practices, the ecological self is awakened as we immediately experience interpenetration with that pine tree which is "really a pine tree." Everyday mindfulness draws us out of our deluded, narrow selves through the experience of co-enlightenment.

But Dogen's recommendations are intensely personal as well. Each mindful act is an act of personal ontological commitment. The movement in Dogen's thought is to undercut the public/private, personal/impersonal distinctions on which Fox's classification rests.

Dogen would also challenge the way Fox makes the distinction between ontological and cosmological identification. Ontologically based identification, "Refers to experiences of commonality with all that is that are brought about through deep-seated realization of the fact *that* things are." Though this view, which he associates with Zen Buddhism, cannot be adequately expressed in words, it points toward the experience of "this state of being, this sense of commonality with all that is simply by virtue of the fact *that* it is, at a certain moment. Things *are!* There is something rather than nothing! Amazing!"

In comparison, "Cosmologically based identification refers to experiences of commonality with all that is that are brought about through deep-seated realization of the fact that we and all other entities are aspects of a single unfolding reality." Fox confirms that "...the inspiration for this concept derives from Gandhi and Spinoza, both of whom explicated their views within the context of a monistic metaphysics, that is, within the context of a cosmology that emphasized the fundamental unity of existence. Gandhi was committed to Advaita Vedanta (i.e., monistic or, more literally, nondual Hinduism).... Spinoza developed a philosophy that conceived of all entities as *modes* of a single substance...."

Despite the apparent distinction, the difference between ontological and cosmological identification is practical rather than theoretical. Fox says, "...it would seem to be much easier to communicate and inspire a cosmologically based sense of identification with all that is rather than an ontologically based identification."[30]

It is simply not true, however, that the distinction between the self in Zen literature (at least as represented by the Zen philosopher most often cited by deep ecologists, Dogen) and the deep ecological, Spinozist, Gandhian (Advaita Vedanta) Self is one of practice rather than theory. Fox appears not to recognize that the holist self which is part of a "monistic metaphysics" is not the relational self!

Fox's characterization of the Zen self reads more like a description of the first premise of the medieval Christian cosmological argument for the existence of a holist God than Dogen: "Things *are*! There is something rather than nothing! Amazing!" The basic Buddhist commitment to the impermanence, the emptiness, of all being, is not the same as the Christian challenge to give a metaphysical explanation for why there is something rather than nothing. Dogen's call to mindfulness about ordinary things is phenomenological. He is simply saying, "Be present to your true self!" The demand for a metaphysical explanation for the existence of something rather than nothing only makes sense in an abstractionist metaphysics that marginalizes ordinariness. Ordinary things, according to such a metaphysic, "demand an explanation," an explanation that only terminates in the whole.

Dogen, Deep Ecology and Ecofeminism. In a recent article Warwick Fox charged that Jim Cheney's version of ecofeminism is incoherent because it is anthropocentric. Expansion of self occurs for Cheney through a "personal," gendered context rather than through cosmological identification with the whole. Fox's conclusion is, "The cosmological/transpersonal voice is a 'different voice' from the personal voice, but it does not seem to respect gender boundaries."[31] A transformative ecophilosophy is not inherently feminist for Fox.

Just as Dogen's philosophy of self resists classification as *either* personal or ontological, so ecofeminism is not merely a personal approach to self-realization. This fails to see that for feminists "the personal is the political." Women have been marginalized through the public/private dualism. Their lives have been considered less important than men's lives because they are constructed as merely homely, domestic, and private. Feminists[32] do not protest this by claiming that their lives ought to be constructed as public. This just reinforces the public/private distinction, and further marginalizes the domain of the ordinary. Rather, their theoretical aspirations are nondualistic. They argue that the public/private distinction cannot be maintained as it has been espoused by the Western liberal (atomic) self. The kind of self required by the public/private distinction does not exist. In basing his criticism on a version of the public/private split, Fox affirms a dualistic stance when he claims to reject it.

The public/private dualism is one of many dualistic pairs that have marginalized contexts of ordinariness. Plato's metaphor of the cave set the tone for Western philosophy by depicting ordinary life as a mere shadowy reflection of the Good and the True. Ways of experiencing the world that are shaped by ordinary, everyday practices are invisible to philosophers trained in these conceptual hierarchies. Practices such as growing and eating food, care for the land, cleaning and maintenance of the home, and daily care for children and others—in short, care for the environment, broadly conceived—have often been regarded as sub-philosophical, as not worthy of a philosopher's interest.

This split between the extraordinary and the ordinary has long been gender-based. One need only look at the cosmology of the Pythagoreans for a set of conceptual dualisms that has played a devastating role in marginalizing the ordinariness of women's lives: "limit and unlimited, odd and even, one and plurality, right and left, male and female, resting and moving, straight and crooked, light and darkness, good and bad, square and oblong."[33] We have been taught that the ordinary is "lower," "female," "bodily," "animal," "natural," irrational," "bad," and "dark."

A transformative ecophilosophy must affirm as a core project the revaluation of the ordinary. It must provide new language that does not equate "ordinary" with "bad" as a tautology. This is not a feminist concern for women alone. In refusing to maintain the ordinary-extraordinary hierarchical dualism, an ecophilosophy of this sort can also lead the way in liberating men from the conceptual dualisms that have resulted in violence against nature. While these dualisms have tended to privilege men by marginalizing women and nonhuman animals, the kinds of power that these dualisms have afforded men—power that comes from being constructed as "rational," "nonbodily," and "active"—are precisely the kinds of power that have alienated men from the rest of nature. A transformative ecophilosophy should argue that men must give up their traditional forms of power, power that derives from normative hierarchies.

Early in his career Dogen was forceful in advocating the view that women are as capable of enlightenment as men. It is possible he realized that the kinds of ordinary activities through which enlightenment can come—and about which Dogen wrote in minute detail—are just those sorts of activities (in Japan as elsewhere) that are typically regarded as "women's work": cleaning, cooking, care for nature, care for others. The radical point is that for Dogen enlightenment occurs precisely through the kinds of homely activities that have been expected of women, those activities that are constructed as marginal.

My point is not the essentialist point that women "by nature" are closer to the rhythms of ecological awareness. Many feminists have been clear in pointing out that this association only strengthens sexist categories by reifying them as if they were metaphysical: women then are constructed as bodily, nonrational creatures who *should* be engaged in manual rather than intellectual practices.[34] Nor is my point that all women possess eco-wisdom. Clearly women, as well as men, are implicated in the degradation of nature.

I am, rather, making points about the ways in which *gender* is constructed in sexist cultures (not a point about individuals), and about the kinds of actual *practices* that have been defined by patriarchal and naturist cultures as "women's work," (or "animals'" work). These are the kinds of marginalized practices that such cultures make available precisely to those who are constructed as women (or animals). Women have been expected to perform those roles that sexist societies have marginalized as lower, less important, on the conceptual hierarchy, roles that philosophers shaped by those cultures have regarded as sub-philosophical.

The insight provided by ecofeminism is that women who have engaged in these practices, who have been expected to practice compassionate entrance into others' worlds, have expert knowledge about the ordinary practices through which an ecoself is awakened.[35] As Sara Ruddick has said about the practice of mothering, for example, "Caretakers are immersed in the materials of the physical world." Because of this, "caring labor" is regarded with disdain and marginalized by intellectuals. Yet, its very standpoint as "subjugated knowledge" produces a "superior" version of experience.[36] Because of the practices in which they have engaged, women have first-hand experience with "the presence of things as they are."

Taking daily practices as guides to philosophical reflection reveals that it is not the project of ecophilosophy to connect us to the "environment" (as if we could be disconnected), or to provide abstract rules for our interaction with the "environment" (when we are already environmentally engaged at every moment of our ordinary lives). The ordinary lives of women and men are already grounded in practices that are morally, spiritually, and physically healthy.

This is why I prefer to say that we can be "awakened" to the presence of an ecological self in ordinary practices. The ecological self is not "realized," brought into being from nonexistence in an atomic self. The issue is not whether something new can be created, but whether we can become aware of these ordinary practices and respond to them mindfully. Activities such as "eating a meal or drinking green tea," or seeing the ordinary everywhere around us—seeing "the donkey's jaw," as Dogen says—are daily routines that mark the ways in which we are already, and inevitably, ecological beings despite the distortions of dualist, hierarchical, homocentric thinking.

I am certainly not claiming an absolute coincidence of Dogen's views with ecofeminism. But I am asserting that they intersect at enough points that it is possible to understand them as united in opposition to both the narrow Cartesian self and the deep ecological identification of part with whole. Both are normatively nonhierarchical in their commitments to undercut traditional conceptual hierarchies that have marginalized women and nature; both are nondualist but maintain difference. Both, I might add, are in a position to reinterpret the idea of a bioregion in terms of ordinariness: a bio-region is that "home" in which we can be our ordinary selves.

Warwick Fox has recalled that the word "ecology" is derived from the Greek word "oikos" meaning "the family household and its daily maintenance."[37] A truly transformative eco-philosophy must work to make this original meaning common knowledge. ~~

*My appreciation to Kansai Gaidai University. It was during the year spent in residence there that the ideas expressed in this essay began to take shape. Thanks also to John Powers for his comments on an early version of this paper. Diacritical remarks have been removed to facilitate translation from Apple to DOS formats.

The Necessity of the Ontological Argument

~

Joseph N. Uemura

"I have never heard of anyone who would die for the ontological argument."
—Albert Camus

*T*he ontological argument is true. For human minds, it always has been true, and, indeed, it always must be true. Of course, I am reminded that philosophy is, oddly enough, not ever refuted. Rather, if not currently in favor, it is usually and generally ignored, not much talked about, damned by faint praise, or simply laughed out of court. The ontological argument usually suffers from all of these fates. In fact, it has so many philosophical enemies, one quickly gains the impression that it must be right!

Here, I would like to argue that, indeed, it strikes me as being so. Let me try to do this in three short steps: First, I shall relate a brief personal account of my experience. Next, I shall give a short historical look at the argument from Parmenides to Hartshorne. Finally, I shall present a small encomium on the argument such as may assure her a serious place in the minds of sensitive and thoughtful human beings.

I

When I entered college almost fifty years ago, I met the ontological argument rather casually. It was sort of a "blind date," and I can say that my eyes were open, but my mind was not. For, I did not know much of the meaning of anything, let alone of "necessity" or "ontology," I could, of course, repeat the words, but I did not understand them.

Professors Dickinson and Sampson did their level best with me. They repeated the argument carefully and clearly. They also repeated the standard academic refutation with equal care and clarity. When I parroted back both the argument and its historic refutation, I got my routine "A," got out, and my "mind" was none the worse or better for the experience. It went something like this:

A. The argument: If there is absolute being, then it must necessarily exist.

B. The refutation: Superficially true; yet we cannot accept a mere logical proof, which assumes its premises to be true, but cannot show that they exist. So, e.g., Gaunilo cannot assume his perfect island to exist.

The upshot: The ontological argument is true, but trivial! So, obviously, I could remember it, but is was not very important.

Graduate school was no different. Sometimes it was clothed in theological clothing—which made it all the worse—something like this:

A. The argument: "If God were absolutely perfect in every way, and if perfection entailed existence, then God must necessarily exist."

B. The refutation: Again, logically true, but it "begs the question," a *petitio principii*. Also, "Existence is not a predicate, a property," and therefore it cannot be entailed by anything possessing it.

Tillich, at Columbia, would say about the same thing in this way: "In theology, we cannot reach the Ground of Being with logical arguments." This, translated from the German and, in the words of the mystical Mr. Kant, means that Pure Reason cannot give you any knowledge of "existence," and Critical Reason can only give you regulative "belief" in the existence of God.

When I started teaching in 1953, I was quite convinced that the ontological argument, like a perfect siren, sounded and appeared to be most enticing; but, in my sophomoric agnosticism, I "knew" it should not be trusted in the hard-headed world of philosophical reality. Of course, the only problem with this was that, in teaching the philosophers I most respected during the next forty years, I discovered that they not only recounted the argument, but found it to be necessary to their philosophies. I found that *without* a clear understanding and affirmation of this argument, it is *hopeless* to try to understand the greatest of philosophers. I also discovered that, to my astonishment, one, actually, cannot do ontology or philosophy itself without the argument, and the affirmation of its truth. As Kant, in his best and earliest work, once said: "That which mingles these pure principles with the empirical does not deserve the name of philosophy!" Of course, Kant, "in order to make room for faith," changed his mind in his *Kritik*. *Sic transit gloria empirici.*

II

Now, a brief look at how intellectual history has presented the argument, from Parmenides to Hartshorne. In the first place, Parmenides should be credited with the first version of the ontological argument. Parmenides said, too simply, that, "Whatever is, is," and "Whatever is not, is not." And, "Never can what is, not be" and "Never can what is not, be." If these are all so, then it follows that "whatever is" is both "thinkable and sayable." But, "whatever is not" is neither "thinkable nor sayable."

To put it differently, if there is no object of thought, then one cannot think of it. And if there is no object of thought, then one cannot speak of it. Or, again, if thinking is possible, then there must necessarily be an object of thought. Those who cannot think that thought has an object, of course, cannot think of the existence of a necessary object. They can only "think" empirically, for example, which Parmenides would not consider thinking at all!

To this, Plato would have quickly added that Parmenides is mistaken only in the fact that he, indeed, does think about an object of thought when he thinks about "what is not." So, one must show how it is possible to think and speak truly about something which is also "not the case." "What is not" must still necessarily possess an object of thought.

Plato, in his *Sophist*, holds that one can only do this dialectically, whereby one can speak truly about "what is not," by the proper mixing of words appropriate to what is true and, most crucially, to what is false. Plato does this routinely in many of his dialogues. For instance, one can show what necessarily exists concerning "what is pious" in *Euthyphro* by showing several things that are "not pious," e.g., "filial piety," "scriptural piety," "what the gods love," etc.

To put it more bluntly and elliptically, as Socrates often does, one needs to ask what "virtue" is, in itself, but also what it is *not*. One cannot just give examples of virtuous things, or beautiful objects. One must establish virtue or beauty themselves. What is "equality," for instance in the *Phaedo*, and what is "not equality," when it seems that nothing in the world appears to be "equal" to anything else. Nothing makes any sense if these necessary thoughts are denied. Or, again, if language is without any ontology, Aristotle would say, nothing can be known, or thought, or said.

Aristotle agreed with Plato although he had to put it in his own unique manner. He said that two rules without which all knowledge of any being would be impossible would be: (1) The law of non-contradiction, and (2) the law against infinite regress. In ordinary English, the first means that any thing must be consistent with itself throughout; and the second means that any thing must be self-identical throughout. Otherwise, we simply cannot know anything, think anything, or speak anything, about the world, or about ourselves in such a world. Unfortunately, Aristotle also said, trying his best to say something new that Plato had not already said, that this is not "dialectical," and allowed so many *Schwaermerei* to inhabit the world that necessity was hardly recognizable in due course when the Medievalists got hold of him.

Actually, Augustine basically agreed with Plato concerning the ontological argument, beginning with (1) his negative proof of his self-existence (his *si fallor sum*, "if I err, I exist") which ends affirmatively; then (2) it is better and more thinkable to live than to exist; (3) it is better to think than merely to live, or to exist; (4) it is better to think correctly at all times and places than merely once-in-a-while; (5) it is divine to think always correctly and necessarily; (6) that than which nothing better or higher can be thought necessarily is divine. (*De Libero Arbitrio*, II)

The medieval theological formulation of the ontological argument came with Anselm of Canterbury, d. 1109, and is commonly regarded as standard:

> Thou art a being than which nothing greater can be conceived.... It is one thing for an object to be in the understanding and another to understand that the object exists. ...And assuredly that, than which nothing greater can be conceived, cannot exist in the understanding alone. For, suppose it exists in the understanding alone: then it can be conceived to exist in reality, which is greater. ...Hence, there is no doubt that there exists a being than which nothing greater can be conceived, and it exists both in the understanding and in reality. ...And it assuredly exists so truly that it cannot be conceived not to exist. (*Proslogion*, chs. II-III)

It is in this formulation that great discussions have taken place. The greatest objection was made by Gaunilo, who claimed to speak in behalf of the Biblical Fool, "who said in his heart, there is no God." (Psalm xiv,1)

Anselm claimed, of course, that the Fool could only show himself, truly, to be a fool just as he denied that God exists. For the Fool would understand what he was saying when he speaks of God, and would be contradicting his own idea of God when he denies God's existence, saying God is and is not in the same breath. Of course, others have spoken in behalf of the Fool ever since Gaunilo: St. Thomas,

Immanuel Kant, and Bertrand Russell to name a few. But, as Gaunilo must separate mind and world in denying Anselm, so must they all who follow him.

Because they thoroughly believed in the primacy of mind, Descartes and Spinoza made the ontological argument the cornerstone of their metaphysics. In their own words, they agreed that, "There is an essence that entails existence," that, "something cannot come from nothing," and "causes are equal to, or greater than their effects." Or, as Descartes put it, "I cannot have a real idea of perfect being without an adequate reason for it." (*Meditation*, III) Of course, many have said one can have many "rampant, speculative, and strange" ideas of "perfect being" such that Gaunilo's "perfect island" may be "thought." But without a necessary object for thinking, such "ideas" are fantasies, hallucinations, or drug-induced imaginations. Clearly, one cannot have a real idea of perfect being without an adequate reason.

Most recently, Charles Hartshorne has defended a strange version of the ontological argument in his *Logic of Perfection* (1961). Although Hegel defended the ontological argument during the past century, few recent philosophers since Kant, d. 1804, have taken it seriously. So, it was a bit of a surprise that Hartshorne took it up, and defended it in its "modal form" In plain language, the argument holds that God is either logically necessary or logically impossible, since logical contingency could not be divine. But, since God has *not* been shown to be either logically impossible, or self-contradictory, God must be logically necessary.

In philosophical circles, discussion of this "modal proof" has been quite popular during the past twenty-five years. And, it has been defended by minds such as Norman Malcolm, Alvin Plantinga, and many others. Theologians, on the other hand, seem not to want to discuss it at all!

Naturally, the basic objection to the modal argument has been that there seem to be two meanings (at least) of the word, "necessary," i.e., Hartshorne and others seem to use it both as "logically necessary" at times, and "ontologically necessary" at other times. And that, of course, has always been the issue!

III

In the two foregoing sections, I have presented several different forms of the ontological argument in the specific ways in which they have occurred in my personal experience as well as in the general cultural history of philosophy. The precise form of the argument makes a superficial, but not a substantial difference. The primary consideration is, actually, ontological reality or the existence of necessity.

Now, the various objections to such demonstrations are as old as philosophy itself, beginning with the Sophists and Skeptics of the past, and continuing to the same among us, today. The sophists and skeptics of all times have not changed much. Both "use reason to deny reason." And neither think that philosophy can ever be a "question of pure thinking" even when "thinking" is the only instrument in their own arsenal. Sophists, I contend, are those who, in various ways, will assert that "all is true," because "truth is subjective," and "everyone is entitled to their version." Proof is impossible. So, if any belief is meaningful, of course, nothing is. Skeptics, on the other hand, will say, in many ways, that "everything is false," and while anyone can claim anything, they agree that proof of anything is impossible, "truth is subjective," and nothing is meaningful. Aristotle, of course, found these same sophists and skeptics would render knowledge, science, and philosophy impossible. And even Camus would say that both, "all is true" and "all is false" are self-refuting and absurd, in spite of saying that he had never known anyone who would die for the ontological argument (Camus knew not Socrates, of course!).

Perhaps the most popular objection to the ontological argument is that of Hume (*Dialogues Concerning Natural Religion*, IX). Here, Hume puts in the mouth of Cleanthes his "decisive refutation" of the argument, saying, "In matters of fact...a contrary does not imply a contradiction," and there is "no being whose existence is demonstrable." What does this mean? To Hume, it meant that while the contrary of '2+2=4' *is* the contradiction '2+2=5,' the contrary of 'any particle of matter exists,' is 'any particle of matter can be annihilated,' and is not a contradiction.

Of course, the flaw in Hume's "refutation" is simply that the contrary of 'any particle of matter exists' is 'any particle of matter does not exist,' which is obviously a contradiction. The apparent move from the "rational realm" (mathematics) to the seemingly "empirical realm" (world) does not alter the rational *necessity* entailed in both.

The serious objections, however, from Heraclitus to the Academics, from St. Thomas to Immanuel Kant, from Bertrand Russell to John Hick, seem to rest their cases upon very dubious assumptions concerning that necessity in mind, reason, and logic. In Heraclitus, for instance, the *logos* both is and is not always changing. "One cannot step into the same river twice," we all have heard from our childhood. Aristotle, at times, invites the same interpretation when he says, "There is a sense in which one can and a sense in which one cannot step into the same river twice," and one wonders as to where his "necessities" have disappeared. Thomas, of course, taking this interpretation of Aristotle seriously felt that the rational ontological argument could not be sustained, although the empirical arguments constituting the *via negativa* (cosmological, teleological, moral, etc.) could. Thomas did not perceive that the contingent empirical arguments depended upon the existence of necessity as demonstrated in the ontological argument. So, Kant agrees with Thomas and denigrates and belittles the mind, splitting it off from existence, and then wondering why Pure Reason "fails" him. Russell, taking his lead from Kant, agrees that "existence" is a "property" and not a "predicate" and keeps language and the world quite separate, and finally repairing to "mysticism" to heal the rift he himself has created.

The upshot of all of these equivocations and separations is that each objection, in some curious way or another, impugns, belittles, denigrates, and separates the human mind and its logic, language, and reason, from existence and the world of being. These thinkers use the mind and its reasoning, the way human beings *connect* with the world, in order to separate and *disconnect* our minds from the world, from reality.

The ontological argument, on the other hand, is an argument that seeks to unite our minds with the world that we know, to unify the knower with the known, logic and ontology, the necessary and the contingent. It shows that if one separates the mind and its objects, one only blurs the distinctions between the mind and its natural objects. And when that occurs, one can no longer tell the difference between fact and fancy, image and imagination, knowledge and opinion, reality and hallucination. When that distinction falls, the entire world becomes populated only with ghosts, goblins, and golems. For, these "refutations" of the ontological argument can only succeed by limiting our minds by excision, detachment, and distortion. And as John Dewey once said, "I have never understood the philosophical disposition to self-mutilation!"

Conclusion

So, we have been given a philosophical choice: (1) The ontological argument can be logically demonstrated from well-acknowledged premises and conclusions, admitted to being rationally and logically correct. (2) However, if one limits the nature of "reason" (Kant), or if one weakens "reason" to include all manner of spiritual entities (Thomas), or if one disparages and denigrates "reason" to apply to, or make room for, any opinion of belief (Heraclitus, Hume), one can freely reject "reason" and the "logic" of the ontological argument, and "consign it to the flames" claiming that it yields "nothing but sophistry and illusion."

Given such a choice, Spinoza chose to give the argument first place in his greatest work, *The Ethics*. "For reason," said Spinoza, "is the light of the mind, and without her all things are dreams and phantoms," a ringing denial of Camus' claim. It is altogether reasonable that I should agree. ❧

A Decalogue for a Pedagogue

I. Thou shalt have several other gods before thee;
God, for instance.

II. Thou shalt always remember that thou art just
a teacher, merely an occasion,
not the substance, of another's mind.

III. Thou shalt teach, not play politics,
neither academic nor administrative.

IV. Thou shalt teach all of thy students,
not just the best, the worst, nor the rest.

V. Thou shalt be objective, even though
they all say it is impossible.

VI. Thou shalt be honest, even though one must
admit to all one's errors;
for thou art too old to be infallible,
and too tired to be a chameleon.

VII. Thou shalt serve the needs of thy students,
not their wants.

VIII. Thou shalt create a devotion to thy science,
not to thyself.

IX. Thou shalt deepen the faith of thy students,
whatever it may be.

X. Thou shalt be cheerful, for misanthropy and
misology are truth's natural enemies.

Contributors

Albert A. Anderson is Professor of Philosophy and Chair of the Arts and Humanities Division at Babson College. He took his B.A. in 1960 at Morningside College, his M.A. in 1963 and his Ph.D. in 1971 at Boston University. His most recent publication is "Three Kinds of Goodness," *Studies in Higher Education* (Vol. 16, No.3, 1991). Currently he is working on *Living Poetically: Peter Handke's Aesthetic* (a translation of Handke's essays) and *Dialectic: The Philosophy of Universalism.*

Ronald E. Beanblossom is Professor of Philosophy and Religion at Ohio Northern University. He earned his B.A. in 1964 at Morningside College, his M. Div. in 1967 at Union Theological Seminary (NY), his M.A. in 1970 and Ph.D. in 1971 at the University of Rochester. He held the Sara A. Ridenour Endowed Chair for the Humanities in 1989-90. He co-edited *Thomas Reid's Inquiry and Essays* (Hackett) and authored "Kant's Quarrel with Reid: The Role of Metaphysics," *History of Philosophy Quarterly.*

Duane L. Cady is Professor of Philosophy and Department Chair at Hamline University. He received his B.A. in 1968 from Hamline University, his A.M. in 1970 and Ph.D. in 1971 from Brown University. He was Visiting Scholar, Westminster College, Oxford, England in 1988. He is author of *From Warism to Pacifism: A Moral Continuum* (Temple University Press, 1989), as well as various journal articles on ethics and history of philosophy.

Deane Curtin is Professor of Philosophy and Department Chair at Gustavus Adolphus College. He finished his B.A. in 1973 at Hamline University and his Ph.D. in 1978 at the University of Iowa. He was an NEH fellow in Florence, Italy, in 1983 and Visiting Professor at Kansai Gaidai University, Osaka, Japan in 1988. He has published in the areas of philosophy of art, philosophy of the environment and feminist philosophy.

Christopher Dreisbach is Associate Professor of Philosophy at The College of Notre Dame of Maryland. He earned his B.A. in 1979 at Hamline University, his M.A. in 1981 and his Ph.D. in 1987 at The Johns Hopkins University. He is co-author of *Study Guide to Accompany Barker: Elements of Logic* (McGraw-Hill, 1985, 1988) and *TUTORIALS: A Software Package to Accompany Copi's Introduction to Logic* (Macmillan, 1988), both with Robert Cavalier. He is editor of *R.G. Collingwood: A Bibliographic Checklist* (Philosophy Documentation Center, forthcoming).

Robert N. Hull is Adjunct Instructor in Philosophy at Missouri Western State College. He completed his B.A. in 1981 at Hamline University, his M.A. in 1983, M. Phil. in 1987 and Ph.D. in 1991 at the University of Kansas. His publications include "Skepticism, Enigma and Integrity: Horizons of Affirmation in Nietzsche's Philosophy," *Man and World* (October, 1990), "Epistemology and the Autodevaluation of Morality: Toward an Atheoretical Nietzsche," *Southwestern Philosophy Review* (Spring, 1992), and "Beyond Epistemology: Nietzsche and the Need for Epistemic Criteria," *Auslegung* (Spring, 1992).

Richard Kyte is a Candidate for the Ph.D. at The Johns Hopkins University. He received his B.A. in 1984 at Hamline University and his M.A. in 1990 at The Johns Hopkins University.

Martha Phillips is Instructor of Philosophy at The College of St. Catherine. She earned her B.A. in 1975 at Hamline University, her M.A. in 1979 at Bryn Mawr College, and she is currently working on her Ph.D. at the University of Minnesota.

Joseph Norio Uemura is Paul Robert and Jean Shuman Hanna Professor of Philosophy at Hamline University. He received his B.A. in 1946 at the University of Denver, his Th.M. in 1949 at Iliff School of Theology and his Ph.D. in 1958 at Columbia University. He is a member of Phi Beta Kappa and was a Danforth Faculty Associate, 1961-75. He received the Merrill E. Burgess Award for Teaching, 1969, was Iliff Alumnus of the Year, 1978, and received Bailey Writing Awards in 1980 and 1987 as well as the Conger Prize for Research in Humanities, 1987. His publications include *Seven Dialogues on Goodness*, 1986, and *Six Dialogues of Plato: An Interpretation*, 1991.

Peter W. Wakefield is an independent scholar and student of ancient Greek Philosophy living in Washington, D.C. He received his B.A. in 1980 at Hamline University and his Ph.D. at Brown University in 1989.

Thomas A. Wilson is Instructor in Philosophy (part-time) at North Harris County College, Houston. He finished his B.A. in 1969 at Hamline University, his M.A. in 1977 at The University of Toledo, and his Ph.D. in 1985 at Southern Illinois University. His publications include "On Time and Motion as Natural Phenomena," *Kinesis* (Vol. X, Spring 1980), "The Is/Ought Gap and the Open Question Argument," *Darshana International* (Vol. 23, October 1983) and "Russell's Later Theory of Perception," *Russell: Journal of the Russell Archives V* (1985).

Dennis Wittmer is Assistant Professor of Management at the University of Denver. He completed the B.A. degree in 1968 at Morningside College, M.A. in 1975,

M.P.A. in 1978 and Ph.D. in 1992 at Syracuse University. He is author of "Serving the People or Serving for Pay: Reward Preferences Among Government, Hybrid Sector and Business Managers," *Public Productivity and Management Review*, (Vol. 14, No. 4, 1991) and "Ethics and Public Management: Some Experimental Results," *Journal of Public Administration Research and Theory* (forthcoming, 1992).

Notes

On Forms

[1] Plato accepts both reasons, but the latter involves problematic assumptions about the nature of God. Since the former argument is also all Plato needs to defend his point, I will rely only on it in my explication and defense of Plato.

[2] Cf. Julia Annas, *Introduction to Plato's 'Republic* (Oxford, Carendon Press, 1981), 199.

[3] G.E.L. Owen, "Dialectic and Eristic in the Treatment of the Forms," in Martha Nussbaum, ed., *Logic, Science, and Dialectic* (Ithaca, Cornell Press, 1986), 230-31.

[4] Cf. Richard Patterson, *Image and Reality in Plato's Metaphysics*, (Indianapolis, Hackett, 1985) 80.

[5] Cf. Ferguson, "Plato's Simile of Light; part 2," *Classical Quarterly*. (1922): 17.

[6] As a start only, cf. *Gorgias* 481c-d, 482a-b; *Republic* 500c, 501c; also v. Patterson, *IRPM*, 203, n. 9; N. Kretzman, "Plato on the Correctness of Names" *Am. Phil. Q.* (1971): 128-129; D. Gallop, *Plato: Phaedo* (Oxford: Clarendon Pr., 1975), 141 (note on *Phaedo* 79e8-80a9).

Phaedo 72e-74a: What Is the Point

[1] Also, the reader knows Simmias in exactly the same way she knows Cebes: through the image in speech (fails to satisfy criterion #2).

The Positive Argument in Plato's *Theaetetus*

[1] I am grateful to Professor Joseph N. Uemura for helpful comments on an earlier draft of this paper. Beyond this, I am grateful to Joe for bringing Socrates to life in his classroom during my undergraduate days and for hours of conversation as my teacher, advisor, colleague and friend since 1966. Still, he cannot be held responsible for mistakes remaining here.

[2] Frederick Copleston, *A History of Philosophy*, Vol. I, Part I, *Greece and Rome*. (Garden City, New York: Image Books, 1946, this edition 1962), p. 166.

[3] James George Frazer, *The Growth of Plato's Ideal Theory*. (London: Macmillan and Co., Ltd., 1930), p. 31.

[4] R. S. Bluck, *Plato's Life and Thought*. (London: Routledge & Kegan Paul, Ltd., 1949), p. 122.

[5] I. M. Crombie, *An Examination of Plato's Doctrines*, Vol. II, *Plato on Knowledge and Reality*. (London: Routledge & Kegan Paul, Ltd., 1963), p. 105.

[6] Glenn R. Morrow, "Plato and the Mathematicians: An Interpretation of Socrates' Dream in the Theaetetus (201e-206c)," *The Philosophical Review*, Vol. LXXIX, No. 3 (July, 1970), p. 330.

[7] Plato, *Theaetetus* 201d (all references to the *Theaetetus*, unless otherwise noted, are from the Fowler translation in *Plato VII: Theaetetus, Sophist*. Cambridge, Mass: Harvard

University Press, 1921).

[8] Plato, *Theaetetus* 201d, translated by F. M. Cornford, *Plato's Theory of Knowledge.* (London: Kegan Paul, Trench & Trubner, Ltd., 1935).

[9] Plato, *Theaetetus* 201d, translated by B. Jowett, *The Dialogues of Plato.* (New York, NY: Macmillan & Co., 1892).

[10] Plato, *Theaetetus* 206c.

[11] Morrow, op. cit., 309.

[12] Plato, *Theaetetus* 206d.

[13] Ibid., 206e.

[14] Ibid., 208c.

[15] William B. Bondeson, "The Dream of Socrates and the Conclusion of the *Theaetetus*," *Apeiron* Vol. 3, No. 1 (July, 1969), p. 11.

[16] Morrow, op. cit., 310.

[17] Plato, *Theaetetus* 152c.

[18] Morrow, op. cit., 311.

[19] Plato, *Republic* 477a.

[20] Plato, *Republic* 508d.

[21] Plato, *Republic* 508d.

[22] Cornford, op. cit., 28.

[23] Ibid., 162.

[24] John Herman Randall, Jr., *Plato: Dramatist of the Life of Reason.* (New York: Columbia University Press, 1970), p. 126.

[25] Cornford, op. cit., 162.

[26] Plato, *Theaetetus* 146e.

[27] Richard Robinson, "Forms and Error in Plato's Theaetetus," *The Philosophical Review*, Vol. LIX (1950), p. 14. This is not to say that Cornford is mistaken in his view that, for Plato, knowledge is the apprehension of Forms (though he probably is mistaken since, as Gilbert Ryle points out in *Plato's Progress*, Cambridge, the Cambridge University Press, 1966, p. 15, the discussion, in the *Theaetetus*, of the *second* proposed definition of knowledge has proved two things: "First, that even about eternal and immutable objects, like the number 7, we can be in a state of mere opinion. For it can erroneously seem to us that, say, 7 + 5 = 11. Secondly, that about mundane happenings like crimes or accidents an eyewitness can have knowledge, where the jurors can achieve nothing better than opinion. Knowledge and opinion, even true opinion, do indeed differ, but not in having different provinces." At any rate, the point *here* is that Cornford's view is not implied by the *Theaetetus*).

[28] Morrow, op. cit., 313.

[29] Ibid.

[30] Plato, *Theaetetus* 148d.

[31] Morrow, op. cit., 314.

[32] Ibid., 316-320.

[33] Morrow's example.

[34] Plato, *Phaedo* 100b.

35 Ibid., 101de.

36 G. M. A. Grube, *Plato's Thought.* (Boston, Mass.: Beacon Press, 1935), p. 25-26.

37 Plato, *Republic* 510cd.

38 Ibid., 511b.

39 Ibid., 533cd.

40 Crombie, op. cit., 109.

41 Plato, *Theaetetus* 201d-202c (in Morrow, op. cit., 326).

42 Morrow, op. cit., 327.

43 Ibid., 328.

44 Ibid.

45 Plato, *Republic* 533cd.

46 Plato, *Theaetetus* 202d.

47 Ibid., 203c.

48 Morrow, op. cit., 329.

49 Ibid., 331.

50 Plato, *Republic* 511b.

51 Plato, *Theaetetus* 201c.

52 Ibid.

53 Ryle, "Plato," *The Encyclopedia of Philosophy*, Vol. VI, ed. Paul Edwards, (New York: The Macmillan Co. & the Free Press, 1967), p. 328.

The Ethics of Being

1 David Hume, *An Enquiry Concerning Human Understanding* Indianapolis: Hackett Publishing Company, 1977 [1748], pp. 5-6.

2 Ibid., p. 114.

3 Ibid., p. 11.

4 Ibid.

5 Kant's analysis of traditional theology is most clearly and fully presented in the *Critique of Pure Reason.* Cf. the Transcendental Dialectic, Chapter III (esp. A 584=B612 ff).

6 Willard Van Orman Quine, "Two Dogmas of Empiricism," *From a Logical Point of View*, Second Edition, (New York: Harper & Row, 1961 [1953]), p. 41.

7 Ibid., p. 20.

8 "My present suggestion is that it is nonsense, and the root of much nonsense, to speak of a linguistic component and a factual component in the truth of any individual statement. Taken collectively, science has its double dependence upon language and experience; but this duality is not significantly tradeable into the statements of science taken one by one" (Ibid., p. 42).

9 Ibid.

10 Quine's battle with what he calls "Platonism" is his substitute for metaphysics. This can be seen in "On What There Is" (*From a Logical Point of View*) and later in *Word and Object* (Cambridge, Mass.: MIT Press, 1960), esp. Chapter VII. Like Hume he seeks to replace the old metaphysics with the dialectic between competing "conceptual schemes" (phenomenal-

ism and physicalism)—cf. *From a Logical Point of View*, pp. 16ff. He identifies "a shift toward pragmatism" (Ibid., p. 20) which turned out to be prophetic, as has become clear with the subsequent popularity of Richard Rorty and his followers.

11 Ibid., p. 42.

12 G. E. Moore, *Principia Ethica* (Cambridge, England: Cambridge University Press, 1962 [1903]).

13 Ibid., p. 13. Consider also the following discussion in Chapter II: "The theories I propose to discuss may be divided into two groups. The naturalistic fallacy always implies that when we think 'This is good,' what we are thinking is that the thing in question bears a definite relation to some one other thing. But this one thing by reference to what is good is defined, may be either what I call a natural object—something of which the existence is admittedly an object of experience—or else it may be an object which is only inferred to exist in a supersensible real world... It should be observed that the fallacy, by reference to which I define 'Metaphysical Ethics,' is the same in kind, and I give it but one name, the naturalistic fallacy" (Ibid., pp. 38-39).

14 "If I am asked 'What is good' my answer is that good is good, and that is the end of the matter. Or if I am asked 'How is good to be defined?' my answer is that it cannot be defined, and that is all I have to say about it" (Ibid., p. 6).

15 Cf. Plato, *Gorgias*, trans. Donald J. Zeyl (Indianapolis: Hackett Publishing Company, 1987), pp. 495a to 503a.

16 Ibid., 494c.

17 J. Baird Callicott, *In Defense of the Land Ethic: Essays in Environmental Philosophy* (Albany: State University of New York Press, 1989), p. 21.

18 Cf. Ibid., pp. 25ff.

19 "Indeed, two of the same analogies figuring in the conceptual foundations of the Leopold land ethic appear in Plato's value theory. From the econological perspective, according to Leopold as I have pointed out, land is like an organic body or like a human society. According to Plato, body, soul, and society have similar structures and corresponding virtues. The goodness of each is a function of its structure organization and the relative value of the parts or constituents of each is calculated according to the contribution made to the integrity, stability, and beauty of each whole" (Ibid., p. 28).

20 Callicott cites Plato's proposals in *The Republic* for "requiring infanticide for a child whose only offense was being born without the sanction of the state, making presents to the enemy of guardians who allow themselves to be captured alive in combat, and radically restricting the practice of medicine to the dressing of wounds and the curing of seasonal maladies on the principle that the infirm and chronically ill not only lead miserable lives but contribute nothing to the good of the polity (Ibid., pp. 28-29).

21 Ibid., p. 29.

22 Ibid.

23 Cf. Ibid., pp. 78-79.

24 Oiron agrees with Joseph Uemura and Duane Cady who interpret *The Republic* as anti-utopian rather than as offering a blueprint for a totalitarian society. Uemura states this thesis clearly, distinctly, and bluntly: "Plato meant to cure us of utopias, not to create one."

(*Six Dialogues of Plato: An Interpretation* [Denver, Colorado: Andy Cleary, Publisher], 1991), p. 87. Also see Duane Cady, "Individual Fulfillment (Not Social Engineering) in Plato's *Republic*" in *Idealistic Studies*, vol. XIII, no. 3, (September, 1983).

25 I first encountered this argument approximately 25 years ago in a paper he wrote called "Plato's *Republic*: An Antidote to Any Future Utopia." In a piece published in 1988, Duskin Clay also identifies three cities in *The Republic*: (1) the healthy city, (2) the city that "is the product of the appetite for gain and self-aggrandizement," and (3) "the Kallipolis, the city of *The Republic* (Duskin Clay, "Reading *The Republic*," in *Platonic Writings, Platonic Readings*, ed. Charles L. Griswold, Jr. (New York: Routledge, Chapman & Hall, Inc., 1988), p. 25.

26 Ibid., p.92.

27 Ibid., p. 93.

28 Moore, p. 7.

29 Plato, *The Republic*, trans. Richard W. Sterling and William C. Scott (New York: W.W. Norton Company, 1985), 505a.

30 Ibid., 505b.

31 Ibid.

32 Ibid., 506b.

33 Ibid., 506c.

34 Ibid., 507b.

35 Ibid.

36 Ibid., 508b-c.

37 Cf. Kant, *Grounding for the Metaphysics of Morals*, p. 400 and again on p. 452, where this dualism is explicitly developed. The notion of "two worlds" is further articulated at 453, and the is/ought distinction is treated even more clearly at 454, specifically in terms of a categorical ought which "presents a synthetic *a priori* proposition."

38 Plato, *The Republic*, 508e.

39 Ibid.

40 Ibid., 509a.

41 Ibid., 509b.

42 Ibid.

43 Ibid., 509c.

44 Plato, *The Sophist*, trans. Harold North Fowler (Cambridge, Mass.: Harvard University Press, 1967), 254d.

45 Ibid., 511b-c.

The Developmental Relationship Between Moral Reasoning and Motivation

1 See Frankena, "Obligation and Motivation in Recent Moral Philosophy" in A. I. Melden (ed.) *Essays in Moral Philosophy* (Seattle: University of Washington Press, 1958) for an early discussion of internalism and externalism and of the many versions of these views. Thomas Nagel in *The Possibility of Altruism* (N.J.: Princeton University Press, 1970) presents an historical overview of the controversy and an argument for internalism.

2 I am indebted to the article by Thomas E. Wren, "The Possibility of Convergence between Moral Psychology and Metaethics" in T. E. Wren (ed.) *The Moral Domain* (Cambridge, Mass.: MIT Press, 1990), where he discusses the relevance of the internalist/externalist debate to theories of moral development.

3 Lawrence Kohlberg, *Essays on Moral Development*, Vol. 1, *The Philosophy of Moral Development* (San Francisco: Harper and Row, 1981).

4 "Moral Internalization: Current Theory and Research" in L. Berkowitz (ed.) *Advances in Experimental Social Psychology*, Vol. 10 (New York: Academic Press, 1977), p. 85.

5 See Justin Aronfreed, "The Concept of Internalization" in D. A. Goslin (ed.) *Handbook of Socialization Theory and Research* (Chicago: Rand McNally, 1969), p. 264.

6 Hoffman, op. cit., p. 86.

7 *Philosophical Investigations*, 185ff.

8 Wittgenstein, 241, 242.

9 See John McDowell, "Non-Cognitivism and Rule-Following" in S. Holtzman and C. Leich (eds.) *Wittgenstein: To Follow a Rule* (London: Routledge and Kegan Paul, 1981).

10 Op. cit., p. 14.

11 In Anna Freud's writings this is known as "primary narcissism" and is distinguished from Sigmund Freud's notion of narcissism by the realization that the infant does not only lack a conception of the other but of the self as well. Piaget refers to this as "a dualism" and attributes the idea to the American psychologist, J. M. Baldwin.

12 F. H. Bradley, *Ethical Studies* (Oxford: Clarendon Press, 2nd ed. 1927), p. 172; quoted in Richard Wollheim, "The Good Self and the Bad Self," *Proceedings of the British Academy* 61, 1975.

13 Bradley, op. cit., p. 283.

14 "On the Source of the Authority of the State," in *The Collected Philosophical Papers of G. E. M. Anscombe, Volume III: Ethics, Religion and Politics* (Minneapolis: University of Minnesota Press, 1981), p. 139.

15 Anscombe takes this expression from Hume, who described promises as "naturally unintelligible."

16 Psychoanalytic theorists tend to emphasize 'introjection,' 'identification,' and 'incorporation' as the principal types of internalization. See, for instance, Roy Schafer, *Aspects of Internalization* (New York: International Universities Press, 1968). Social learning theorists, on the other hand, speak of 'modeling,' 'reinforcement,' 'conditioning,' etc. Since I am interested only in the specifically moral significance of internalization, I will limit my discussion of types of internalization to 'acceptance.'

17 *Wise Choices, Apt Feelings* (Cambridge, Mass: Harvard University Press, 1990), p. 75.

18 My use of these terms differs from Gibbard's in that he contrasts acceptance and internalization as manifestations of distinct and often conflicting motivational systems, acceptance of norms belonging to what he calls the "normative control system" and internalization of norms belonging to the "animal control system." (Gibbard, op. cit., p. 56) This paper, however, is concerned to demonstrate that at least in the early stages of moral development there is only one motivational system that is described by internalization and that acceptance

is one type or aspect of internalization among others, namely, the internalization of a norm through conceiving it to be justified.

[19] Moral norms are not the only norms that can be justified by certain concepts. There are, for example, norms of prudence and etiquette that are similar to moral norms in that their internalization is explained in terms of concepts that justify them, which is to say that they are internalized by means of acceptance.

[20] See Anscombe, "Rules, Rights and Promises" in op. cit., p. 101.

[21] One way in which this account may prove useful is in explaining the frequency of failings such as moral weakness and self-deception among mature moral agents and the relative infrequency of such failings among children.

Rachels' Defense of Active Euthanasia: A Critique

[1] James Rachels, in Wade L. Robison and Michael S. Pritchard (ed.), *Medical Responsibility*. New Jersey: The HUMANA Press, 1979, pp. 153-168.

[2] Ibid., p. 156.

[3] Ibid., p. 154.

[4] Ibid.

[5] Ibid., p. 158.

[6] Ibid., p. 159.

[7] Ibid.

[8] Ibid., pp. 161-162.

[9] Ibid., p. 161.

[10] Ibid., p. 156.

[11] Ibid.

[12] Rachels has discussed this criticism briefly in "Euthanasia," *Philosophy and Public Affairs*, 6:2 (Winter 1977), 111-112. His response is basically that we have evidence that shows that killing in one context does not necessarily lead to killing in another, and he mentions ancient Greek and Eskimo societies (and killing in self-defense in our own) to back this up. In my view he fails to consider the central thrust of the criticism, in that he does not discuss what reasons he may have for believing that the moral values comprising our reverence for life would not be undermined by permitting active euthanasia. Instead, he says that since the acceptance of killing in self-defense has not led to a breakdown of respect for life, neither would active euthanasia. I am not convinced that the cases are analogous. After all, only one involves saving a life. And, who is to say that *accepting* killing in self-defense does not already suggest, if not a breakdown, perhaps a very slight diminution of respect for life. In any event, his response, curiously, does not mention the case I discuss next.

[13] Leo Alexander, "Medical Science Under Dictatorship," *The New England Journal of Medicine*, July, 1949. See also Robert Lifton, *The Nazi Doctors*. New York: Basic Books, 1986.

[14] Lucy Dawidowicz, *The War Against The Jews 1933-1945*. New York: Holt, Rinehart and Winston, 1975, p. 133.

[15] John Stuart Mill, *On Liberty*. New York: Bantam, 1961.

[16] To put it in terms that are helpful to those familiar with Plato's *Republic*, our real prob-

lem is not Thrasymachus but Kephalus.

[17] The students who participated in the study included 307 part-time students. Among the part-time students were teachers, office workers, and state employees.

[18] Helge Hilding Mansson, "Justifying the Final Solution," *Omega*, Vol. 3, No. 2, p. 87.

[19] Ibid., p. 85.

Ethical Perception and Managerial Decision Making

[1] A previous version of this paper was presented at the Conference on the Study of Government and Ethics, Park City, Utah, June, 1991.

Retention and Advising: Paternalism, Agency and Contract

[1] This is a revised version of a paper presented at the Noel/Levitz 1990 National Conference on Student Retention, July 9, 1990.

[2] For perceptions see Beal and Noel (43), Finney (2,7), and Heard (15). Cf. Holm (90) who found the advisor had little perceived effect on retention of "adult" students in a personalized learning program. For demonstrations see Atkins (8,22) and Brophy (38,41,43) who cite several works, Crockett (244-46), Gordon (127), and Tinto (152). Forrest (71) argues that the significance is probable but not certain.

[3] This is not to discount the possible role of the advisor as counselor and confidant, but only to distinguish the basic duties of an advisor from those of a counselor (see Dressel 158). Some writers are not careful about this distinction (e.g. Brophy 12, 122).

[4] Less prosaically we may, with Walsh, place the focus of advising on the students' development of their academic selves (447).

[5] This paper assumes that the relationship between advisor and advisee is either a professional-client relationship or close enough to one not to require entering the debate about what constitutes a professional. But cf. Bayles (7).

[6] Furthermore, the question whether friendship between a teacher and a student is ever appropriate merits a discussion all its own, thus we shall not confront the issue here. The more general contract model should be of sufficient interest for our purposes (cf Cahn 36).

[7] In fact advisors may even be in danger of malpractice suits (Hollander 9-10).

Dewey's Theory of Aesthetics and Art

[1] Cf., Philip M. Zeltner, *John Dewey's Aesthetic Philosophy* (Amsterdam: B.R. Gritner, B.V., 1975). I owe the determination of this scheme of classification to Zeltner's excellent book. The development of this format is, however, my own.

[2] John Dewey, *Experience and Nature* (LaSalle, Illinois: Open Court Publishing Company, 1929; Sixth Printing, 1971), p. 4.

[3] John Dewey, *Art as Experience* (New York: Minton, Balch & Company, 1934), p. 13.

[4] Lewis E. Hahn, "Dewey's Philosophy and Philosophic Method," *Guide to the Works of John Dewey*, ed. Jo Ann Boydston (Carbondale, Illinois: Southern Illinois University Press, 1970; Arcturus Books edition, 1972), 15-60, p. 29.

[5] John Dewey, *Experience and Nature*, op. cit., p. 291.

[6] Ibid., pp. 210-211.

[7] Ibid., p. 211.

[8] Ibid., p. 247.

[9] John Dewey, *The Quest for Certainty* (New York: Minton, Balch & Company, 1929), pp. 237-238.

[10] John Dewey, *Experience and Nature*, op. cit., p. 288.

[11] John Dewey, *Art as Experience*, op. cit., p. 37.

[12] Ibid., p. 38.

[13] Ibid., p. 39.

[14] Ibid., p. 40.

[15] John Dewey, *Experience and Nature*, op. cit., p. 288.

[16] Ibid., p. 290.

[17] S. Morris Eames, *Pragmatic Naturalism* (Carbondale, Illinois: Southern Illinois University Press, 1977), p. 161.

[18] John Dewey, *Art as Experience*, op. cit., pp. 41-42.

[19] Ibid., p. 65.

[20] Ibid., p. 65.

[21] Ibid., pp. 65-66.

[22] Ibid., p. 67.

[23] Ibid., pp. 67-68.

[24] Ibid., p. 69.

[25] P.G. Whitehouse, "The Meaning of 'Emotion' in Dewey's Art as Experience," *The Journal of Aesthetics and Art Criticism*, XXXVII (Winter 1978), 149-156, p. 152.

[26] Cf., S. Morris Eames, *Pragmatic Naturalism*, op. cit., and cf., Bertram Morris, "Dewey's Theory of Art," *Guide to the Works of John Dewey*, op. cit., 156-182.

[27] P.G. Whitehouse, op. cit., p. 154.

[28] Ibid., p. 155.

[29] Ibid., p. 155.

[30] Ibid., pp. 155-156.

[31] John Dewey, *Art as Experience*, op. cit., pp. 52-53.

[32] Ibid., p. 106.

[33] Ibid., pp. 107-108.

[34] Ibid., pp. 26-27.

[35] Ibid., p. 109.

[36] Ibid., p. 109.

[37] Ibid., p. 114.

[38] Ibid., p. 114.

[39] Ibid., pp. 115-117.

[40] Ibid., p. 117.

[41] Ibid., p. 163.

[42] Ibid., p. 166.

[43] Ibid., pp. 178-179.

[44] Ibid., pp. 298-299.

45 Ibid., p. 301.

46 Ibid., p. 301.

47 Ibid., pp. 303-304.

48 Ibid., p. 306.

49 Ibid., p. 307.

50 Ibid., pp. 308-309.

51 Ibid., p. 310.

52 Ibid., p. 312.

53 Ibid., p. 314.

54 Ibid., pp. 317-318.

55 Ibid., pp. 319-320.

56 Ibid., p. 349.

James and Reid: Meliorism *vs* Metaphysics

1 William James, "The Dilemma in Philosophy," *Pragmatism*, ed. Bruce Kuklich (Indianapolis: Hackett Publishing Company, 1981), p. 10.

2 "Pragmatism and Humanism," *Pragmatism*, p. 120.

3 Immanuel Kant, *Critique of Pure Reason*, tr. Norman Kemp Smith (New York: St. Martin's Press, 1929), p. 41.

4 Ibid., p. 29.

5 William James, "The Will to Believe," in *Essays in Pragmatism*, ed. Alburey Castell (New York: Hafner Publishing Co., 1948), p. 95.

6 Cf. John Passmore, *A Hundred Years of Philosophy* (New York: Basic Books, 1966), p. 261.

7 Ibid., p. 261.

8 William James, "The Present Dilemma in Philosophy," *Pragmatism, op. cit.*, p. 7.

9 William James, "What Pragmatism Means," *Pragmatism*, pp. 25-26.

10 Ibid., p. 28.

11 Immanuel Kant, *Critique of Pure Reason, op. cit.*, pp. 23-24.

12 William James, "The Sentiment of Rationality," *Essays in Pragmatism, op. cit.*, p. 33. The mention of "meaningfulness" and "verifiability" is due to James' effort to distance himself from positivism. Kant would only contend that metaphysical claims, though meaningful, are unknowable because they transcend experience.

13 *Thomas Reid's Inquiry and Essays*, ed. Ronald E. Beanblossom and Keith Lehrer (Indianapolis: Hackett Publishing Company, 1983), p. 11.

14 Ibid., p. 12.

15 Ibid., p. 12.

16 Ibid., p. 288-293.

17 William James, "What Pragmatism Means," *Pragmatism, op. cit.*, p. 29.

18 Ibid., p. 29.

19 William James, "Pragmatism and Humanism," *Pragmatism, op. cit.*, p. 115.

20 Ibid., p. 115.

21 Ibid., p. 116.

22 Immanuel Kant, *Critique of Pure Reason, op. cit.*, p. 115.

23 William James, "Common Sense," *Pragmatism, op. cit.*, p. 82.

24 William James, "Pragmatism and Humanism," *Pragmatism*, p. 113.

25 Cf. Ronald E. Beanblossom, "Kant's Quarrel With Reid: The Role of Metaphysics," in *History of Philosophy Quarterly*, Vol. 5, 1988, pp. 53-62.

26 William James, "What Pragmatism Means," *Pragmatism op. cit.*, p. 29.

27 William James, "The One and the Many," *Pragmatism*, p. 62.

28 Ibid., p. 69.

29 Ibid., p. 68.

30 Thomas Reid, *Inquiry and Essays, op. cit.*, p. 71.

31 William James, "The One and the Many," *Pragmatism, op. cit.*, p. 71.

32 Ibid., p. 73.

33 Thomas Reid, *Inquiry and Essays, op. cit.*, p. 291.

34 William James, "Pragmatism and Humanism" *Pragmatism, op. cit.*, p. 115.

35 William James, "The One and the Many," *Pragmatism*, p. 73.

36 William James, "What Pragmatism Means," *Pragmatism*, p. 29.

37 Ibid., p. 28.

38 William James, "Pragmatism and Humanism," *Pragmatism, op. cit.*, p. 120.

39 William James, "The Sentiment of Rationality," *Essays in Pragmatism, op. cit.*, p. 33.

40 William James, "The Moral Philosopher and the Moral Life," *Essays in Pragmatism*, p. 69.

41 Ibid., p. 70.

42 Ibid., p. 72.

43 William James, "The Dilemma of Determinism," *Essays in Pragmatism, op. cit.*, p. 56.

44 Ibid., p. 57.

45 Ibid., p. 58.

46 Ibid., p. 47.

47 Ibid., p. 38.

48 Ibid., p. 38.

49 Ibid., p. 59.

50 Ibid., p. 59.

51 Thomas Reid, *Inquiry and Essays, op. cit.*, p. 7.

52 Ibid., pp. 257-266.

53 Ibid., pp. 265-266.

54 Ibid., p. 86.

55 William James, "The Sentiment of Rationality," *Essays in Pragmatism, op. cit.*, p. 27.

56 Thomas Reid, *Inquiry and Essays, op. cit.*, p. 10.

57 Ibid., p. 336.

58 Ibid., pp. 18-19.

59 Ibid., p. 11.

60 William James, "The Will to Believe," *Essays in Pragmatism, op. cit.*, p. 98.

61 William James, "Conclusions on Varieties of Religious Experience," *Essays in Pragmatism*, p. 120.

62 William James, "Pragmatism and Religion," *Pragmatism, op. cit.,* p. 134.

63 William James, "The Moral Philosopher and the Moral Life," *Essays in Pragmatism, op. cit.,* p. 71.

Seeing a Donkey's Jaw, Drinking Green Tea: Self and Ordinariness in Ecophilosophy

1 See Jim Cheney, "Eco-feminism and Deep Ecology," *Environmental Ethics,* 9 (1987): 115-145, Ariel Kay Salleh, "Deeper Than Deep Ecology: The Eco-Feminist Connection," *Environmental Ethics,* 6 (1984): 339-45, and Val Plumwood, "Self, and Gender: Feminism, Environmental Philosophy, and the Critique of Rationalism," *Hypatia,* 6 (1, 1991): 3-27.

2 As will become clear, not all deep ecological formulations of Self *are* holist and hierarchical. Fundamentally different positions have been classed under the heading of deep ecological Self.

3 While Dogen is not well known in the West, translations of his works are readily available. The complete Japanese text is *Dogen Zenji Zenshu,* ed. Okubo Doshu (Tokyo: Chikuma Shobu, 1969-1970). Among the notable translations are: *Flowers of Emptiness: Selections from Dogen's Shobogenzo,* ed. and trans. Hee-Jin Kim (Lewiston, N.Y.: 1985); *How to Raise an Ox,* ed. and trans. Francis Dojun Cook (Los Angeles: Center Publications, 1978); *Moon in a Dewdrop: Writings of Zen Master Dogen,* ed. and trans. Tanahashi Kazuaki, et. al. (San Francisco: North Point Press, 1985); *Shobogenzo Zen Essays by Dogen,* ed. and trans. Thomas Cleary (Honolulu: University of Hawaii Press, 1986); *Shobogenzo,* trans. Kosen Nishiyama (Tokyo: Nakayama Shobo), 1988); *Sounds of Valley Streams: Enlightenment in Dogen's Zen,* ed. and trans. Francis H. Cook (Albany, N.Y.: State University of New York Press, 1989); *Zen Master Dogen: An Introduction with Selected Writings,* ed. Yokoi Yuho (New York: Weatherhill, 1976). Norman Waddell and Abe Masao have translated several of the important fascicles from *Shobogenzo* in *The Eastern Buddhist:* "Bendowa." *The Eastern Buddhist,* 4 (1, 1971),"Ikka Myoju." *Eastern Buddhist,* 4 (2, 1971),"Shobogenzo Genjokoan." *Eastern Buddhist,* 5 (2, 1972), "Zenki and Shoji." *Eastern Buddhist,* 5 (1, 1972), "Sammai O zammai." *Eastern Buddhist,* 7 (1, 1974), " "*Shobogenjo* Buddha-nature," *Eastern Buddhist,* 8 (2, 1975): 9 (1, 1976); 9 (2 1976); and Norman Waddell trans., "Uji." *Eastern Buddhist,* 12 (1, 1979).

The notable secondary literature includes: David Appelbaum, "On Turning a Zen Ear," *Philosophy East and West,* 33 (2, 1983): 115-122; Steven Heine, *Existential and Ontological Dimensions of Time Heidegger and Dogen,* (Albany, N.Y.: State University of New York Press, 1985); David Loy, "The Path of No-path: Sankana and *Dogen* on the Paradox of Practice." *Philosophy East and West,* 38 (2, 1988): 127-146; Carl Olson, "The Human Body as a Boundary Symbol: A Comparison of Merleau-Ponty and *Dogen* " *Philosophy East and West,* 36 (2, 1986): 107-120; T. P. Kasulis, *Zen Action Zen Person,* (Honolulu: The University of Hawaii Press, 1981); Hee-Jin Kim, *Dogen Kigen: Mystical Realist,* (Tucson: The University of Arizona Press, 1987, revised from 1975 ed.); James Takashi Kodera, *Dogen's Formative Years in China,* (Boulder: Prajna Press, 1980); William R. LaFleur, ed., *Dogen Studies,* (Honolulu: University of Hawaii Press, 1985); David

Edward Shaner, *The Bodymind Experience in Japanese Buddhism*, (Albany, N.Y.: State University of New York Press, 1985); David E. Shaner, "The Bodymind Experience in *Dogen's* Shobogenzo: A Phenomenological Perspective," *Philosophy East and West*, 35 (1, 1985): 17-35; Joan Stambaugh, *Impermanence is Buddha-nature: Dogen's Understanding of Temporality*, (Honolulu: University of Hawaii Press, 1990); Yasuo Yuasa, *The Body: Toward an Eastern Mind-Body Theory*, trans. Shigenori Nagatomo and Thomas P. Kasulis, (Albany: State University of New York Press, 1987).

[4] See Robert Aitken Roshi, "Gandhi, Dogen and Deep Ecology," *Deep Ecology: Living as if Nature Mattered*, (Salt Lake City: Peregrine Smith Books, 1985), pp. 232-235; Arne Naess, "Through Spinoza to Mahayana Buddhism, or Through Mahayana Buddhism to Spinoza" in *Spinoza's Philosophy of Man: Proceedings of the Scandinavian Spinoza Symposium, 1977*, ed. Jon Wetlesen (Oslo: Universitetsforlaget, 1978) pp. 136-158, and Warwick Fox, *Toward a Transpersonal Ecology: Developing New Foundations for Environmentalism*, (Boston: Shambhala, 1990), p. 268. A collection of essays on Buddhism and the environment is *Dharma Gaia: A Harvest of Essays in Buddhism and Ecology*, ed. Allan Hunt Badiner (Berkeley: Parallax Press, 1990). See especially the essays by Joan Halifax, "The Third Body: Buddhism, Shamanism, & Deep Ecology," Jeremy Hayward, "Ecology and the Experience of Sacredness," Bill Devall, "Ecocentric Sangha," Carla Deicke, "Women and Ecocentricity," and John Seed, "Wake the Dead!"

[5] As Thomas Kasulis has argued persuasively, Dogen's work can be explicated philosophically; he need not be categorized (and dismissed) as a mystic in the popular sense of the word. See "The Zen Philosopher: A Review Article on Dogen Scholarship in English," *Philosophy East and West*, 28 (3, 1978): 353-373. While the claim has been made by Orientalists recently that one or more of the Oriental traditions is particularly relevant to environmental ethics, my contention is that Dogen stands somewhat apart from the traditions from which he emerged in his consciousness of ordinariness. The same universalistic and hierarchical tendencies exist in Eastern philosophy as in Western philosophy; these are the tendencies on which Naess and Fox often depend. I contend that Dogen's departure from Hindu, Chinese Taoist and certain earlier Buddhist philosophies makes him particularly relevant to environmental ethics.

Baird Callicott has encouraged cross-fertilization of Western environmental philosophy with Eastern philosophies as an aid in the search for a transformative moral theory . (See J. Baird Callicott, "Conceptual Resources for Environmental Ethics in Asian Traditions of Thought: A Propaedeutic." *Philosophy East and West*, 37 (2, 1987): 115-130.) The most distinguished examples so far produced by this process of have focused on the potential of early Buddhist and Taoist philosophies. For a collection of writings on the environment by Oriental specialist see J. Baird Callicott and Roger T. Ames, eds. *Nature in Asian Traditions of Thought*, (Albany, N.Y.: State University of New York Press, 1989).

[6] Norman Waddell and Abe Masao in introductory comments to their translation of "*Shobogenzo* Buddha-nature," *The Eastern Buddhist*, 8 (2, 1975): 94.

[7] This idea, however, was not original with Dogen. See William LaFleur's "Sattva: Enlightenment for Plants and Trees in Buddhism," (*CoEvolution Quarterly*, 19 (1978): 47-52) for some fascinating background on this issue.

8 Waddell and Abe, "*Shobogenzo* Buddha-nature," p. 95. Their translation of the second sentence is "All sentient beings-whole being is the Buddha-nature." I have kept the translations parallel here. On the radicalization of Buddha-nature see Heinrich Dumoulin, *Zen Buddhism: A History*, Vol. 2 (Japan) (New York: Macmillan Publishing Company, 1990), pp. 79ff.

9 "*Shobogenzo* Buddha-nature," pp. 91 and 93.

10 "Mountains and Waters Sutra" in *Moon in a Dewdrop: Writings of Zen Master Dogen*, pp. 97-98.

11 Abe Masao, "Dogen on Buddha-nature," *Eastern Buddhist*, 4 (1, 1971): 39. My emphasis.

12 "*Shobogenzo* Buddha-nature," p. 100.

13 "Actualizing the Fundamental Point" (*Genjo Koan*), *Moon in a Dewdrop*, p. 70.

14 "Undivided Activity," (*Zenki*) *Moon in a Dewdrop*, p. 84.

15 See "Body and Mind Study of the Way," (*Shinjin Gakudo*) *Moon in a Dewdrop* for the two ways of studying the Buddha way. Dogen accepts the traditional Buddhist understanding of body as "the four great elements" (earth, water, fire, and air) and the five skandhas (form, feeling, perception, impulses, and consciousness). The five skandhas are the mental and physical aggregates into which the phenomenal world is analyzed. The point of the analysis is to show that there is no substantial self.

16 "Undivided Activity," (*Zenki*) *Moon in a Dewdrop*, p. 85.

17 Ibid., pp. 85-86.

18 See *Zen Action Zen Person*, pp. 87-103. There is no better philosophical introduction to Dogen's thought than Kasulis's book.

19 Takashi James Kodera, *Dogen's Formative Years in China*, p. 37.

20 Nor is there a dualistic preference among everyday activities. Another of the fascicles of the *Shobogenzo* instructs monks on the dharma of face washing, tooth brushing, and proper use of the toothpick. See "Washing the Face" *Senmen*, *Shobogenzo*, trans. Kosen Nishiyama (Tokyo: Nakayama Shobo, 1988) pp. 370-380.

21 *Fushuku-hampo* (Mealtime Regulations), trans. Roshi Jiyu-Kennett, *Zen is Eternal Life*, (Mt. Shasta, CA: Shasta Abbey Press, 1987) , p. 95. In *Cooking, Eating, Thinking: Transformative Philosophies of Food* (with Lisa Heldke), (Bloomington: Indiana University Press, 1992). I argue for a food-based understanding of personhood and values that responds to Dogen's writings on food. A book that takes Dogen's writings of food as central to understanding his philosophy is Kosho Uchiyama, *Refining Your Life: From Zen Kitchen to Enlightenment*, trans. Thomas Wright (New York: Weatherhill, 1983).

22 "Everyday Activity" *(Kajo)*, *Moon in a Dewdrop*, p. 125.

23 "Identification as a Source of Deep Ecological Attitudes" *Deep Ecology*, ed. Michael Tobias (San Diego: Avant Books, 1985), pp. 261 and 263. Though political, Gandhi's understanding of self derives from the Hindu (Advaita Vedanta) idea of self *asatman*. So the alternatives offered by Naess are not really different.

24 David J, Kalupahana, *The Principles of Buddhist Psychology*, (Albany, N.Y.: State University of New York Press, 1987), p. 12.

25 Freya Mathews, "Conservation and Self-Realization: A Deep Ecology Perspective,"

Environmental Ethics, 10 (1988): 349.

[26] Naess is quoted in Warwick Fox, *Toward a Transpersonal Ecology*, p. 230 from an unpublished manuscript "Gestalt Thinking and Buddhism" (1983). See Devall's "Ecocentric Sangha," in *Dharma Gaia* and Snyder's "Blue Mountains Constantly Walking" *The Practice of the Wild*, (San Francisco: North Point Press, 1990), especially p. 103.

[27] Abe Masao, "Dogen on Buddha-Nature," pp. 41-42.

[28] "Undivided Activity" *(Zenki) Moon in a Dewdrop*, pp. 85-86.

[29] Dumoulin, *Zen Buddhism: A History*, p 82. Having shown that the deep ecological Self moves in the direction of the Senika heresy, it is also worth reconsidering the second mistaken theory of self that Dogen warned against, the metaphor of the self as a seed that realizes its potential. In holding that Self is realized through identification with "the whole," some deep ecologists are snared by precisely this dualism. Full realization of the Self occurs at the end of a process as in the experience of the yogi who identifies with the whole of nature, who sees "the same" everywhere. There is in Naess and some other writers an implicit dualism between theory and practice that remains largely unexamined.

[30] Fox, *Toward a Transpersonal Ecology*, pp. 250, 251 and 252, 259 and 260.

[31] Warwick Fox, "The Deep Ecology-Ecofeminism Debate and its Parallels" *Environmental Ethics*, 11 (1, 1989) 12-13.

[32] This is too broad. Actually, liberal feminists accept these dualistic frameworks and work to be included on the masculine side of the dualism. Other forms of feminism seek to undercut the dualisms altogether. See Alison M. Jaggar, *Feminist Politics and Human Nature*, (Totowa, N.J.: Rowman and Allanheld, 1983) especially chapters 3-6 for a discussion of the differences between liberal feminism and other forms of feminism.

[33] *Greek Philosophy: Thales to Aristotle*, ed. Reginald E. Allen (New York: Free Press, 1966), p. 39. Quoted from Aristotle's *Metaphysics*, 985b 23.

[34] See Sherry B. Ortner, "Is Female to Male as Nature Is to Culture?" in *Women, Culture, and Society*, ed. Michelle Zimbalist Rosaldo and Louise Lamphere (Stanford: Stanford University Press, 1974), pp. 67-87.

[35] In "Toward an Ecological Ethic of Care" *Hypatia*, 6 (1, 1991) I explore some of the conditions for an ecofeminist ethic.

[36] Sara Ruddick, *Maternal Thinking:Toward a Politics of Peace*, (New York: Ballantine Books, 1989), pp. 129 and 130.

[37] *Toward a Transpersonal Ecology*, p. 31.